THE UPDATED & EXPANDED ANSWERS BOOK

THE 20 MOST-ASKED QUESTIONS ABOUT CREATION, EVOLUTION, & THE BOOK OF GENESIS ANSWERED!

THE ANSWERS BOOK

UPDATED & EXPANDED

THE 20 MOST-ASKED QUESTIONS ABOUT CREATION, EVOLUTION, & THE BOOK OF GENESIS ANSWERED!

Don Batten (ed.)
Ken Ham
Jonathan Sarfati
Carl Wieland

Answers In Genesis

ISBN: 0-94990-623-9

Scripture quotations from the Modern King James Version or King James Version (AV).

Cover design by Brandon Vallorani

Illustrations by Steve Cardno, Dan Lietha, Brendon O'Loughlin or Robert Smith, unless otherwise noted.

First printing: December 1999

Printed in Australia by Triune Press, Brisbane.

Please visit our website for further information on the Christian world-view and the Creation/Evolution issue.

www.AnswersinGenesis.org

Acknowledgments

Many people helped in the production of this book. Dr Andrew Snelling, one of the authors of the original *Answers Book*, made helpful suggestions at various points in the new edition. Dr Werner Gitt provided much of the text of Chapter 9. Dr John Baumgardner helped with parts of the chapter on continental drift. Michael Oard also contributed significantly to the chapter on the Ice Age. Dr Russell Humphreys helped with various aspects of the chapters on distant stars in a young universe and carbon dating.

Dr Len Morris, Rev. Jock Butteriss and Warren Nunn checked the first draft of the *Answers Book* and made many helpful suggestions. Russell Grigg and Dr Tas Walker proof-read a later pre-publication draft and made helpful suggestions and corrections.

Brendon O'Loughlin helped with various aspects of the layout and the index, and created many of the special figures and images used in the book. Brenda Alder also helped with layout. Special thanks to Robert Smith for his charcoal drawings.

Other people who have helped with advice on various points are: Dr David Catchpoole, David Jolly, and Professors Douglas Kelly and David Menton.

Abbreviations

AiG: Answers in Genesis
CEN Technical Journal: Creation Ex Nihilo Technical Journal
ICC: International Conference on Creationism
Ma: *mega annum,* or millions of years

Metric conversions

1 centimetre (cm)	0.4 inches
1 metre (m)	3.3 feet
1 kilometre (km)	0.62 miles
1 square kilometre (km^2)	0.39 square miles
1 cubic kilometre	0.24 cubic miles
1 tonne	0.98 tons or 1.1 US ('short') tons
0 °C	32 °F
30 °C	86 °F
-20 °C	-4 °F

Contents

... be ready always to give an answer to everyone who asks you a reason of the hope in you, with meekness and fear; having a good conscience ...

1 Peter 3:15,16

Chapter 1

Does God exist?

Is there objective evidence that God exists? What are the consequences of atheism? Where did God come from? Can we know God personally?

THE Bible begins with the statement: *'In the beginning God created the heavens and the earth'* (Gen. 1:1). God's existence is assumed, self-evident. In Psalm 14:1 we are told, *'The fool has said in his heart, There is no God! They acted corruptly; they have done abominable works, there is none who does good.'*

Here we see that the Bible connects corrupt thoughts about God — especially denying His very existence — with corrupt morals. And it is true that, if there is no God, no Creator who sets the rules, then we are set adrift morally. When the children of Israel forgot their Creator in the times of the Judges, when they had no one leading them in being faithful to God, *'... every man did that which was right in his own eyes'* (Judges 21:25), and chaos reigned.

We see the same thing happening today. Countries where the people once honoured God, recognising that *'God was in Christ reconciling the world to Himself'* (2 Cor. 5:19), experienced unprecedented security and prosperity. Those same countries today are crumbling as people turn their backs on God. *'Righteousness lifts up a nation, but sin is a shame to any people'* (Prov. 14:34).

As nations turn their backs on God, living as if He does not exist, sin abounds — political corruption, lying, slander, public displays of debauchery, violent crime, abortion, theft, adultery, drug-taking, drunkenness, gambling and greed of all kinds. Economic woes follow as taxes increase and governments borrow money to pay for bigger and bigger police forces, jails, and social security systems to patch up the problems.

Romans chapter one reads like a commentary on today's world:

[18]For the wrath of God is revealed from Heaven against all ungodliness and unrighteousness of men, who hold the truth in unrighteousness, [19]because the thing which may be known of God is clearly revealed within them, for God revealed it to them. [20]For the unseen things of Him from the creation of the world are clearly seen, being understood by the things that are made, even His eternal power and Godhead, so they are without excuse. [21]Because, knowing God, they did not glorify Him as God, neither were they thankful. But they became vain in their imaginations, and their foolish hearts were darkened. [22]Professing to be wise, they became fools [23]and changed the glory of the incorruptible God into an image made like corruptible man, and birds, and four-footed animals, and creeping things. [24]Therefore God also gave them up to uncleanness through the lusts of their hearts, to dishonour their own bodies between themselves. [25]For they changed the truth of God into a lie, and they worshiped and served the created thing more than the Creator, who is blessed forever. Amen. [26]For this cause, God gave them up to dishonourable affections. For even their women changed the natural use into that which is against nature. [27]And likewise also the men, leaving the natural use of the woman, burned in their lust toward one another; males with males working out shamefulness, and receiving in themselves the recompense which was fitting for their error. [28]And even as they did not think fit to have God in their knowledge, God gave them over to a reprobate mind, to do the things not right, [29]being filled with all unrighteousness, fornication, wickedness, covetousness, maliciousness; being full of envy, murder, quarrels, deceit, evil habits, becoming gossips, [30]backbiters, haters of God, insolent, proud, braggarts, inventors of evil things, disobedient to parents, [31]without discernment, covenant-breakers, without natural affection, unforgiving, unmerciful; [32]who, knowing the righteous order of God, that those practising such things are worthy of death, not only do them, but have pleasure in those practising them.

Many of those in the highest positions in government and education in the once great Christian nations the Bible would call 'fools'. They claim to be wise. But by denying the very existence of God, or His relevance to them today, they have become 'fools'.

Underpinning this abandonment of faith in God is the widespread acceptance of evolutionary thinking — that everything made itself by natural processes; that God is not necessary. There is 'design', such people will admit, but no Designer is necessary. The designed thing designed itself! This thinking, where the plain-as-day evidence for God's existence (Rom. 1:19–20) is explained away, leads naturally to atheism (belief in no god) and secular humanism (man can chart his own course without God). Such thinking abounds in universities and governments today.

Some of the greatest evil seen has been perpetrated by those who have adopted an evolutionary approach to morality — Lenin, Hitler, Stalin, Mao Zedong, Pol Pot. Atheistic evolutionist Sir Arthur Keith acknowledged of Hitler:

> 'The German Führer ... consciously sought to make the practice of Germany conform to the theory of evolution.'[1]

Many millions have suffered terribly and lost their lives because of this atheistic way of thinking. Atheism kills, because without God there are no rules — anything goes! Atheists are at the forefront of efforts to legitimize abortion, euthanasia, drug-taking, prostitution, pornography and promiscuity. All these things cause misery, suffering and death. Atheism is the philosophy of death.

Now atheists love to point to atrocities committed by supposed 'Christians' — the Crusades and Northern Ireland are favourites. If the people committing these terrible deeds were indeed Christians, they were/are being **inconsistent** with their own standard of morality (e.g., *'do not murder'*, *'love your enemies'*). However, Stalin, for example, was being **consistent** with

---

[1] Keith, A., 1947. *Evolution and Ethics,* Putman, New York, p. 230.

his, because, being an atheist (after reading Darwin), he had no objective basis for any standard of morality. Keith (above) admitted that Hitler was also consistent with his evolutionary philosophy.

Christianity says *'God is love'*, *'love one another'* and *'love your enemies'*. Such love is self-sacrificing. Consequently, Christians have been at the forefront in helping the sick, looking after the orphaned and the aged, feeding the hungry, educating the poor, and opposing exploitation through such things as child labour and slavery.

Atheism, with its evolutionary rationale, says 'love' is nothing more than self-interest in increasing the chances of our genes surviving in our offspring or our close relatives. In the 'struggle for survival of the fittest', where is the basis for compassion? Hitler's death camps grew out of his desire for the 'Aryan race' to win the battle for 'the preservation of favoured races in the struggle for life'.[2]

However, not only is atheism destructive, it is logically flawed at its very roots because there must be a Creator, as we shall see.

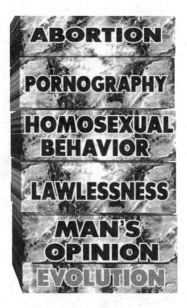

A Supreme Creator who gave Law provides a solid foundation for morality and meaning whereas evolution-made-everything provides no such basis.

---

[2] The subtitle of Darwin's *On the Origin of Species*.

Biblical evidence for the existence of a divine author

The Bible, as well as proclaiming the existence of God, also bears witness that God exists, because only divine inspiration can explain the existence of this most remarkable of books. The characteristics that point to divine authorship are:[3-5]

The Bible's amazing unity. Despite being penned by more than 40 authors from over 19 different walks of life over some 1,600 years, the Bible is a consistent revelation from the beginning to the end. Indeed the first and last books of the Bible, Genesis and Revelation, dovetail so perfectly — telling of 'Paradise Lost' and 'Paradise Regained' respectively — that they speak powerfully of their divine authorship (compare for example Gen. 1–3 and Rev. 21–22).

The Bible's amazing preservation. In spite of political and religious persecution, the Bible remains. The Roman Emperor Diocletian, following an edict in AD 303, thought he had destroyed every hated Bible. He erected a column over the ashes of a burnt Bible to celebrate his victory. Twenty-five years later, the new emperor, Constantine, commissioned the production of 50 Bibles at the expense of the government! In the eighteenth century, the noted French infidel, Voltaire, forecast that within a century there would be no Bibles left on the earth. Ironically, 50 years after he died, the Geneva Bible Society used his old printing press and his house to produce stacks of Bibles. The Bible is today available in far more languages than any other book.

The Bible's historical accuracy. Nelson Glueck, famous Jewish archaeologist, spoke of what he called 'the almost incredibly accurate historical memory of the Bible, and particularly so when it is fortified by archaeological fact'.[6] William F. Albright, widely recognised as

---

[3] The basic concept for this section comes from Willmington, H.L., 1981. *Willmington's Guide to the Bible,* Tyndale House Publishers, Wheaton, IL, USA., pp. 810–824.

[4] Geisler, N.L. and Nix, W.E., 1986. *A General Introduction to the Bible,* Moody Press, Chicago.

[5] McDowell, J., 1972. *Evidence that Demands a Verdict,* Vol. 1, Campus Crusade for Christ, San Bernadino, CA.

[6] Cited in Ref. 5, p. 68.

one of the great archaeologists, stated:
> 'The excessive scepticism shown toward the Bible by important historical schools of the eighteenth and nineteenth centuries, certain phases of which still appear periodically, has been progressively discredited. Discovery after discovery has established the accuracy of innumerable details, and has brought increased recognition to the value of the Bible as a source of history.'[6]

Sir William Ramsay, regarded as one of the greatest archaeologists ever, trained in mid-nineteenth century German historical scepticism and so did not believe that the New Testament documents were historically reliable. However, his archaeological investigations drove him to see that his scepticism was unwarranted. He had a profound change of attitude. Speaking of Luke, the writer of the *Gospel of Luke* and the *Acts of the Apostles,* Ramsay said, 'Luke is a historian of the first rank ... he should be placed along with the greatest of historians.'[7]

At many specific points archaeology confirms the Bible's accuracy.[8] There are many particulars where sceptics have questioned the Bible's accuracy, usually on the basis of there being no independent evidence (the fallacy of arguing from silence), only to find that further archaeological discoveries have unearthed evidence for the biblical account.[5]

The Bible's scientific accuracy. Some examples: that the earth is round (Isa. 40:22); the earth is suspended in space without support (Job 26:7); the stars are countless[9] (Gen. 15:5); the hydrologic cycle;[10] sea currents;[10] living things reproduce after their kind;[11] many insights into health, hygiene,[12] diet,[13] physiology (such as the importance of

---

[7] Ramsay, W., 1953. *Bearing of Recent Discoveries on the Trustworthiness of the New Testament,* Baker Books, Grand Rapids, Michigan, p. 222.

[8] For comprehensive information on the Bible and archaeology, see <http://www.christiananswers.net>

[9] People of old thought that the stars could be counted — there were about 1200 visible stars. Ptolemy (AD 150) dogmatically stated that the number of stars was exactly 1056. See Gitt, W., 1997. Counting the stars. *Creation* **19**(2):10–13.

[10] Sarfati, J., 1997. The wonders of water. *Creation* **20**(1):44–46.

[11] Batten, D., 1996. Dogs breeding dogs? That's not evolution. *Creation* **18**(2):20–23.

[12] Wise, D.A., 1995. Modern medicine? It's not so modern! *Creation* **17**(1):46–49.

[13] Emerson, P., 1996. Eating out in Eden. *Creation* **18**(2):10–13.

blood, e.g. Lev. 17:11); the first and second laws of thermodynamics (e.g. Isa. 51:6), and many other things.[14]

The Bible's prophetic accuracy. The Bible states that the accurate foretelling of events is the province of God. God said:

I have foretold the former things from the beginning; and they went out of My mouth; and I made them hear; I acted suddenly; and they came about. ... I declared it to you from the beginning. Before it happened I revealed it to you; lest you should say, 'My idol has done them, and my graven image, and my molten image, has commanded them.' (Isa 48:3,5)

One will search in vain for one line of accurate prophecy in other religious books, but the Bible contains many specific prophecies. McDowell[6] documents 61 prophecies regarding Jesus alone. Many of these, such as His place, time, and manner of birth, betrayal, manner of death, burial, etc., were beyond His control. McDowell also thoroughly documents 12 detailed, specific prophecies regarding Tyre, Sidon, Samaria, Gaza and Ashkelon, Moab and Ammon, Petra and Edom, Thebes and Memphis, Nineveh, Babylon, Chorazin- Bethsaida Capernaum, Jerusalem and Palestine. He shows how these prophecies were not 'post-dictions' (that is, written after the event).

The probability of all these things coming to pass by chance is effectively zero. Only the wilfully ignorant (2 Peter 3:5) could deny this evidence that God must have inspired these prophecies.

The Bible's civilizing influence. The Bible's message elevated the blood-drinking 'barbarians' of the British Isles to decency. It is the basis of English common law, the American Bill of Rights and the constitutions of great democracies such as the United Kingdom, the United States, Canada, Australia and New Zealand.

The Bible has inspired the noblest of literature — from Shakespeare, Milton, Pope, Scott, Coleridge and Kipling, to name a few — and the art of such as Leonardo da Vinci, Michelangelo, Raphael and Rembrandt. The Bible has inspired the exquisite music of Bach, Handel, Haydn, Mendelssohn and Brahms. Indeed, the decline in acceptance of the biblical world-view in the West has been paralleled

---

[14] See Morris, H.M., 1984. *The Biblical Basis of Modern Science,* Baker Book House, Grand Rapids, Michigan.

by a decline in the beauty of art.[15]

Today the message of the Bible still transforms. Animistic tribal groups in the Philippines are today still being delivered from fear, and former cannibals in Papua New Guinea and Fiji now live in peace, all because of the Gospel.

The Bible's absolute honesty. Someone has said 'The Bible is not a book that man could write if he would, or would write if he could'. The Bible does not honour man, but God. The people in the Bible have feet of clay; they are shown 'warts and all'. Against the backdrop of their sinfulness and unfaithfulness, God's holiness and faithfulness shine through.

The Gospel has transformed the lives of animistic people.

Even the heroes of the faith (Heb. 11) have their failures recorded, including Noah (Gen. 9:20–24), Moses (Num. 20:7–12), David (2 Sam. 11), Elijah (1 Kings 19), and Peter (Matt. 26:74). On the other hand, the enemies of God's people are often praised — for example, Artaxerxes (Neh. 2), Darius the Mede (Dan. 6), and Julius (Acts 27:1–3). These are clear indications that the Bible was not written from a human perspective.

The Bible's life-transforming message. In San Francisco, a man once challenged Dr Harry Ironside to a debate on 'Agnosticism[16] versus Christianity'. Dr Ironside agreed, on one condition: that the agnostic first provide evidence that agnosticism was beneficial enough to defend. Dr Ironside challenged the agnostic to bring one man who had been a 'down-and-outer' (a drunkard, criminal, or such) and one woman who had been trapped in a degraded life (such as prostitution), and show that both of these people had been rescued from their lives of degradation though embracing the philosophy of agnosticism. Dr Ironside undertook to bring 100 men and women to the debate who

---

[15] Schaeffer, F., 1968. *Escape from Reason,* Inter-Varsity Press, London.

[16] Agnosticism is another form of unbelief that denies the truth of God's Word by claiming that we cannot know if God exists. It is in practice little different from atheism.

had been gloriously rescued through believing the Gospel the agnostic ridiculed. The sceptic withdrew his challenge to debate Dr Ironside.

The message of the Bible mends lives broken by sin, which separates us from our holy Creator. In contrast, agnosticism and atheism, like all anti-God philosophies, destroy.

Other evidence for the Creator-God of the Bible[17]

The universal tendency of things to rundown and to fall apart shows that the universe had to be 'wound up' at the beginning. It is not eternal. This is totally consistent with *'In the beginning God created the heaven and the earth.'* (Gen. 1:1).

The changes we see in living things are not the sorts of changes that suggest that the living things themselves came into being by any natural, evolutionary, process. Evolution from molecules to man needs some way of creating new complex genetic programs, or information. Mutations and natural selection lead to loss of information.

The fossils do not show the expected transitions from one basic kind of organism to another. This is powerful evidence against the belief that living things made themselves over eons of time.

Evidence that the universe is relatively 'young' also contradicts the belief that everything made itself over billions of years. Because the events are so improbable, lots of time is thought to help the cause of the materialists.

The traditions of hundreds of indigenous peoples from around the world — stories of a global Flood, for example — corroborate the Bible's account of history, as does linguistic and biological evidence for the closeness of all human 'races'.

The explosion in knowledge of the intricate workings of cells and organs has shown that such things as the blood clotting system could not have arisen by a series of accidental changes. The instructions, or information, for specifying the complex organisation of living things is not in the molecules themselves (as it is with a crystal), but is imposed from outside. All this demands an intelligent Creator who vastly exceeds our intelligence.

---

[17] For more details on these evidences, see the Appendix to this chapter.

The myth of atheism and science

Many today think that science is anti-God. Atheists encourage this view by claiming that their way of thinking is 'scientific'. In claiming this, they are merely re-defining science to exclude God. In fact, science began to flourish only when the biblical view of creation took root in Europe as the Reformation spread its influence. The presuppositions that enabled a scientific approach to investigating the world — that the created universe is real, consistent, understandable, and possible to investigate, for example — came from the Bible. Even non-Christian historians of science such as Loren Eiseley have acknowledged this.[18] Consequently, almost every branch of science was either founded, co-founded, or dramatically advanced, by scientists who believed in the Bible's account of Creation and the Flood.[19,20] And there are many scientists today who believe the Bible.[21]

Is it science?

Science has given us many wonderful things: men on the moon, cheap food, modern medicine, electricity, computers, and so on. All these achievements involve doing experiments in the present, making inferences from these results and doing more experiments to test those ideas. Here, the inferences, or conclusions, are closely related to the experiments and there is often little room for speculation. This type of science is called process, or operational, science, and has given us many valuable advances in knowledge that have benefited mankind.

However, there is another type of science that deals with the past, which can be called historical, or origins, science. When it comes to working out what happened in the past, science is limited because we cannot do experiments directly on past events, and history cannot be repeated. In origins science, observations made in the present are used to make inferences about the past. The experiments that can be

[18] Eiseley, L., 1969. *Darwin's Century: Evolution and the Man who Discovered it.* Doubleday, New York, p. 62.

[19] Morris, H.M., 1982. *Men of Science, Men of God,* Master Books, Colorado Springs, USA.

[20] Lamont, A., 1995. *21 Great Scientists Who Believed the Bible,* Answers in Genesis, Brisbane, Australia.

[21] Ashton, J., 1999. *In Six Days: Why 50 Scientists Choose to Believe in Creation,* New Holland Publishers, Sydney, Australia.

done in the present that relate to the past are often quite limited, so the inferences require a deal of guesswork. The further in the past the event being studied, the longer the chain of inferences involved, the more guesswork, and the more room there is for non-scientific factors to influence the conclusions — factors such as the religious belief (or unbelief) of the scientist. So, what may be presented as 'science' regarding the past may be little more than the scientist's own personal world-view. The conflicts between 'science' and 'religion' occur in this historical science, not in operational science. Unfortunately, the respect earned by the successes of operational science confounds many into thinking that the conjectural claims arising from origins science carry the same authority.

When it comes to historical science, it is not so much the evidence in the present that is debated, but the inferences about the past. Scientists who believe the record in the Bible, which claims to be the Word of God,[22] will come to different conclusions from those who ignore the Bible. Wilful denial of God's Word (2 Peter 3:3–7) lies at the root of many disagreements over 'historical science'.

OPERATIONAL SCIENCE | HISTORICAL SCIENCE

---

[22] Psalm 78:5, 2 Timothy 3:14–17, 2 Peter 1:19–21. God, who inspired the Bible, has always existed, is perfect and never lies (Titus 1:2). See also Psalm 119 to understand the importance of God's Word.

Who created God?[23]

The sceptic asks of Christians, 'If God created the universe, then who created God?' But God *by definition* is the *uncreated* creator of the universe, so the question 'Who created God?' is illogical, just like 'To whom is the bachelor married?'.

So a more sophisticated questioner might ask, 'If the universe needs a cause, then why doesn't God need a cause? And if God doesn't need a cause, why should the universe need a cause?' The following reasoning stands up to scrutiny:

- Everything **which has a beginning** has a cause.[24]
- The universe has a beginning.
- Therefore the universe has a cause.

It is important to stress the words in **bold type**. The universe requires a cause because it had a beginning, as will be shown below. God, unlike the universe, had no beginning, so does not need a cause. In addition, Einstein's general relativity, which has much experimental support, shows that time is linked to matter and space. So time itself would have begun along with matter and space at the beginning of the universe. Since God, by definition, is the creator of the whole universe, He is the creator of time. Therefore He is not limited by the time dimension He created, so He has no beginning in time. Therefore He does not have, or need to have, a cause.

In contrast, there is good evidence that the universe had a beginning. This can be shown from the *Laws of Thermodynamics,* the most fundamental laws of the physical sciences.

1st Law: The **total** amount of mass-energy in the universe is **constant**.

2nd Law: The amount of energy in the universe **available for work** is running down, or *entropy*[25] is increasing to a maximum.

If the total amount of mass-energy is limited, and the amount of usable energy is decreasing, then the universe cannot have existed forever, otherwise it would *already* have exhausted all usable energy

---

[23] This section is based upon Sarfati, J., 1998. If God created the universe, then who created God? *CEN Technical Journal* **12**(1):20–22.

[24] Actually, the word 'cause' has several different meanings in philosophy. But here the word refers to the *efficient cause*, the chief agent causing something to be made.

[25] Entropy is a measure of disorder, or of the decrease in usable energy.

and reached what is known as 'heat death'. For example, all radio-active atoms would have decayed, every part of the universe would be the same temperature, and no further work would be possible. So the best solution is that the universe must have been created with a lot of

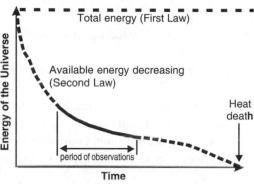

The amount of available energy in the universe is always decreasing, clear evidence that it had a beginning.

usable energy, and is now running down.[26]

Now, what if the questioner accepts that the universe had a beginning, but not that it needs a cause? But it is self-evident that things that begin have a cause — no one really denies it in their heart. All science, history and law enforcement would collapse if this law of cause and effect were denied.[27] Also, the universe cannot be self-caused — nothing can create itself, because it would need to exist before it came into existence, a logical absurdity.

---

[26] Oscillating (yoyo) universe ideas were popularized by atheists like the late Carl Sagan and Isaac Asimov, solely to avoid the notion of a beginning, with its implications of a Creator. But the laws of thermodynamics undercut that argument — as each one of the hypothetical cycles would exhaust more and more usable energy. This means every cycle would be larger and longer than the previous one, so looking back in time there would be smaller and smaller cycles. So the multicycle model could have an infinite future, but can only have a finite past. Also, there is far too little mass to stop expansion and allow cycling in the first place, and no known mechanism would allow a bounce back after a hypothetical 'big crunch'.

[27] Some physicists assert that quantum mechanics violates this cause/effect principle and can produce something from nothing, but this is not so. Theories that the universe is a quantum fluctuation must presuppose that there was *something* to fluctuate — their 'quantum vacuum' is a lot of matter-antimatter potential — not 'nothing'. Also, if there is no cause, there is no explanation why *this particular universe* appeared at a *particular time*, nor why it was a universe and not, say, a banana or a cat which appeared. This universe can't have any properties to explain its preferential coming into existence, because it would not have *any* properties until it actually came into existence.

In summary

- The universe (including time itself) can be shown to have had a beginning.
- It is unreasonable to believe something could begin to exist without a cause.
- The universe therefore requires a cause, just as Genesis 1:1 and Romans 1:20 teach.
- God, as creator of time, is outside of time. Therefore, He had no beginning in time, has always existed, and so does not need a cause.[28,29]

Whichever way you look at it — the evidence from the Bible, the incredibly complex, organised information in living things, or the origin of the universe — belief in an all-powerful, all-knowing Creator God, as revealed in the Bible, not only makes sense, but is the only viable explanation.

The Christian knows God!

To one who is a genuine Christian, there is no doubt about God's existence. The Bible says,

For as many as are led by the *Spirit of God, they are the sons of God. For you have not received the spirit of bondage again to fear, but you have received the Spirit of adoption by which we cry, Abba, Father! The Spirit Himself bears witness with our spirit that we are the children of God.* (Rom. 8:14–16)

The Bible here says that Christians have a personal relationship with God. This is the testimony of those who have realised their sinfulness in the sight of Almighty God and the dire consequences of their sin, have repented of their sin, and have accepted the forgiveness of God made possible through Jesus' death and resurrection. All such genuine Christians have received the Holy Spirit of God and so have assurance that they are 'children of God'. They can indeed know that they have eternal life (1 John 5:13).

---

[28] See Craig, William L., 1984. *Apologetics: An Introduction,* Moody, Chicago, and *The Existence of God and the Beginning of the Universe,* at <http://www.leaderu.com/truth/>.

[29] Geisler, N.L., 1976. *Christian Apologetics,* Baker Books, Grand Rapids, Michigan. But beware of the unfortunate (and unnecessary) friendliness towards the unscriptural 'big bang' theory.

Appendix: Non-biblical evidence for the Creator God of the Bible

1. Natural law

There is a universal tendency for all systems of matter/energy to run down.[30] Available energy is dissipated and order is lost. Without either a programmed mechanism or intelligent action, even open systems[31] will tend from *order to disorder*, from information to non-information, and towards less availability of energy. This is the reason why heat flows from hot to cold, and why the sun's energy will not make a dead stick grow (as opposed to a green plant, which contains specific, pre-programmed machinery to direct the energy to create a special type of order known as *specified complexity*).

Applied to the origin of the first life, this denies that such specified complexity can possibly arise *except* from *outside information impressed on to matter* (see pp. 19–20). Applied to the whole universe, which is acknowledged as winding down to 'heat death' (that is, 'cosmos to chaos'), this implies a fundamental contradiction to the 'chaos to cosmos, all by itself' essence of evolutionary philosophy.[32,33]

So, the universe had to be 'wound up' at the beginning and it could not have existed eternally. This requires some agent outside the universe to wind it up — just as a clock cannot wind itself!

2. Living things

Observed changes in living things head in the wrong direction to support evolution from protozoan to man (macro-evolution).

Selection from the genetic information already present in a population (for example, DDT resistance in mosquitoes) causes a net *loss* of genetic information in that population. A DDT-resistant mosquito is adapted to an environment where DDT is present, but the population has lost genes present in the mosquitoes that were not

---

[30] This is an aspect of the Second Law of Thermodynamics — see pp. 12–13.
[31] Those able to exchange energy/matter with their surroundings.
[32] Thaxton, C.B., Bradley, W.L. and Olsen, R.L., 1984. *The Mystery of Life's Origin,* Lewis and Stanley, Dallas, Texas. These experts in thermodynamics show that thermodynamics is a huge problem for the naturalistic origin of life.
[33] Wilder-Smith, A.E., 1981. *The Natural Sciences Know Nothing of Evolution,* Master Books, San Diego, CA.

resistant to DDT because they died and so did not pass on their genes. So natural selection and adaptation involve *loss* of genetic information.

From information theory and a vast number of experiments and observations, we know that mutations (copying mistakes) are incapable of causing an *increase* in information and functional complexity.[34] Instead, they cause 'noise' during the transmission of genetic information, in accordance with established scientific principles of the effect of random change on information flow, and so destroy the information.[35] Not surprisingly, several thousand human diseases are now linked to mutations.

This decrease in genetic information (from mutations, selection/ adaptation/speciation and extinction) is consistent with the concept of original created gene pools — with a large degree of initial variety — being depleted since.

Since observed 'micro' changes — such as antibiotic resistance in bacteria and insecticide resistance in insects — are informationally downhill, or at best horizontal, they cannot accumulate to give the required (up-hill) changes for 'macro' evolution, regardless of the time period.[36]

These small changes are erroneously used as 'proofs of evolution' in biology courses, yet they cannot be extrapolated to explain amebato-man evolution. Such extrapolation is like arguing that if an unprofitable business loses only a little money each year, given enough years it will make a profit. The observed changes do, however, fit a Creation/Fall model well.

3. Fossils

Although Darwin expected millions of transitional fossils to be found, none have been found, except for a mere handful of disputable ones. Evolutionist Dr Colin Patterson of the British Museum of Natural History responded as follows to a written question asking why he failed to include illustrations of transitional forms in a book he wrote on evolution:

'... I fully agree with your comments on the lack of direct

---

[34] Spetner, L., 1997. *Not by Chance! Shattering the Modern Theory of Evolution,* The Judaica Press, Inc.,Brooklyn, NY.

[35] This is similar to the noise added in the copying of an audio cassette tape. The copy is never better than the master.

[36] Lester, L.P., and Bohlin, R.G., 1989. *The Natural Limits of Biological Change,* Probe Books, Dallas, Texas.

illustration of evolutionary transitions in my book. If I knew of any, fossil or living, I would certainly have included them. You suggest that an artist should be used to visualise such transformations, but where would he get the information from? I could not, honestly, provide it, and if I were to leave it to artistic licence, would that not mislead the reader?

'I wrote the text of my book four years ago. If I were to write it now, I think the book would be rather different. Gradualism is a concept I believe in, not just because of Darwin's authority, but because my understanding of genetics seems to demand it. Yet Gould and the American Museum people are hard to contradict when they say there are no transitional fossils. As a palaeontologist myself, I am much occupied with the philosophical problems of identifying ancestral forms in the fossil record. You say that I should at least "show a photo of the fossil from which each type of organism was derived." I will lay it on the line — there is not one such fossil for which one could make a watertight argument.'[37]

Even the often-claimed transition between reptiles and birds, *Archaeopteryx,* shows no sign of the crucial scale-to-feather or leg-to-wing transition. While it is always possible to maintain faith in evolution by belief in unobservable mechanisms,[38] the evidence of such a *systematic* paucity of the anticipated evolutionary 'links' on a global scale is powerful, positive support for biblical creation, regardless of any argument about how and when fossils may have formed.

An artist's impression of Archaeopteryx

---

[37] Letter (written April 10, 1979) from Dr Colin Patterson, then Senior Palaeontologist at the British Museum of Natural History in London, to Luther D. Sunderland, as quoted in Sunderland, L.D., 1984. *Darwin's Enigma*, Master Books, San Diego, USA, p. 89. Patterson subsequently tried to play down the significance of this very clear statement.

[38] Such as 'punctuated equilibrium', or other secondary assumptions.

4. The age of things

The evidence for a 'young' earth/universe is, by definition, evidence for biblical creation, as naturalistic evolution, if it were at all possible, would require eons. There is much evidence that the universe is relatively young,[39] such as the decay of the earth's magnetic field, including rapid paleomagnetic reversals,[40] fragile organic molecules in fossils supposedly many millions of years old,[41] not enough helium in the atmosphere,[42] not enough salt in the sea,[43] carbon-14 in coal and oil supposedly millions of years old (see Chapter 4), polystrate fossils that extend through strata supposedly representing many millions of years, inter-tonguing of non-sequential geological strata,[44] small number of supernova remnants,[45] magnetic fields on 'cold' planets, and much more (see pp. 77–78).

Elapsed time extending back beyond one's own lifetime cannot be directly measured, so all arguments for either a long or a short age are necessarily indirect and must depend on acceptance of the assumptions on which they are inevitably based.

Young-earth arguments make sense of the fact that many fossils show well-preserved soft parts. This requires rapid deposition and rapid hardening of the encasing sediment for such fossils to exist. Observations of multiple geologic strata and canyons, for example, forming rapidly under catastrophic conditions in recent times, indicate that the entrenched slow-and-gradual, vast-age thinking may well be markedly in error.[46,47]

[39] Morris, J.D., 1994. *The Young Earth,* Master Books, Colorado Springs, CO.

[40] Sarfati, J., 1998. The earth's magnetic field: evidence that the earth is young. *Creation* 20(2):15–17.

[41] For example, Wieland, C., 1997. Sensational dinosaur blood report. *Creation* 19(4):42–43.

[42] Sarfati, J., 1998. Blowing old-earth beliefs away. *Creation* 20(3):19–21.

[43] Sarfati, J. 1998. Salty seas. *Creation* 21(1):16–17.

[44] That is, where there are 'missing' layers in between, according to the standard geologic column and the millions of years time-scale, suggesting that the missing layers do not represent the many millions of years claimed. See Snelling, A., 1992. The case of the missing geologic time. *Creation* 14(3):31–35.

[45] Sarfati, J., 1997. Exploding stars point to a young universe. *Creation* 19(3):46–48.

[46] *Mount St Helens: Explosive Evidence for Catastrophe in Earth's History,* Video featuring Dr Steve Austin, Creation Videos.

[47] See Chapter 4, 'What about carbon dating?'

5. Cultural-anthropological evidence

Hundreds of world-wide traditions among indigenous peoples about a global Flood, each with features in common with the biblical account, provide evidence of the reality of that account. Also widespread, but less so, are accounts of a time of language dispersal. Linguistic and biological evidence has recently revealed a hitherto unrealised genetic closeness among all the 'races' of people (see Chapter 18), consistent with a recent origin from a small population source. This denies the previously widely held belief that human races evolved their characteristic features during long periods of isolation. Molecular studies suggest that, relatively recently, one woman provided the mitochondrial DNA which gave rise to the sequences in all people alive today.[48] Such evidence may be squeezed into an evolutionary model, but it was not a direct prediction of it. However, it is directly consistent with biblical creation.

6. Design and complexity

Incredibly complex coordinated biological systems are known in which no conceivable part-coordinated, part-functioning, simpler arrangement would be other than a liability.[49] Some examples are the blood-clotting mechanism, the bacterial flagellum (used for propulsion), the photosynthetic apparatus, and the pupal transformation of caterpillars to butterflies. Examples abound in living things.

The immense complexity of the human brain, its creativity and power of abstract reasoning, with capacities vastly beyond that required for sheer survival, is perhaps the most 'obvious' evidence for intelligent creation.

At the molecular level, the organisation that characterizes living things is inherently different from, for example, a crystal arrangement. The function of a given protein, for instance, depends upon the

The highly integrated transformation of a caterpillar to a pupa to a butterfly defies evolution's (small) step-wise change as an explanation for its existence.

---

[48] Wieland, C., 1998. A shrinking date for 'Eve'. *CEN Technical Journal* **12**(1):1–3.

[49] Behe, M.J., 1996. *Darwin's Black Box,* The Free Press, New York.

assembly sequence of its constituents. The coded information required to generate these sequences is *not* intrinsic to the chemistry of the components (as it is for the structure of a crystal) but extrinsic (imposed from outside).

During reproduction, the information required to make a living organism is impressed upon material substrates to give a pre-programmed pattern, by systems of equal (or greater) complexity (in the parent organism/s) which themselves had the same requirement for their formation. Without pre-programmed machinery, no spontaneous, physico-chemical process is known to generate such information-bearing sequences — this requires the operation of outside intelligence.

The most reasonable inference from such observations is that outside intelligence was responsible for a vast original store of biological information in the form of created populations of fully functioning organisms.[49] Such intelligence vastly surpasses human intelligence — again consistent with the concept of God as revealed in the Bible.

---

[49] Gitt, W., 1997. *In the Beginning Was Information,* Christliche Literatur-Verbreitung, Bielefeld, Germany (the German edition was published in 1994).

Chapter **2**

Did God really take six days?

Are the days of creation ordinary days? Could they be long periods of time? Why six days? Does the length of the days really affect the Gospel? How can there be 'days' without the sun on the first three days? Does Genesis 2 contradict Genesis 1? How are we meant to understand the Bible?

Why is it important?

IF the days of creation are really 'geologic ages' of millions of years, then the Gospel message is undermined at its foundation because it puts death, disease, thorns and suffering before the Fall. This idea also shows an erroneous approach to Scripture — that the Word of God can be interpreted on the basis of the fallible theories of sinful people.

It is a good exercise to read Genesis chapter one and try to put aside outside influences that may cause you to have a pre-determined idea of what the word 'day' may mean. Just let the words of the passage speak to you.

Taking Genesis 1 in this way, at face value, without doubt it seems to say that God created the universe, the earth, the sun, moon and stars, plants and animals, and the first two people, within six ordinary (approximately 24 hour) days. Being really honest, one would have to admit that you could *never* get the idea of millions of years from reading this passage.

However, the majority of Christians (including many Christian leaders) in the Western world either do not insist that these days of creation were ordinary days, or they accept and teach that they must have been long periods of time — even millions or billions of years.

How does God communicate?

God communicates through language. When he made the first man Adam, he had already 'programmed' him with a language, so there could be communication. Human language consists of words used in a specific context that relates to the entire reality around us.

Thus, God can reveal things to man, and man can communicate with God, as these words have meaning and convey an understandable message. If this were not so, how could any of us communicate with each other, or with God, or God with us?

> *The entrance of Your words gives light; it gives understanding to the simple.* **(Psalm 119:130)**

Why 'long days'?

Romans 3:4a: ... *let God be true, and every man a liar.*

In *every* instance where someone has not accepted the 'days' of creation to be ordinary days, it is because they have **not** allowed the words of Scripture to speak to them in context, as the language requires for communication. They have been influenced by ideas from *outside* of Scripture. Thus they have set a precedent that could allow any word to be reinterpreted by the preconceived ideas of the person reading the words. Ultimately, this will lead to a communication breakdown, as the same words in the same context could mean different things to different people.

The Church Fathers: Most 'church fathers' accepted the days as ordinary days.[1] It is true that some of the early church fathers did not teach the 'days' of creation as ordinary days — but many of them had been influenced by Greek philosophy, which caused them to interpret the days as allegorical. They reasoned that the creation 'days' were related to God's activities, and God being timeless meant that the 'days' could not be related to human time.[2] In contrast to today's allegorizers, they could not accept that God took *as long as* six days.

---

[1] Van Bebber, M. and Taylor, P.S., 1994. *Creation and Time: A Report on the Progressive Creationist Book by Hugh Ross,* Films for Christ, Mesa, Arizona.
[2] Hasel, G.F., 1994. The 'days' of creation in Genesis 1: literal 'days' or figurative 'periods/epochs' of time? *Origins* **21**(1):5–38.

Thus the non-literal 'days' resulted from extra-biblical influences (i.e. influences *outside* the Bible), not from the words of the Bible!

This approach has affected the way people interpret Scripture to this day. As the man who started the Reformation said:

'The Days of Creation were ordinary days in length. We must understand that these days were actual days (*veros dies*), contrary to the opinion of the Holy Fathers. Whenever we observe that the opinions of the Fathers disagree with Scripture, we reverently bear with them and acknowledge them to be our elders. Nevertheless, we do not depart from the authority of Scripture for their sake.'[3]

Today's church leaders: Many church leaders today do *not* accept the creation days as ordinary Earth-rotation days. However, when their reasons are investigated, we find that influences from *outside* of Scripture (particularly belief in a billions-of-years-old universe) are the ultimate cause.

Again and again, such leaders admit that Genesis 1, taken in a straightforward way, seems to teach six ordinary days. But they then say that this cannot be, because of the age of the universe, or because of some other extra-biblical reason!

Consider the following representative quotes from Bible scholars who are considered to be conservative, yet do not accept the days of creation as ordinary days:

'From a superficial reading of Genesis 1, the impression would seem to be that the entire creative process took place in six twenty-four-hour days ... this seems to run counter to modern scientific research, which indicates that the planet Earth was created several billion years ago...'[4]

'...we have shown the possibility of God's having formed the earth

> **Genesis 1, taken in a straightforward way, seems to teach ordinary days.**

---

[3] Luther, M., as cited in Plass, E.M., 1991. *What Martin Luther Says, a Practical In-Home Anthology for the Active Christian,* Concordia Publishing House, St. Louis, Missouri, p. 1523.

[4] Archer, G.L., 1994. *A Survey of Old Testament Introduction,* Moody Press, Chicago, Illinois, pp. 196–197.

and its life in a series of creative days representing long periods. In view of the apparent age of the earth, this is not only possible — it is probable.'[5]

It is as if these theologians view 'nature', as a '67th book of the Bible', albeit with more authority than the 66 written books. Consider the words of Charles Haddon Spurgeon in 1877:

C.H. Spurgeon

'We are invited, brethren, most earnestly to go away from the old-fashioned belief of our forefathers because of the supposed discoveries of science. What is science? The method by which man tries to conceal his ignorance. It should not be so, but so it is. You are not to be dogmatical in theology, my brethren, it is wicked; but for scientific men it is the correct thing. You are never to assert anything very strongly; but scientists may boldly assert what they cannot prove, and may demand a faith far more credulous than any we possess. Forsooth, you and I are to take our Bibles and shape and mould our belief according to the ever-shifting teachings of so-called scientific men. What folly is this! Why, the march of science, falsely so called, through the world may be traced by exploded fallacies and abandoned theories. Former explorers once adored are now ridiculed; the continual wreckings of false hypotheses is a matter of universal notoriety. You may tell where the learned have encamped by the debris left behind of suppositions and theories as plentiful as broken bottles.'[6]

Those who would use historical science (as propounded by people who by-and-large ignore God's written revelation) to interpret the Bible, to teach us things about God, have things back to front. Because we are fallen, fallible creatures, we need God's written Word,

---

[5] Boice, J.M., 1982. *Genesis, An Expositional Commentary* Vol. 1, Genesis 1:1–11, Zondervan Publishing House, Grand Rapids, Michigan, p. 68.

[6] Spurgeon, C.H., 1877. *The Sword and the Trowel,* p. 197.

illuminated by the Holy Spirit, to properly understand natural history. The respected systematic theologian Berkhof said,[7]

'...Since the entrance of sin into the world, man can gather true knowledge about God from His general revelation only if he studies it in the light of Scripture, in which the elements of God's original self-revelation, which were obscured and perverted by the blight of sin, are republished, corrected, and interpreted. ... Some are inclined to speak of God's general revelation as a second source; but this is hardly correct in view of the fact that nature can come into consideration here only as interpreted in the light of Scripture.'

In other words, Christians should build their thinking on the Bible, not on 'science'.

The 'days' of Genesis one

What does the Bible tell us about the meaning of 'day' in Genesis 1? A word can have more than one meaning, depending on the context. For instance, the English word 'day' can have perhaps 14 different meanings. For example, consider the following sentence: 'Back in my father's day, it took ten days to drive across the Australian Outback during the day.' Here the first occurrence of 'day' means 'time' in a general sense. The second 'day', where a number is used, refers to an ordinary day, and the third refers to the daylight period of the 24-hour period. The point is that words can have more than one meaning, depending on the context.

Christians should base their thinking on the Bible.

To understand the meaning of 'day' in Genesis 1, we need to determine how the Hebrew word for 'day', *yom,* is used in the context of Scripture. Consider the following:

● A typical concordance will illustrate that *yom* can have a range of meanings: a period of light as contrasted to night, a 24-hour period, time, a specific point of time, or a year.

● A classical, well-respected Hebrew-English lexicon[8] (a one-way

---

[7] Berkhof, Louis, Introductory volume to *Systematic Theology,* pp. 60, 96.
[8] Brown, Driver and Briggs, 1951. *A Hebrew and English Lexicon of the Old Testament,* Clarendon Press, Oxford, p. 398.

dictionary) has seven headings and many subheadings for the meaning of *yom* — but defines the creation days of Genesis 1 as ordinary days under the heading 'day as defined by evening and morning'.

● A number, and the phrase 'evening and morning', are used for each of the six days of creation (Genesis 1:5,8,13,19,23,31).

● Outside Genesis 1, *yom* is used with a number 410 times, and each time it means an ordinary day[9] — why would Genesis 1 be the exception?[10]

● Outside Genesis 1, *yom* is used with the word 'evening' or 'morning'[11] 23 times. 'Evening' and 'morning' appear in association, but without *yom*, 38 times. All 61 times the text refers to an ordinary day — why would Genesis 1 be the exception?[12]

● In Genesis 1:5, *yom* occurs in context with the word 'night'. Outside of Genesis 1, 'night' is used with *yom* 53 times — and each time it means an ordinary day. Why would Genesis 1 be the exception? Even the usage of the word 'light' with *yom* in this passage determines the meaning as ordinary day.[13]

> **The Hebrew word for 'day', *yom*, is used in several ways in Genesis 1 that show that the days were ordinary days.**

● The plural of *yom,* which does not appear in Genesis 1, ***can be*** used to communicate a longer time period, e.g. 'in those days'.[14] Adding a number here would be nonsensical. Clearly, in Exodus 20:11 where a number is used with *days*, it unambiguously refers to six Earth-rotation days.

---

[9] Some say that Hosea 6:2 is an exception to this, because of the figurative language. However, the Hebrew idiomatic expression used, 'After two days ... in the third day ...', meaning 'in a short time', only makes sense if 'day' is understood in its normal sense. See Ref. 1, pp. 74–5, for a more details.

[10] Stambaugh, James, 1996, The days of creation: A semantic approach. *Proc. Evangelical Society's Far West Region Meeting,* The Master's Seminary, Sun Valley, California, April 26, p.12.

[11] The Jews start their day in the evening (sundown followed by night) — obviously based on the fact that Genesis begins the day with the 'evening.'

[12] Stambaugh, Ref. 10, p. 15.

[13] Stambaugh, Ref. 10, p. 72.

[14] Stambaugh, Ref. 10, pp. 72–73.

● There are words in biblical Hebrew (such as *olam* or *qedem*) that are very suitable for communicating long periods of time, or indefinite time, but ***none*** of these words are used in Genesis 1.[15] Alternatively, the days or years could have been compared with grains of sand if long periods were meant.

● Dr James Barr (Regius Professor of Hebrew, at Oxford University), who himself does not believe Genesis is true history, nonetheless admitted as far as the language of Genesis 1 is concerned that:

'… so far as I know, there is no professor of Hebrew or Old Testament at any world-class university who does not believe that the writer(s) of Gen. 1 11 intended to convey to their readers the ideas that (a) creation took place in a series of six days which were the same as the days of 24 hours we now experience (b) the figures contained in the Genesis genealogies provided by simple addition a chronology from the beginning of the world up to later stages in the biblical story (c) Noah's Flood was understood to be world-wide and extinguish all human and animal life except for those in the ark.'[16]

Martin Luther

In like manner, nineteenth century liberal Professor Marcus Dods, New College, Edinburgh, said:

'… if, for example, the word "day" in these chapters does not mean a period of twenty-four hours, the interpretation of Scripture is hopeless.'[17]

[15] Stambaugh, Ref. 10, pp. 73–74, Grigg, Russell, 1996. How long were the days of Genesis 1? *Creation* **19**(1):23–25.

[16] Barr, James, 1984, Letter to David C.C. Watson, April 23.

[17] Dods, M., 1888. *Expositor's Bible,* T & T Clark, Edinburgh, p. 4., as cited by Kelly, D.F., 1997. *Creation and Change,* Christian Focus Publications, Fearn, U.K., p. 112.

CONCLUSION: If we are prepared to let the words of the language speak to us in accord with the context and normal definitions, without being influenced by outside ideas, then the word for 'day' in Genesis 1 — which is qualified by a number, the phrase *'evening and morning'*, and for day one the words *'light and darkness'* — **obviously** means an ordinary day (about 24 hours).

In Martin Luther's day, some of the church fathers were saying that God created everything in only one day, or in an instant. Martin Luther wrote:

'When Moses writes that God created Heaven and Earth and whatever is in them in six days, then let this period continue to have been six days, and do not venture to devise any comment according to which six days were one day. But, if you cannot understand how this could have been done in six days, then grant the Holy Spirit the honor of being more learned than you are. For you are to deal with Scripture in such a way that you bear in mind that God Himself says what is written. But since God is speaking, it is not fitting for you wantonly to turn His Word in the direction you wish to go.'[18]

John Calvin

Similarly, John Calvin stated: '...albeit the duration of the world, now declining to its ultimate end, has not yet attained six thousand years... God's work was completed not in a moment but in six days.'[19]

Luther and Calvin were the backbone of the Protestant Reformation that called the Church back to Scripture — *Sola Scriptura* (Scripture alone). Both of these men were adamant that Genesis 1 taught six ordinary days of creation — only thousands of years ago.

---

[18] Plass, Ref. 3, p. 1523.
[19] McNeil, J.T. (ed.), 1960. *Calvin: Institutes of the Christian Religion 1,* The Westminster Press, pp. 160–161, 182.

Why six days?

Exodus 31:12 says that God commanded Moses to say to the Children of Israel:

¹⁵Six days may work be done, but on the seventh is the sabbath of rest, holy to the LORD. Whoever does any work in the Sabbath day, he shall surely be put to death. ¹⁶Therefore the sons of Israel shall keep the Sabbath, to observe the Sabbath throughout their generations, for an everlasting covenant. ¹⁷It is a sign between Me and the sons of Israel forever. For in six days the LORD made the heavens and the earth, and on the seventh day He rested, and was refreshed. (Ex. 31:15–17)

Then God gave Moses two tablets of stone upon which were written the commandments of God, written by the finger of God (Ex. 31:18).

Because God is infinite in power, and wisdom, there's no doubt he could have created the universe and its contents in no time at all, or six seconds, or six minutes, or six hours — after all, *with God nothing shall be impossible* (Luke 1:37).

However, the question to ask is, 'Why did God take so long? Why as long as six days?' The answer is also given in Exodus 20:11, and that answer is the basis of the fourth commandment:

For in six days the LORD made the heavens and the earth, the sea, and all that is in them, and rested the seventh day. Therefore the LORD blessed the Sabbath day, and sanctified it.

The seven-day week has no basis outside of Scripture. In this Old Testament passage, God commands His people, Israel, to work for six days and rest for one — that is why He deliberately took as long as six days to create everything. He set the example for man. Our week is patterned after this principle. Now if He created everything in six thousand, or six million years, followed by a rest of one thousand or one million years, then we would have a very interesting week indeed!

Some say that Exodus 20:11 is only an analogy in the sense that man is to work and rest — not that it was to mean six literal ordinary days followed by one literal ordinary day. However, Bible scholars have shown that this commandment 'does not use analogy or archetypal thinking but that its emphasis is "stated in terms of the imitation of God or a divine precedent that is to be followed"'.[20] In other words, it was to be six literal days of work, followed by one literal day of rest, just as God worked for six literal days and rested for one.

Some have argued that *'the heavens and the earth'* is just Earth and perhaps the solar system, not the whole universe. However, this verse clearly says that God made **everything** in six days — six consecutive ordinary days, just like the commandment in the previous verse to work for six consecutive, ordinary days.

The phrase 'heaven(s) and earth' in Scripture is an example of a figure of speech called a *merism*, where two opposites are combined into an all-encompassing single concept, in this case the totality of creation. A linguistic analysis of the words 'heaven(s) and earth' in Scripture shows that they refer to the totality of all creation (the Hebrews did not have a word for 'universe'). For example, in Genesis 14:19 God is called *'Creator of heaven and earth.'* In Jeremiah 23:24 God speaks of himself as filling *'heaven and earth'*. See also Gen. 14:22, 2 Kings 19:15, 2 Chron. 2:12, Ps. 115:15, 121:2, 124.8, 134.3, 146.6, Is. 37:16.

Thus there is no scriptural warrant for restricting Ex. 20:11 to the earth and its atmosphere, or the solar system alone. So Ex. 20:11 does show that the whole universe was created in six ordinary days.

Implication

As the days of creation are ordinary days in length, then by adding up the years in Scripture (assuming no gaps in the genealogies[21]) the age of the universe is only about six thousand years.[22]

---

[20] Hasel, Ref. 2, p. 29

[21] Whitcomb, J.C. and Morris, H.M., 1961. *The Genesis Flood,* Presbyterian and Reformed Publ. Co., Phillipsburg, New Jersey. Appendix II, p. 481–483. They allow for the possibility of gaps in the genealogies because the word 'begat' can skip generations. However, they point out that even allowing for gaps would give a maximum age of around 10,000 years.

[22] Pierce, L., 1998. The forgotten archbishop. *Creation* **20**(2):42–43. Ussher carried out a very scholarly work in adding up all the years in Scripture to obtain a date of creation of 4004 BC. Ussher has been mocked for stating that

Objections to literal days in Genesis 1

Objection 1: 'Science' has shown the earth and universe are billions of years old, therefore the 'days' of creation **must** be long periods (or indefinite periods) of time.

Answer:

a) The age of the earth as determined by man's fallible methods is based on unproved assumptions, so it is not proven that the earth is billions of years old.[23-29]

b) This unproved age is being used to force an interpretation on the language of the Bible. Thus, man's fallible theories are allowed to interpret the Bible. This ultimately undermines the use of language to communicate.

c) Evolutionary scientists claim the fossil layers over the earth's surface date back hundreds of millions of years. As soon as one allows millions of years for the fossil layers — then one has accepted death, bloodshed, disease, thorns and suffering before Adam's sin.

---

creation occurred on October 23rd — he obtained this date by working backwards using the Jewish civil year and accounting for how the year and month etc., were derived over the years. Thus he didn't just pull this date out of the air, but gave a scholarly mathematical basis for it. This is not to say this is the correct date, as there are assumptions involved, but the point is his work is not to be scoffed at. Ussher did *not* specify the hour of the day for creation as some sceptics assert. Young's *Analytical Concordance*, under 'creation', lists many other authorities, including extra-biblical ones, who all give a date for creation of less than 10,000 years ago.

[23] Morris, H.M. and Morris, J.D., 1989. *Science, Scripture, and the Young Earth,* Institute for Creation Research, El Cajon, California. pp. 39–44.

[24] Morris, J.D., 1996. *The Young Earth,* Master Books, Green Forest, Arkansas, pp. 51–67.

[25] Austin, S.A., 1994. *Grand Canyon: Monument to Catastrophe*, Institute for Creation Research., Santee, California. pp. 111–131.

[26] Humphreys, D.R., 1996. *Starlight and Time*, Master Books, Green Forest, Arkansas. Appendix C. 'Progress Towards a Young-Earth Relativistic Cosmology' *Proc. 3rd ICC,* Pittsburg, PA., pp. 83–133.

[27] Wieland, C., 1993. Creation in the physics lab (interview with Dr Russell Humphreys). *Creation* **15**(3):20–23.

[28] Taylor, I.T., 1984. *In the Minds of Men*, TFE Publ., Toronto, pp. 295–322.

[29] See also Chapter 4, 'What about carbon dating?' and Chapter 1, pp. 11–12.

The Bible makes it clear[30–35] that death, bloodshed, disease, thorns and suffering are a consequence of sin.[36] In Genesis 1:29–30, God gave Adam and Eve and the animals plants to eat (this is reading Genesis and taking it at face value, as literal history, as Jesus did in Matt. 19:3–6). In fact, there is a theological distinction made between animals and plants. Human beings and higher animals are described in Genesis 1 as having a *'nephesh'*, or life principle. (This is true of at least the vertebrate land animals as well as the birds and fish: Gen. 1:20,24.) Plants do not have this *'nephesh'*— they are not 'alive' in the same sense animals are. They were given for food.

Man was permitted to eat meat only after the Flood (Gen. 9:3) — this also makes it obvious that the statements in Genesis 1:29–30 were meant to inform us that man and the animals were vegetarian to start with. Also in Genesis 9:2 we are told of a change God made in the way animals react to man.

God warned Adam in Genesis 2:17, that if he ate of the *'tree of the knowledge of good and evil'*, he would *'die'*. The Hebrew grammar actually means, *'dying, you will die'*. In other words, it would be the commencement of a process of physical dying. It also clearly involved spiritual death (separation from God).

After Adam disobeyed God, the Lord clothed Adam and Eve with *'coats of skins'* (Gen. 3:21).[37] To do this He must have killed and shed

---

[30] Ham, K., 1987. *The Lie: Evolution,* Master Books, Green Forest, Arkansas, Introduction, pp. xiii–xiv.

[31] Ham, K., 1996. The necessity for believing in six literal days. *Creation* **18**(1):38–41.

[32] Ham, K., 1996. The wrong way round! *Creation* **18**(3):38–41.

[33] Ham, K., 1997. Fathers, promises and Vegemite. *Creation* **19**(1):14–17.

[34] Ham, K., 1997. The narrow road. *Creation* **19**(2):47–49.

[35] Ham, K., 1997. Millions of years and the 'doctrine of Balaam'. *Creation* **19**(3):15–17.

[36] Gill, John, 1760. *A Body of Doctrinal and Practical Divinity,* Republished by Primitive Baptist Library, 1980, p. 191. This is not just a new idea from modern scholars. In 1760, John Gill in his commentaries insisted there was no death, bloodshed, disease or suffering before sin.

[37] All Eve's progeny, except the God-man Jesus Christ, were born with original sin (Rom. 5:12,18–19), so Eve could not have conceived when she was sinless. So the Fall must have occurred fairly quickly, before Eve had conceived any children (they were told to *'be fruitful and multiply'*).

the blood of at least one animal. The reason for this can be summed up by Hebrews 9:22:

And almost all things are by the law purged with blood; and without shedding of blood is no remission.

God requires the shedding of blood for the remission of sins. What happened in the garden was a picture of what was to come in Jesus Christ, who shed His blood on the cross as *the Lamb of God, who takes away the sin of the world* (John 1:29).

Now if the garden were sitting on a fossil record of dead things millions of years old, then there was the shedding of blood before sin.

This would destroy the foundation of the atonement. The Bible is clear: the sin of Adam brought death and suffering into the world. As Romans 8:19–22 tells us, the whole of creation *'groans'* because of the effects of the Fall of Adam, and will be liberated *'from the bondage of corruption into the glorious liberty of the children of God'* (verse 21). Also, bear in mind that thorns came into existence after the Curse. Because there are thorns in the fossil record, it had to be formed after Adam and Eve sinned.

The pronouncement of the death penalty on Adam was both a curse and a blessing. A curse because death is horrible and continually reminds us of the ugliness of sin; a blessing because the consequences of sin — separation from fellowship with God — need not be eternal. Death stopped Adam and his descendants from living in a state of sin, with all its consequences, forever. And because death was the just penalty for sin, Jesus Christ suffered physical death, shedding His blood, to release Adam's descendants from the consequences of sin. The Apostle Paul discusses this in depth in Romans 5 and 1 Corinthians 15.

Revelation chapters 21 and 22 make it clear that there will be a *'new heaven and a new earth'* one day where there will be *'no more death'* and *'no more curse'* — just like before sin changed everything. If there are to be animals as part of the new earth, obviously they will not be dying or eating each other, or eating the redeemed people!

Thus, adding the supposed millions of years to Scripture destroys the foundations of the message of the cross.

Objection 2: According to Genesis 1, the sun was not created until day four. How could there be day and night (ordinary days) without the sun for the first three days?

Answer:

a) Again, it is important for us to let the language of God's Word speak to us. If we come to Genesis 1 without any outside influences, as has been shown, each of the six days of creation appears with the Hebrew word *yom* qualified by a number, and the phrase *'evening and morning'*. The first three days are written the **same** way as the next three. So if we let the language speak to us — all six days were ordinary Earth days.

b) The sun is not needed for day and night! What is needed is light and a rotating Earth. On the first day of creation, God made light (Gen. 1:3). The phrase *'evening and morning'* certainly implies a rotating Earth. Thus if we have light from one direction, and a spinning Earth, there can be day and night.

Where did the light come from? We are not told,[38] but Genesis 1:3 certainly indicates it was a created light to provide day and night until God made the sun on day four to rule the day He had made. Revelation 21:23 tells us that one day the sun will not be needed, as the glory of God will light the heavenly city.

Perhaps one reason God did it this way was to illustrate that the sun did not have the priority in the creation that people have tended to give it. The sun did not give birth to the earth as evolutionary theories postulate; the sun was God's created tool to rule the day that God had made (Gen. 1:16).

Down through the ages people, such as the Egyptians, have worshipped the sun. God warned the Israelites in Deuteronomy 4:19 not to worship the sun like the pagan cultures around them did. They were commanded to worship the God who made the sun — not the sun that was *made* by God.

Evolutionary theories (the 'big bang' hypothesis for instance) state that the sun came before the earth, and that the sun's energy on the earth eventually gave rise to life. Just as in pagan beliefs, the sun is, in a sense, given credit for the wonder of creation.

It is interesting to contrast the speculations of modern cosmology with the writings of the early church father, Theophilus:

'On the fourth day the luminaries came into existence. Since God has foreknowledge, he understood the nonsense of the foolish philosophers who were going to say that the things produced on earth came from the stars, so that they might set God aside. In order therefore that the truth might be demonstrated, plants and seeds came into existence before stars. For what comes into existence later cannot cause what is prior to it.'[39]

---

[38] Some people ask why God did not tell us the source of this light. However, if God told us everything, we would have so many books we would not have time to read them. God has given us all the information we need to come to the right conclusions about the things that really matter.

[39] Lavallee, L., 1986. The early church defended creation science. *Impact*, No. 160, p. ii. Quote from, *Theophilus, 'To Autolycus'*, 2.8, Oxford Early Christian Texts.

Objection 3: 2 Peter 3:8 states *'that one day is with the Lord as a thousand years'*, therefore, the days of creation could be long periods of time.

Answer:

a) This passage has *no* creation context — it is *not* referring to Genesis or the six days of creation.

b) This verse has what is called a 'comparative article' — 'as' or 'like' — which is not found in Genesis 1. In other words, it is *not* saying a day *is* a thousand years — it is comparing a real, literal day to a real, literal thousand years. The context of this passage is the Second Coming of Christ. It is saying that to God, a day is *like* a thousand years, because God is outside of time. God is not limited by natural processes and time as humans are. What may seem like a long time to us (waiting for the Second Coming) is nothing to Him. What to us may seem to be a long time, or a short time, is nothing to God, either way.

c) The second part of the verse reads *'and a thousand years as one day'*, which in essence cancels out the first part of the verse for those who want to equate a day with a thousand years! Thus it cannot be saying a day is a thousand years or vice versa.

d) Psalm 90:4 states: *'For a thousand years in your sight* are *as yesterday when it is past, and* as *a watch in the night.'* Here a thousand years is being compared with a 'watch in the night' (4 hours[40]). As the phrase *'watch in the night'* is joined in a particular way to *'yesterday'* — it is saying that a thousand years is being compared with a short period of time — not simply to a day.

e) If one used this passage to claim that 'day' in the Bible means a thousand years, then to be consistent, one would have to say that Jonah was in the belly of the fish three thousand years, or that Jesus has not yet risen from the dead!

Objection 4: Insisting on six solar days for creation limits God, whereas allowing God billions of years does not limit Him.

---

[40] The Jews had three watches during the night (sunset to 10 p.m.; 10 p.m.–2.00 a.m.; 2.00 a.m.–sunrise), but the Romans had four watches, beginning at 6.00 p.m.

Jonah-3000 years in the whale?!

Answer:

Actually, insisting on six ordinary Earth days of creation is not limiting *God,* but limiting *us* to believing that God actually did what He tells us in His Word. Also, if God created everything in six days, like the Bible says, then surely this reveals the power and wisdom of God in a profound way — Almighty God did not *need* eons of time! However, the billions of years scenarios diminish God by suggesting that mere chance could create things, or that God needed huge amounts of time to create things.

Objection 5: Adam could not have accomplished all that the Bible states in one day (day six). He could not have named all the animals, for instance; there was not enough time.

Answer:

Adam did not have to name *all* the animals — only those God brought to him. For instance, Adam was commanded to name *'every beast of the field'* (Genesis 2:20), not *'beast of the earth'* (Genesis 1:25). The phrase *'beast of the field'* is most likely a subset of the larger group *'beast of the earth'*. He did not have to name *'everything that creeps upon the earth'* (Genesis 1:25), or any of the sea creatures. Also the number of 'kinds' would be much less than the number of 'species' in today's classification (see pp. 169–171).

When critics say that Adam could not name the animals in less than one day, what they really mean is they do not understand how they could do it, so Adam could not. However, our brain has suffered from six thousand years of the Curse — it has been greatly affected by the Fall. Before sin, Adam's brain was perfect.

When God made Adam, He must have programmed him with a perfect language. Today we program computers to 'speak' and 'remember'. How much more could our Creator God have created Adam as a mature human (he was not born as a baby needing to learn to speak), having in his memory cells a perfect language with a perfect understanding of each word. (That is why Adam understood what God meant when he said he would 'die' if he disobeyed, even though he had not seen any death.) Adam may also have had a 'perfect' memory (something like a photographic memory, perhaps).

It would have been no problem for this first perfect man to make up words and name the animals God brought to him and remember the names — in far less than one day.[41]

Objection 6: Genesis chapter 2 is a different account of creation, with a different order, so how can the first chapter be accepted as teaching six literal days?

Answer:

Actually, Genesis chapter 2 is not a *different* account of creation. It is a *more detailed* account of day six of creation. Chapter 1 is an overview of the whole of creation; chapter 2 gives details surrounding the creation of the garden, the first man, and his activities on day six.[42,43]

> **Genesis chapter 2 is not a *different* account of creation — it is a *more detailed* account of the sixth day of creation.**

Between the creation of Adam and the creation of Eve, the KJV/ AV Bible says (Gen. 2:19) *'out of the ground the Lord God formed every beast of the field and every fowl of the air'*. This seems to say that the land beasts and birds were created between Adam and Eve. However, Jewish scholars did not recognize any such conflict with the account in chapter 1, where Adam and Eve were both created after the beasts and birds (Gen. 1:23–25). There is no contradiction, because in Hebrew the precise tense of a verb is determined by the context. It is clear from chapter 1 that the beasts and birds were created before Adam, so Jewish scholars would have understood the verb 'formed' in Genesis 2:19 to mean 'had formed' or 'having formed'. If we translate verse 19 thus: *'Now the Lord God **had** formed out of the*

---

[41] Grigg, R., 1996. Naming the animals: all in a day's work for Adam. *Creation* **18**(4):46–49.

[42] Batten, D., 1996. Genesis contradictions? *Creation* **18**(4):44–45.

[43] Kruger, M.J., 1997. An understanding of Genesis 2:5. *CEN Technical Journal* **11**(1):106–110.

ground all the beasts of the field ... ' the apparent disagreement with Genesis 1 disappears completely.

Regarding the plants and herbs in Genesis 2:5 and the trees in Genesis 2:9 (compare with Gen. 1:12), the plants and herbs are described as *'of the field'* in Genesis chapter 2 and they needed a man to tend them (2:5). These are clearly cultivated plants, not just plants in general (Gen. 1). Also, the trees (2:9) are only the trees planted in the garden, not trees in general.

In Matthew 19:3–6 Jesus Christ quotes from both Genesis 1:27 and Genesis 2:24 when referring to the **same man and woman** in teaching the doctrine of marriage. Clearly, Jesus saw them as **complementary** accounts, **not** contradictory ones.

Objection 7: There is no *'evening and morning'* for the seventh day of the creation week (Gen. 2:2), thus we must still be in the 'seventh day', so none of the days can be ordinary days.

Answer:

Look again at the previous section entitled 'Why six days?' (p. 29). Exodus 20:11 makes it clear that there were seven literal days — six for work, and one for rest.

Also, God stated that He *'rested'* from his work of creation (not that He **is resting**!). The fact that He rested from his work of creation, does not preclude Him from continuing to rest from this activity. God's work now is different — it is a work of sustaining His creation, and of reconciliation and redemption because of man's sin.

The word *yom* is qualified by a number (Gen. 2:2,3), so the context still determines it is an ordinary solar day. Also, God blessed this seventh day and made it holy. In Genesis 3:17–19 we read of the curse on the earth because of sin. Paul refers to this in Romans 8:22. It does not make sense that God would call this day holy and blessed if he cursed the ground on this 'day'. We live in a sin-cursed Earth — we are not in the seventh blessed holy day!

Note: In arguing that the seventh day is not an ordinary day because it is not associated with *'evening and morning'* like the other days, proponents are tacitly agreeing that the other six days are ordinary days because they are defined by an evening and a morning!

Some have argued that Hebrews 4:3–4 implies that the seventh day is continuing today. However, verse 4 reiterates that God rested

(past tense) on the seventh day. Also, only those who have believed in Christ will enter that rest, showing that it is a spiritual rest, which is compared with God's rest since the creation week. It is not some sort of continuation of the seventh day (otherwise *everyone* would be 'in' this rest).[44]

Hebrews does *not* say that the seventh day of creation week is continuing today, merely that His rest is continuing. If someone says on Monday that he rested on Friday and is still resting, this would not suggest that Friday continued through to Monday!

Objection 8: Genesis 2:4 states *'In the day that the Lord God made the earth and the heavens'*. As this refers to all six days of creation, it shows that the word day does not mean an ordinary day.

Answer:

The Hebrew word *yom* as used here is *not* qualified by a number, the phrase *'evening and morning',* light, or darkness. In this context, the verse really means 'In the time God created' (referring to the creation week) or, 'When God created'.

Other problems with long days and similar interpretations

● If the plants made on day three were separated by millions of years from the birds and nectar bats (created day 5), and insects (created day six) necessary for their pollination, then such plants could not have survived. This problem would be especially acute for species

[44] Anon., 1999. Is the seventh day an eternal day? *Creation* **21**(3):44–45.

with complex symbiotic relationships (each depending on the other; e.g. Yucca plant and moth[45]).

● Adam was created on day six, lived through day seven, and then died when he was 930 years old (Gen. 5:5). If each day were a thousand years, or millions of years, this would make no sense of Adam's age at death!

● Some have claimed that the word for 'made' (*asah*) in Exodus 20:11 actually means 'show'. They propose that God showed or revealed the information about creation to Moses during a six-day period. This allows for the creation itself to have occurred over millions of years. However, 'showed' is not a valid translation for *asah*. Its meaning covers 'to make, manufacture, produce, do' etc., but not 'to show' in the sense of reveal.[46] Where *asah* is translated as 'show' — for example, *'show kindness'* (Gen. 24:12), it is in the sense of 'to do' or 'make' kindness.

● Some have claimed that because the word *asah* is used for the creation of the sun, moon and stars on day 4, and not the word *bara* which is used in Genesis 1:1 for create, that this means God only revealed the sun, moon and stars at this stage. They insist the word *asah* has the meaning of 'revealed'. In other words, the luminaries were supposedly already in existence, and were only revealed at this stage. However, *bara* and *asah* are used in Scripture to describe the same event. For example, *asah* is used in Exodus 20:11 to refer to the creation of the heavens and the earth, but *bara* is used to refer to the creation of the heavens and the earth in Genesis 1:1. The word *asah* is used concerning the creation of the first people in Genesis 1:26 — they did not previously exist. And then they are said to have been created *(bara)* in Genesis 1:27. There are many other similar examples. *Asah* has a broad range of meanings involving 'to do' or 'to make', which includes *bara* creation (see Chapter 3 for more on *asah* and *bara*).

● Some accept that the days of creation are ordinary days as far as

---

[45] Meldau, F.J., 1972. *Why We Believe in Creation Not in Evolution,* Christian Victory Publ. Co., Denver, Colorado, pp. 114–116.
[46] Nothing in Gesenius' *Lexicon* supports the interpretation of *asah* as 'show'. See Taylor, Charles V., 1997, Revelation or creation? on the Answers in Genesis website <http://www.answersingenesis.org/>.

the language of Genesis is concerned, but not as literal days of history as far as man is concerned. This is basically the view called the 'Framework Hypothesis'.[47,48] This is a very complex view which has been thoroughly refuted by scholars.[49–51]

The real purpose of the 'Framework Hypothesis' can be seen in the following quote from an article by one of its proponents:

'To rebut the literalist interpretation of the Genesis creation "week" propounded by the young-earth theorists is a central concern of this article.'[48]

● Some people want the days of creation to be long periods in an attempt to harmonize evolution or billions of years with the Bible's account of origins. However the order of events according to long-age beliefs does not agree with that of Genesis. Consider the following table:

Contradictions between the order of creation in the Bible and evolution / day-ages.

Bible account of Creation	Evolutionary / long-age speculation
Earth before the sun and stars	Stars and sun before Earth
Earth covered in water initially	Earth a molten blob initially
Oceans first, then dry land	Dry land then the oceans
Life first created on the land	Life started in the oceans
Plants created before the sun	Plants came long after the sun
Land animals created after birds	Land animals existed before birds
Whales before land animals	Land animals before whales

[47] Kline, M.G., 1957–1958. Because it had not rained. *Westminster Theological Journal* **20**:146–157.

[48] Kline, M.G., 1996. Space and time in the Genesis cosmology. *Perspectives on Science & Christian Faith* **48**(1).

[49] Kruger, Ref. 43, pp. 106–110.

[50] Pipa, J.A., 1996. From chaos to cosmos: a critique of the Framework Hypothesis. Presented at the Far-Western Regional Annual Meeting of The Evangelical Theological Society, USA, April 26, 1996.

[51] Wayne Grudem's *Systematic Theology,* pp. 302–305, summarises the Framework Hypothesis and its problems and inconsistencies.

Clearly, those who do not accept the six literal days are the ones reading into the passage their own preconceived ideas.

Long-age compromises

Other than the 'gap theory', which is covered in the next chapter, the major compromise positions that try to harmonise long ages and/ or evolution with Genesis fall into two categories:

1. 'theistic evolution', wherein God supposedly directed the evolutionary process of millions of years, or even just set it up and let it run, and

2. 'progressive creation' where God supposedly intervened in the processes of death and struggle for survival to create millions of species at various times over the millions of years.

All long-age compromises reject Noah's Flood as a global Flood — it could only be a local event, because the fossil layers are accepted as evidence for millions of years. A global Flood would have destroyed this record and produced another! Therefore these positions cannot allow a catastrophic global Flood that would form layers of fossil bearing rocks over the earth. This of course goes against Scripture, which obviously teaches a global Flood (Gen. 6–9).[52]

Does it really matter?

Yes, it does matter what a Christian believes concerning the days of creation in Genesis 1. Most importantly, all schemes which insert eons of time into or before creation undermine the Gospel by putting death, bloodshed, disease, thorns and suffering before sin and the Fall, as explained above (see Answer to Objection 1 above, p. 31). Here are two more reasons:

1. It is really a matter of how one approaches the Bible, in principle. If we do not allow the language to speak to us in context, but try to make the text fit ideas outside of Scripture, then ultimately the meaning of any word in any part of the Bible depends on man's interpretation — which can change according to whatever outside ideas are in vogue.

2. If one allows 'science' (which has wrongly become synonymous with evolution and materialism) to determine our understanding of

---

[52] Van Bebber, M. and Taylor, P.S., 1994. Ref. 1. pp. 55–59. See also Ref. 21, pp. 212–330. Also see Chapter 10 'Was the Flood Global?'

Scripture, then this can lead to a slippery slope of unbelief through the rest of Scripture. For instance, 'science' would proclaim that a person cannot be raised from the dead. Does this mean we should 'interpret' the resurrection of Christ to reflect this? Sadly, some do just this, saying that the resurrection simply means that Jesus' teachings live on in His followers!

When people accept at face value what Genesis is teaching, and accept the days as ordinary days, they will have no problem accepting and making sense of the rest of the Bible.

Martin Luther once said:

'I have often said that whoever would study Holy Scripture should be sure to see to it that he stays with the simple words as long as he can and by no means departs from them unless an article of faith compels him to understand them differently. For of this we must be certain: no clearer speech has been heard on Earth than what God has spoken.'[53]

Pure words

God's people need to realize that the Word of God is something very special. It is not just the words of men. As Paul said in 1 Thessalonians 2:13, *you received* it *not* as *the word of men, but as it is, truly the word of God.*

Proverbs 30:5–6 states that '*Every word of God* is *pure ... do not add to His words, lest He reprove you and you be found a liar.*' The Bible cannot be treated as just some great literary work. We need to '*tremble at his word*' (Isa. 66:5) and not forget that

All Scripture is God-breathed, and is profitable for doctrine, for reproof, for correction, for instruction in righteousness, that the man of God may be perfected, thoroughly equipped for every good work. (2 Timothy 3:16–17)

In the original autographs, every word and letter in the Bible is there because God put it there. Let us listen to God speaking to us through His Word, and not arrogantly think we can tell God what He really means!

'*Every word of God* is *pure*' (Proverbs 30:5)

---

[53] Plass, Ref. 3, p. 93.

Chapter 3

What about the 'gap' and 'ruin-reconstruction' theories?

What is the 'gap theory'? Where did it come from? Does it help? Is it biblical? What are its consequences?

MANY people have tried to place a gap of indeterminate time between the first two verses of Genesis chapter 1. There are many different versions as to what supposedly happened in this 'gap' of time. Most versions of the 'gap' theory place millions of years of geologic time (including billions of fossil animals) in between these first two verses of Genesis. This is the 'ruin-reconstruction' version of the gap theory.

However, this undermines the Gospel as it allows for death, bloodshed, disease and suffering before Adam's sin. Because most 'gap' theorists have accepted the millions of years dating for the fossil record, they have thus allowed the fallible theories of scientists to determine the meaning of Scripture.

Some put the fall of Satan in this supposed period. But any rebellion of Satan during this gap of time contradicts God's description of His completed creation on day six as all being *'very good'* (Gen. 1:31).

All versions of the gap theory impose outside ideas on Scripture and thus open the door for further compromise.

These are the verses where there is supposed to be a gap:

In the beginning God created the heavens and the earth. And the earth was without form, and empty; and darkness was *upon the face of the deep. And the Spirit of God moved on the face of the waters.* (Genesis 1:1–2)

Where did the 'gap theory' come from?

There have been many attempts over the years to harmonize the Genesis account of Creation with accepted geology (and its teaching of billions of years for the age of the earth), such as 'theistic evolution' and 'progressive creation.'

The gap theory was another significant attempt by Christian theologians to reconcile the time-scale of world history found in Genesis with the popular belief that geologists provide 'undeniable' evidence that the world is exceedingly old (currently said to be about 4.6 billion years).

Thomas Chalmers (1780–1847), a notable Scottish theologian and first Moderator of the Free Church of Scotland, was perhaps the man most responsible for the gap theory.[1] The idea can be traced back to the rather obscure writings of the Dutchman Episcopius (1583–1643), and was first recorded from one of Chalmers' lectures in 1814.[2] Rev. William Buckland, a geologist, did much to popularize the idea.

Although Chalmers' writings give very little information about the gap theory,[3] many of the details are obtained from other writers such as the 19th century geologist, Hugh Miller, who quoted from Chalmers' lectures on this subject.[4]

This ruin-reconstruction view is held by many who use Bible study aids such as the *Scofield Reference Bible, Dake's Annotated Reference Bible* and *The Newberry Reference Bible.*

The most notably influential 19th century writer to popularize this view was G.H. Pember, in his book *Earth's Earliest Ages,*[5] first published in 1884. Numerous editions of this work were published, with the 15th edition appearing in 1942.[6]

---

[1] Fields, W.W., 1976. *Unformed and Unfilled,* Burgeners Enterprises, Collinsville, Illinois, p. 40.

[2] Taylor, I.T., 1984. *In The Minds Of Men: Darwin and the New World Order,* TFE Publishing, Toronto, Canada, p.363.

[3] Chalmers, T., 1857. *Natural Theology,* Selected works of Thomas Chalmers, Vol.5 of 12. Edited by William Hanna, Thomas Constable, Edinburgh. All Chalmers basically states concerning the gap theory in these writings is: 'The detailed history of creation in the first chapter of Genesis begins at the middle of the second verse.' p.146.

[4] Miller, H., 1867. *The Testimony of the Rocks,* Boston, Gould and Lincoln, New York, p.143

[5] Pember, G.H., 1900. *Earth's Earliest Ages*, H. Revell Company, New York.

[6] Taylor, Ref. 2, p.363.

The 20th century writer who published the most academic defence of the gap theory was Arthur C. Custance in his work, *Without Form and Void*.[7]

The basic reason for developing and promoting the gap theory can be seen from the following very telling quotes:

Scofield Study Bible: 'Relegate fossils to the primitive creation, and no conflict of science with the Genesis cosmogony remains.'[8]

Dake's Annotated Reference Bible: 'When men finally agree on the age of the earth, then place the many years (over the historical 6,000) between Genesis 1:1 and 1:2, there will be no conflict between the Book of Genesis and Science.'[9]

The above quotes are typical of the many compromise positions — accepting so-called 'science'[10] and its long ages for the earth, and incorporating this into Scripture.

A testimony of struggle

Pember's struggle with long 'geologic ages' has been the struggle of many Christians, ever since the idea of millions of years for the fossil record became popular in the early 19th century. Many respected Christian leaders of today wrestle with this same issue.

Recounting Pember's struggle helps us understand the implications of the gap theory. The following is based on or quoted from his book *Earth's Earliest Ages*.[5]

Pember, like today's conservative Christians, defended the authority of Scripture. He was most adamant that one had to start *from* Scripture alone, and *not* bring preconceived ideas *to* Scripture, thus changing

---

[7] Custance, A.C., 1970. *Without Form and Void*, published by the author at Brookville, Canada.

[8] Scofield, C.I., (Editor) 1945. *The Scofield Study Bible,* Oxford University Press, New York. (Originally published as *The Scofield Reference Bible*, this edition is unaltered from the original of 1909).

[9] Dake, F.H., 1961. *Dake's Annotated Reference Bible*, Dake Bible Sales, Inc., Lawrenceville, Georgia, p.51.

[10] Many people now equate the teaching of millions of years and evolution with 'science'. However, these teachings are **not** 'science' in the empirical (repeatable, testable) sense. Scientists have only the present to work with. To connect the present to the past involves interpretations based on unprovable assumptions.

its meaning. He boldly chastened people who came to the Bible 'filled
with myths, philosophies, and prejudices, which they could not
altogether throw off, but retained, in part at least, and mingled —
quite unwittingly, perhaps — with the truth of God.' (page 5). He
describes how the church is weakened when man's philosophies are
used to interpret God's Word:

> 'For, by skilfully blending their own systems with the truths of
> Scripture, they so bewildered the minds of the multitude that but
> few retained the power of distinguishing the revelation of God from
> the craftily interwoven teachings of men.' (page 7)

> 'And the result is that inconsistent and unsound interpretations have
> been handed down from generation to generation, and received as
> if they were integral parts of the Scriptures themselves; while any
> texts which seemed violently opposed were allegorized,
> spiritualized, or explained away, till they ceased to be troublesome,
> or perchance, were even made subservient.' (page 8)

He then warns Christians:

> 'For, if we be observant and honest, we must often ourselves feel
> the difficulty of approaching the sacred writings without bias, seeing
> that we bring with us a number of stereotyped ideas, which we
> have received as absolutely certain, and never think of testing, but
> only seek to confirm.'

What happened with Pember should warn us that, no matter how
great a theologian we may be, or how respected and knowledgeable a
Christian leader, as finite sinful human beings we cannot easily empty
ourselves of preconceived ideas. We see that Pember did exactly what
he preached against, and did not realize it. Such is the ingrained nature
of the 'long ages' issue. He did not want to question Scripture (he
accepted the six literal days of creation), but he did not question the
long ages either (perhaps he just took the word of Chalmers, who was
a highly respected Christian). So he struggled with what to do. Many
of today's respected Christian leaders show the same struggle in their
commentaries as they then capitulate to 'progressive creation' or even
'theistic evolution'.[11]

---

[11] Ham, K., 1997. Millions of Years and the 'Doctrine of Balaam'. *Creation*
19(3):15–17.

Pember recognized that a fossil record of death, decay and disease before sin was totally inconsistent with the Bible's teaching:

'For, as the fossil remains clearly show not only were disease and death — inseparable companions of sin — then prevalent among the living creatures of the earth, but even ferocity and slaughter.'

He understood there could be no carnivores before sin:

'On the Sixth Day God pronounced every thing which He had made to be very good, a declaration which would seem altogether inconsistent with the present condition of the animal as well as the vegetable kingdom. Again: He gave the green herb alone for food "to every beast of the field, and to every fowl of the air, and to every thing that creepeth upon the earth." There were, therefore, no carnivora in the sinless world.' (page 35)

Pember taught from Isaiah that the earth will be restored to what it was like at first. There will be no more death, disease, or carnivorous activity. However, because he had accepted the long ages for the fossil record, what was he to do with all this death, disease and destruction in this record?

'Since, then, the fossil remains are those of creatures anterior to Adam, and yet show evident tokens of disease, death, and mutual destruction, they must have belonged to another world, and have a sin-stained history of their own ...' (page 35).

Thus, in trying to reconcile the long ages with Scripture, Pember justifies the gap theory:

'There is room for any length of time between the first and second verses of the Bible. And again; since we have no inspired account of the geological formations, we are at liberty to believe that they were developed just in the order which we find them. The whole process took place in preadamite times, in connection, perhaps, with another race of beings, and, consequently, does not at present concern us.' (page 28).

With this background, let us consider this gap theory in detail. Basically, the gap theory incorporates three strands of thought:

1. A literal view of Genesis.
2. Belief in an extremely long but undefined age for the earth.
3. An obligation to fit the origin of most of the geologic strata and other geologic evidence between Genesis 1:1 and 1:2. Gap theorists

oppose evolution, but believe in an ancient origin of the universe.

There are many variations of the gap theory. According to Fields,[12] the theory can be summarized as follows:

'In the far distant dateless past, God created a perfect heaven and perfect Earth. Satan was ruler of the earth which was peopled by a race of "men" without any souls. Eventually, Satan, who dwelled in a garden of Eden composed of minerals (Ezek. 28), rebelled by desiring to become like God (Isa. 14). Because of Satan's fall, sin entered the universe and brought on the earth God's judgment in the form of a Flood (indicated by the water of 1:2), and then a global ice-age when the light and heat from the sun were somehow removed. All the plant, animal, and human fossils upon the earth today date from this "Lucifer's flood" and do not bear any genetic relationship with the plants, animals and fossils living upon the earth today.'

Some versions of the gap theory state that the fossil record (geologic column) formed over millions of years, and then God destroyed the earth with a catastrophe (Lucifer's flood) that left it 'without form and void'.

Western Bible commentaries written before the eighteenth century, and before the belief in a long age for the earth became popular, knew nothing of any gap between Genesis 1:1 and Genesis 1:2. Certainly some commentaries proposed intervals of various lengths of time for reasons relating to Satan's fall,[13] but none proposed a 'ruin-reconstruction' situation, or pre-Adamite world. In the 19th century, it became popular to believe that geological changes occurred slowly, and roughly at the present rate (uniformitarianism[14]). With increased

---

[12] Ref. 1, p. 7.

[13] Those who try to put the fall of Satan (not connected with millions of years) into this gap, need to consider that if all the angels were a part of the original creation, as Exodus 20:11 indicates and Colossians 1 seems to confirm, then **everything** God had created by the end of the sixth day was 'very good'. There could not have been **any** rebellion before this time. So Satan fell some time after day seven.

[14] The term 'uniformitarian' commonly refers to the idea that geological processes such as erosion and sedimentation have remained essentially the same throughout time, and so the present is the key to the past. But after the

acceptance of uniformitarianism, many theologians urged reinterpretation of Genesis (with ideas such as day-age, 'progressive' creation, theistic evolution, days-of-revelation, etc. — see Chapter 2).

Problems with the Gap Theory

● **It is inconsistent with God creating *everything* in six days, as Scripture states.**

Exodus 20:11 says, *'For in six days the L*ORD *made the heavens and earth, the sea, **and all that is in them**, and rested the seventh day. Therefore the L*ORD *blessed the Sabbath day, and made it holy.'* Thus the creation of the heavens and the earth (Genesis 1:1) and the sea and **all** that is in them (the rest of the Creation) was completed in six days.[15] Where is there time for a gap?

*God created **everything** in six days*

● **It puts death, disease and suffering before the Fall, contrary to Scripture.**

From Romans 5:12, *'Therefore, even as through one man [Adam] sin entered into the world, and death by sin, and so death passed on all men inasmuch as all sinned'*, we understand that there could not have been human sin or death before Adam. The Bible teaches (1 Cor. 15) that Adam was the first man, and as a result of his rebellion (sin), death and corruption (disease, bloodshed and suffering) entered the universe. Before Adam sinned there could not have been any (*nephesh*[16]) animal or human death. Note also that there could not

---

mid-19th century, the concept has been extended. Huxley said, 'Consistent uniformitarianism postulates evolution as much in the organic as in the inorganic world.' It is now assumed that a closed system exists, to which neither God nor any other non-human or non-natural force has access. (from Rendle-Short, J., 1984. *Man: Ape or Image*, Master Books, San Diego, CA, p. 20, note 4).

[15] See Chapter 2 for more details.

[16] The Bible speaks of animals and humans having or being *nephesh* (Heb.), or soul-life, in various contexts suggesting conscious life. The death of a jellyfish, for example, may not be death of a *nephesh* animal. See Chapter 6 (pp. 91–92).

have been a race of men before Adam that died in 'Lucifer's flood' because 1 Corinthians 15:45 tells us that Adam was the 'first' man.

Genesis 1:29,30 teaches us that the animals and man were originally created vegetarian. This is consistent with God's description of the Creation as 'very good'. How could a fossil record which gives evidence of disease, violence, death and decay (fossils have been found of animals apparently fighting and certainly eating each other) be described as 'very good'? Thus, the death of billions of animals (and many humans) as seen in the fossil record must have occurred after Adam's sin. The historical event of Noah's Flood, recorded in Genesis, provides an explanation for the presence of huge numbers of dead animals buried in rock layers laid down by water all over the earth.

Romans 8:22 teaches that *'we know that the whole creation groans and travails in pain together until now.'* Clearly the whole of creation was, and is, subject to decay and corruption because of sin. The fossil record shows disease, decay and death. When gap theorists believe that disease, decay and death existed before Adam sinned, they ignore that this contradicts the teaching of Scripture.[17]

Gap theorists, often unwittingly, put death and suffering before Creation week and the Fall.

The version of the gap theory that puts Satan's fall at the end of the geological ages, just before the supposed pre-Adamic Lucifer's flood, has a further problem — the death and suffering recorded in the fossils

---

[17] See Chapter 2, 'Did God really take six days?' Also, Ham, K., 1987. *The Lie: Evolution,* Master Books, Green Forest, Arkansas. pp.71–82.

must have been God's fault. As it happened before Satan's fall, Satan and sin cannot be blamed for it.[18]

● **The gap theory is logically inconsistent because it explains away what it is supposed to accommodate — supposed evidence for an old Earth.**

Gap theorists accept that the earth is very old. They base this on geologic evidence interpreted with the assumption that the present is the key to the past. This assumption implies that in the past, sediments containing fossils formed at basically the same rate as they do today. This is also used by most geologists and biologists to justify belief in the 'geologic column' as representing billions of years of Earth history. This geologic column has become the showcase of evolution because the fossils are claimed to show 'ascent' from simple to complex forms.

This places gap theorists in a dilemma. Committed to literal creation because of their acceptance of a 'literal' view of Genesis, they cannot accept the conclusions of evolution based on the geologic column. Nor can they accept that the days in the Genesis record correspond to geologic periods. So they propose that God reshaped the earth and re-created all life in six literal days after 'Lucifer's Flood' (which produced the fossils); hence the name 'ruin-reconstruction'. Satan's sin supposedly caused this flood and the resulting judgment upon that sin reduced the previous world to a state of being 'without form and void'.

While the gap theorist may think Lucifer's flood solves the problem, this actually removes the reason for the theory in the first place. If all, or most, of the sediments and fossils were produced quickly in one massive world-wide Lucifer's flood, then the main 'evidence' that the earth is extremely old (based on the assumed slow formation of the sediments) no longer exists.

Also, if the world was reduced to a shapeless chaotic mess, as gap theorists propose, how could a reasonably ordered assemblage of fossils and sediments remain as evidence? Surely with such chaos the fossil record would have been severely disrupted, if not entirely destroyed. (This argument also applies to those who say the fossil record formed over hundreds of millions of years before this so-called 'Lucifer's Flood', which would have severely rearranged things.)

---

[18] Morris, H., 1997. Why the gap theory won't work. *Back to Genesis* No. 107, Institute for Creation Research, San Diego, California.

● **The gap theory does away with the evidence for Noah's Flood.**

If the fossil record was formed by 'Lucifer's flood', then what did the global Flood of Noah do? On this point the gap theorist is forced to conclude that Noah's Flood must have left virtually no trace. To be consistent, the gap theorist would have to defend Noah's Flood as a local event. Custance, one of the major proponents of the gap theory, did this. He even published a paper defending a local flood.[19]

Genesis, however, depicts Noah's Flood as a judgment for man's sin (Gen. 6). Water flooded the earth for over a year (Gen. 6:17 and 7:19–24). Only eight people, and air-breathing land-dwelling animals with them on the Ark, survived (Gen. 7:23). See Chapter 10, 'Was the Flood global?'

Sadly, in relegating the fossil record to the supposed gap, 'gappists' have removed the evidence of God's judgment on the violent pre-Flood world in the graveyard of the Flood. The fossils buried by the Flood should warn us of God's judgment to come on sinful humans (2 Pet. 3:2–14).

If 'Lucifer's flood' created this, then what did Noah's Flood do?

---

[19] Custance, A.C., 1970. The Flood: local or global? *The Doorway Papers,* Vol. 9, Zondervan, Grand Rapids, Michigan.

- **The gap theorist ignores the evidence for a young Earth.**

The true gap theorist also ignores evidence consistent with an age for the earth of less than 10,000 years. There is much evidence for this — the decay, and rapid reversals, of the earth's magnetic field; the quantity of helium in the earth's atmosphere; the amount of salt in the oceans; the wind-up of spiral galaxies; and much more.[20]

- **The gap theory fails to accommodate standard uniformitarian geology with its long ages anyway.**

Today's uniformitarian geologists allow for no world-wide flood of any kind — the imaginary Lucifer's flood, or Noah's real Flood. They also recognize no break between the supposed former created world and the current recreated world.

- **Most importantly, the gap theory undermines the Gospel at its foundations.**

By accepting an ancient age for the earth (based on the standard uniformitarian interpretation of the geologic column), gap theorists leave the evolutionary system intact (which by their own assumptions they oppose).

Even worse, they must also theorize that Romans 5:12 and Genesis 3:3 refer only to spiritual death. But this contradicts other Scriptures (see 1 Cor. 15; Gen. 3:22–23). These passages tell us that Adam's sin led to *physical* death as well as spiritual death. In 1 Corinthians 15 the death of the last Adam (the Lord Jesus Christ) is compared with the death of the first Adam. Jesus suffered physical death for man's sin, because Adam, the first man, died physically because of sin. Genesis 3:22–23 tells us that if Adam and Eve could have partaken of the fruit of the Tree of Life, they would have lived forever, but God decreed that they should die physically because of their sin.

In placing on man the curse of physical death, God provided a way to redeem man through the person of His Son Jesus Christ, who suffered the curse of death on the cross for us. *'He tasted death for every man'* (Heb. 2:9). By becoming the perfect sacrifice for our sin and rebellion, He conquered death. He took the penalty that should rightly have been ours at the hands of a righteous judge, and bore it in His own body on the cross. All who believe in Jesus Christ as Lord and Saviour

---

[20] Humphreys, D.R., 1991. Evidence For a Young World, *Creation* **13**(3):46–50, also available as a pamphlet. See also Chapters 1 and 4 in this book.

are received back to God to spend eternity with Him. That is the message of Christianity. To believe there was death before Adam's sin destroys the basis of the Christian message, because the Bible states that man's rebellious actions led to death and the corruption of the universe (Rom. 8:19–22). Thus the gap theory undermines the foundations of Christianity.

Conclusion

Genesis records a catastrophe that destroyed all organisms that had the 'breath of life in them' except for those preserved in Noah's Ark. Christ refers to Noah's Flood in Matthew 24:37–39, and the Apostle Peter writes that, just as there was once a global judgment of mankind by water, so there will be another world-wide judgment by fire (2 Peter 3).

It is more consistent with the whole framework of Scripture to attribute most fossils to Noah's Flood than to resort to a strained interpretation of the fall of Satan[21] and a totally speculative catastrophe that contributes nothing to biblical understanding, or to science.

> **The gap theory undermines the**
> **foundations of the Gospel.**

Moreover, advocating death before Adam sinned contradicts the clear teaching of Scripture that death came only after Adam sinned and made man's redemption necessary.

A Closer Look at Genesis 1:1–2.

The earliest available manuscript of Genesis 1:1–2 is found in the Greek translation of the Old Testament, the Septuagint (LXX), prepared about 250–200 BC. The LXX does not permit the reading of any 'Ruin-Reconstruction' scenario into these verses, as even Custance admitted. A closer look at these verses reveals that the gap theory imposes an interpretation upon Genesis 1:1–2 which is unnatural, and grammatically unsound. Like many attempts to harmonize the Bible with

---

[21] This also impinges upon the perspicuity of Scripture — that is, that the Bible is clear and understandable to ordinary Christians in all that's important.

uniformitarian geology's supposed long ages of Earth history, the gap theory involves a well-meant but misguided twisting of Scripture.

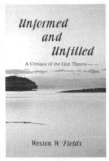

In the following we deal with the five major issues of interpretation bearing on the gap theory. For a much fuller analysis, we recommend the book *Unformed and Unfilled.*[1]

Creating and making (Hebrew: *bara* and *asah*)

It is generally acknowledged that the Hebrew word *bara*, used with 'God' as its subject, means 'to create' — in the sense of the production of something which did not exist before.

However, in the Fourth Commandment God 'made' *(asah)* the heavens and the earth and everything in them in six days (Ex. 20:11). If God made everything in six days then there is clearly no room for a gap. To avoid this clear scriptural testimony against any gap, gap theorists have alleged that *asah* cannot mean 'to create', but to 'form' or even 're-form'. They claim that Exodus 20:11 refers not to six days of creation, but six days of re-forming a ruined world.

Is there such a difference between *bara* and *asah* in biblical usage? A number of verses show that while *asah* may mean 'to do', or 'to make', it can also mean 'to create', the same as *bara*. For example, Nehemiah 9:6 states that God made *(asah)* '*heaven, the heaven of heavens, with all their host, the earth, and all things on it, the seas, and all in them.*'

The reference is obviously to the original *ex nihilo* creation, but the word *asah* is used. (We may safely assume that no 'gappist' will want to say that Nehemiah 9:6 refers to the supposed 'reconstruction', because if it did, the 'gappist' would have to include the geological strata as well, thereby depriving the whole theory of any purpose.)

The fact is that the words *bara* and *asah* are often used interchangeably in the Old Testament; indeed, in some places they are used in synonymous parallelism (e.g. Gen. 1:26,27; 2:4; Ex. 34:10; Isa. 41:20; 43:7).

Applying this conclusion to Exodus 20:11 (cf. 31:17) as well as Nehemiah 9:6, we see that Scripture teaches that God created the universe (everything) in six days, as outlined in Genesis 1.

The grammar of Genesis 1:1-2

Many gap theorists claim that the grammar of Genesis 1:1-2 allows, and even requires, a time-gap between verse 1 and verse 2. Into this gap they place the supposed millions of years of geological time that have shaped the world.

This is a most unnatural interpretation. The most straightforward reading sees verse 1 as a subject-and-verb clause, with verse 2 containing three 'circumstantial clauses' — that is, three statements describing the characteristics of what is described by the principal clause (verse 1). This conclusion is reinforced by the grammarian Gesenius who says that the conjunction *waw* ('and') at the beginning of verse 2 is a '*waw* copulative' (also called a '*waw* disjunctive'), which compares with the old English expression 'to wit'. (Wherever the Hebrew *waw* ('and') is followed by a noun (i.e. *waw* + noun) it is known as a *waw* copulative or disjunctive, and has this meaning.)

This connection of verses 1 and 2 rules out the gap theory, because verse 2 is in fact a description of the state of the originally created earth: *'**And** the earth was without form, and empty'*.

'Was' or 'became'?

Gappists want to translate verse 2 *'the earth **became** (or, had become) without form and empty'*, rather than *'the earth **was** without form and empty'*. At stake is the translation of the Hebrew verb, *haya/hayetah*, 'to be'). Custance claims that of 1,320 occurrences of the verb in the Old Testament, only 24 can certainly be said to bear the meaning 'to be'. He concludes *haya* in Genesis 1:2 must mean 'became' and not simply 'was'.

However, the meaning of a word is controlled by its context. The previous section shows that verse 2 follows on from verse 1 ('to wit…') — a description of what was already mentioned in summary. Furthermore, the *waw* disjunctive (*waw* + noun: *erets*, earth) preceding the verb *haya* (qal perfect tense, 3rd person) defines *haya* as 'was'. It is rendered this way in every major English translation, as well as in the LXX. Other places where this construction is used are also translated as 'was'. For example, Gen. 3:1 would make no sense if translated as 'the serpent *became* more crafty …'.

Conclusion: *became* is not a valid translation of *haya* in Gen. 1:2.

tohu and *bohu*

These delightful words are usually translated 'formless and empty' (Gen. 1:2a). They imply that the original universe was created unformed and unfilled and was, during six days, formed and filled by God's creative actions.

'Gappists' claim that these words imply a process of judgmental destruction, and indicate 'a sinful, and therefore, not an original state of the earth'. However, this imports into Genesis 1 interpretations found in other parts of the Old Testament with very different contexts (namely, Isa. 34:11 and Jer. 4:23).

Tohu and *bohu* appear together only in the three above-mentioned places in the Old Testament. However, *tohu* appears alone in a number of other places and in all cases simply means 'formless'. The word itself does not tell us about the cause of formlessness; this has to be gleaned from the context. Isaiah 45:18 (often quoted by 'gappists') is rendered in the KJV *'he created it not in vain [tohu], he formed it to be inhabited.'* In the context, Isaiah is speaking about Israel, God's people, and His grace in restoring them. He did not choose His people in order to destroy them, but to be their God and they His people. Isaiah draws an analogy with God's purpose in creation: He did not create the world for it to be empty! No, He created it to be formed and filled, a suitable abode for His people. 'Gappists' miss the point altogether when they argue that because Isaiah says God did not create the world *tohu,* it must have **become** *tohu* at some later time. Isaiah 45:18 is about God's **purpose** in creating, not about the original state of the creation.

Though the expression *tohu* and *bohu* in Isaiah 34.11 and Jeremiah 4:23 speaks of a formlessness and emptiness resulting from divine judgment for sin, this meaning is not implicit in the expression itself, but is gained from the particular contexts in which it occurs. It is not valid therefore to infer that same meaning into Genesis 1:2, where the context does not suggest it. As an analogy, we might think of a word like 'blank', in reference to a computer screen. It can be blank because nothing has been typed on the keyboard, or it can be blank because the screen has been erased. The word 'blank' does not suggest, in itself, the reason why the screen is blank. It is likewise with 'formless and empty' — this can be due to the earth not yet being formed and filled, or it could be due to something becoming that way through judgment, for example.

Theologians call the form of use of *tohu* and/or *bohu* in Isaiah 34:11 and Jeremiah 4:23 a 'verbal allusion'. These passages on judgment allude to the formless and empty Earth at the beginning of creation to suggest the extent of God's judgment to come. God's judgment will be so complete that the result will be like the earth before it was formed and filled — formless and empty. This does not imply that the state of the creation in Genesis 1:2 was arrived at by some sort of judgment or destruction as imagined by gappists. As theologian Robert Chisholm Jr wrote, [22] 'By the way, allusion only works one way. It is unwarranted to assume that Jeremiah's use of the phrase in a context of judgment implies some sort of judgment in the context of Genesis 1:2 ... Jeremiah is not interpreting the meaning of Genesis 1:2.'

> **The gap theory imposes an interpretation upon Genesis 1:1–2 which is unnatural, and grammatically unsound.**

'Replenish'

Many gappists have used the word 'replenish' in the KJV translation of Genesis 1:28 to justify the gap theory on the basis that this word means 'refill'. Thus they claim that God told Adam and Eve to 'refill' the earth, implying it was once before filled with people (the 'pre-Adamites').

However, this is wrong. In the Hebrew, the word translated 'replenish', *male*,[23] simply means 'fill' (or 'fulfil' or 'be filled').

The English word 'replenish' meant 'fill' from the 13th to the 17th centuries. Then it changed to mean 'refill.' As the KJV was published in 1611, the translators used the English word 'replenish', which at that time meant only 'fill', not 'refill'.[24]

---

[22] Chisholm, R.B., Jr, (1998). *From Exegesis to Exposition: A Practical Guide to Using Biblical Hebrew,* Baker Books, Grand Rapids, p. 41.

[23] Strong's Concordance, Hebrew word No. 4390.

[24] See Taylor, C., 1996. What does 'replenish the earth' mean? *Creation* **18**(2):44–45, for more details on the history of the meaning of 'replenish'.

The straightforward meaning of Genesis 1:1–2

The gap (or 'ruin-reconstruction') theory is based on a very tenuous interpretation of Scripture.

The simple, straightforward meaning of Genesis 1:1–2 is that when God at the beginning created the earth it was initially formless, empty, and dark, and God's Spirit was there above the waters. It was through His creative energy that the world was then progressively 'formed and filled' during the remaining six days of creation.

Consider the analogy of a potter making a vase. The first thing he does is get a ball of clay. What he has is good, but it is unformed. Next, he shapes it into a vase, using his potter's wheel. Now it is no longer formless. He then might dry it, apply glaze and fire it. Now it is ready to be filled — with flowers and water. At no time could one of the stages be considered evil or bad. It was just not finished — unformed and unfilled. When it was finally formed and filled, it could be described as 'very good'.

God of course did not have to take six days to create everything, but he did this deliberately as a pattern for us — for our seven-day week.

Warning

Many sincere Christians have invented reinterpretations of Scripture to avoid intellectual conflicts with 'scientific' ideas. The gap theory was one such reinterpretation designed to fit in with scientific concepts that arose in the early 1800s and are still popular today.

In reality though, the gap theory was an effective 'anesthetic' that put the church to sleep for over one hundred years. When the children who learned this compromise position went on to higher education, they were shocked to discover that this theory explained nothing. They thus accepted the only remaining 'respectable' theory, evolution (which went hand in hand with millions of years). The results were usually disastrous for their faith.

Today, other compromise positions like 'progressive creation' or 'theistic evolution' have by and large replaced the gap theory.[25]   The

---

[25] A strange modern 'gap' theory is found in *Genesis Unbound,* by J. Sailhamer, Multnomah Books, Oregon, 1996. The author fits the supposed

'gappists', by attempting to maintain a literal Genesis but adhering to the long ages (millions of years), opened the door for greater compromise in the next generation — the re-interpretation of the days, God used evolution, etc.

> **The gap theory anesthetised the church for over one hundred years.**

But whether it be a 'gap theory', 'progressive creation' or 'theistic evolution', the results are the same. These positions may be acceptable in some churches, but the learned in the secular world will, with some justification, mock those who hold them — they see the inconsistencies.

Christians will be derided whatever they believe about Genesis. We can choose to be scoffed at for believing the first book of the Bible as God intended it to be understood, or for believing in a compromise position that undermines the authority of God's Word.

---

millions of years of geologic history into Genesis 1:1, and then claims the six days of creation relate to the promised land! He states his motivation for this novel approach on p. 29: 'If billions of years really are covered by the simple statement, "In the beginning God created the heavens and the earth," then many of the processes described by modern scientists fall into the period covered by the Hebrew term "beginning". Within that "beginning" would fit the countless geologic ages, ice ages, and the many global climatic changes on our planet. The many biological eras would also fit within "the beginning" of Genesis 1:1, including the long ages during which the dinosaurs roamed the earth. By the time human beings were created on the sixth day of the week, the dinosaurs already could have flourished and become extinct — all during the "beginning" recorded in Genesis 1:1.' Many of the problems with the classical gap theory also apply to this attempt to fit millions of years into the Bible.

Chapter 4

What about carbon dating?

How does the carbon 'clock' work? Is it reliable? What does carbon dating really show? What about other radiometric dating methods? Is there evidence that the earth is young?

PEOPLE who ask about carbon-14 (^{14}C) dating usually want to know about the radiometric[1] dating methods that are claimed to give millions and billions of years — carbon dating can only give thousands of years. People wonder how millions of years could be squeezed into the biblical account of history.

Clearly, such huge time periods cannot be fitted into the Bible without compromising what the Bible says about the goodness of God and the origin of sin, death and suffering — the reason Jesus came into the world (see Chapter 2).

Christians, by definition, take the statements of Jesus Christ seriously. He said, *'But from the beginning of the creation God made them male and female'* (Mark 10:6). This only makes sense with a time line beginning with the creation week thousands of years ago. It makes no sense at all if man appeared at the end of billions of years.

We will deal with carbon dating first and then with the other dating methods.

How the carbon clock works

Carbon has unique properties that are essential for life on Earth. Familiar to us as the black substance in charred wood, as diamonds, and the graphite in 'lead' pencils, carbon comes in several forms, or isotopes. One rare form has atoms that are 14 times as heavy as hydrogen atoms: carbon-14, or ^{14}C, or radiocarbon.

Carbon-14 is made when cosmic rays knock neutrons out of atomic

---

[1] Also known as isotope or radioisotope dating.

nuclei in the upper atmosphere. These displaced neutrons, now moving fast, hit ordinary nitrogen (^{14}N) at lower altitudes, converting it into ^{14}C. Unlike common carbon (^{12}C), ^{14}C is unstable and slowly decays, changing back into nitrogen and releasing energy. This instability makes it radioactive.

Ordinary carbon (^{12}C) is found in the carbon dioxide (CO_2) in the air, which is taken up by plants, which in turn are eaten by animals. So a bone, or a leaf of a tree, or even a piece of wooden furniture, contains carbon. When ^{14}C has been formed, like ordinary carbon (^{12}C), it combines with oxygen to give carbon dioxide ($^{14}CO_2$), and so it also gets cycled through the cells of plants and animals.

We can take a sample of air, count how many ^{12}C atoms there are for every ^{14}C atom, and calculate the ^{14}C/^{12}C ratio. Because ^{14}C is so well mixed up with ^{12}C, we expect to find that this ratio is the same if we sample a leaf from a tree, or a part of your body.

In living things, although ^{14}C atoms are constantly changing back to ^{14}N, they are still exchanging carbon with their surroundings, so the mixture remains about the same as in the atmosphere. However, as soon as a plant or animal dies, the ^{14}C atoms which decay are no longer replaced, so the amount of ^{14}C in that once-living thing decreases as time goes on (Figure 1). In other words, the ^{14}C/^{12}C ratio gets smaller. So, we have a 'clock' which starts ticking the moment something dies (Figure 2).

Obviously, this works only for things which were once living. It cannot be used to date volcanic rocks, for example.

The rate of decay of ^{14}C is such that half of an amount will convert back to ^{14}N in $5,730 \pm 40$ years. This is the 'half-life'. So,

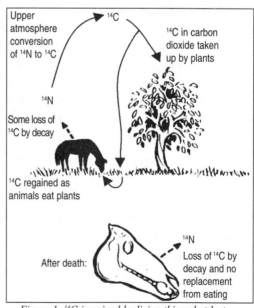

Figure 1. ^{14}C is gained by living things but lost after death.

in two half-lives, or 11,460 years, only one-quarter will be left. Thus, if the amount of ^{14}C relative to ^{12}C in a sample is one-quarter of that in living organisms at present, then it has a theoretical age of 11,460 years. Anything over about 50,000 years old, should theoretically have no detectable ^{14}C left. That is why radiocarbon dating cannot give millions of years. In fact, if a sample contains ^{14}C, it is good evidence that it is **not** millions of years old.

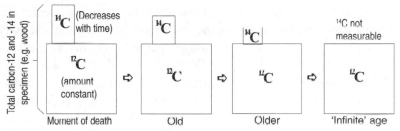

Figure 2. After death, the amount of ^{12}C remains constant, but the amount of ^{14}C decreases.

However, things are not quite so simple. Firstly, plants discriminate against carbon dioxide containing ^{14}C. That is, they take up less than would be expected and so they test older than they really are. Furthermore, different types of plants discriminate differently. This also has to be corrected for.[2]

Secondly, the ratio of $^{14}C/^{12}C$ in the atmosphere has not been constant — for example it was higher before the industrial era when the massive burning of fossil fuels released a lot of carbon dioxide that was depleted in ^{14}C. This would make things which died at that time appear older in terms of carbon dating. Then there was a rise in $^{14}CO_2$ with the advent of atmospheric testing of atomic bombs in the 1950s.[3] This would make things carbon-dated from that time appear younger than their true age.

Measurement of ^{14}C in historically dated objects (e.g. seeds in the graves of historically dated tombs) enables the level of ^{14}C in the atmosphere at that time to be estimated, and so partial calibration of the 'clock' is possible. Accordingly, carbon dating carefully applied to items from historical times can be useful. However, even with such

---

[2] Today, a stable carbon isotope, ^{13}C, is measured as an indication of the level of discrimination against ^{14}C.

[3] Radiation from atomic testing, like cosmic rays, causes the conversion of ^{14}N to ^{14}C.

historical calibration, archaeologists do not regard ^{14}C dates as absolute because of frequent anomalies. They rely more on dating methods that link into historical records.

Outside the range of recorded history, calibration of the [14]C 'clock' is not possible.[4]

Other factors affecting carbon dating

The amount of cosmic rays penetrating Earth's atmosphere affects the amount of ^{14}C produced and therefore the dating system. The amount of cosmic rays reaching the earth varies with the sun's activity, and with the earth's passage through magnetic clouds as the solar system travels around the Milky Way galaxy.

The strength of the earth's magnetic field affects the amount of cosmic rays entering the atmosphere. A stronger magnetic field deflects more cosmic rays away from the earth. Overall, the energy of the earth's magnetic field has been decreasing,[5] so more ^{14}C is being produced now

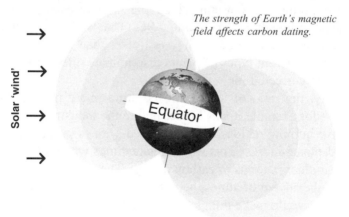

The strength of Earth's magnetic field affects carbon dating.

Solar 'wind'

Equator

---

[4] Tree ring dating (dendrochronology) has been used in an attempt to extend the calibration of carbon-14 dating earlier than historical records allow, but this depends on temporal placement of fragments of wood (from long-dead trees) using carbon-14 dating, assuming straight-line extrapolation backwards. Then cross-matching of ring patterns is used to calibrate the carbon 'clock' — a somewhat circular process which does not give an independent calibration of the carbon dating system.

[5] McDonald, K.L. and Gunst, R.H., 1965. An analysis of the earth's magnetic field from 1835 to 1965. *ESSA Technical Report IER 46-IES,* U.S. Government Printing Office, Washington, D.C., p. 14.

than in the past. This will make old things look older than they really are.

Also, the Genesis Flood would have greatly upset the carbon balance. The Flood buried a huge amount of carbon, which became coal, oil, etc., lowering the total ^{12}C in the biosphere (including the atmosphere — plants regrowing after the Flood absorb CO_2 which is not replaced by the decay of the buried vegetation). Total ^{14}C is also proportionately lowered at this time, but whereas no terrestrial process generates any more ^{12}C, ^{14}C is continually being produced, and at a rate which does not depend on carbon levels (it comes from nitrogen). Therefore the ^{14}C level *relative to ^{12}C* increases after the Flood. So the ^{14}C/^{12}C ratio in plants/animals/the atmosphere before the Flood had to be lower than what it is now.

Unless this effect (which is additional to the magnetic field issue just discussed) were corrected for, carbon dating of fossils formed in the Flood would give ages much older than the true ages.

Creationist researchers have suggested that dates of 35,000–45,000 years should be re-calibrated to the biblical date for the Flood.[7] Such a re-calibration makes sense of anomalous data from carbon dating — for example, very discordant 'dates' for different parts of a frozen musk ox carcass from Alaska and an inordinately slow rate of accumulation of ground sloth dung pellets in the older layers of a cave where the layers were carbon dated.[7]

Also, volcanoes emit much CO_2 depleted in ^{14}C. Since the Flood was accompanied by much volcanism (see Chapters 10, 11, 12, 17), fossils formed in the early post-Flood period would give radiocarbon ages older than they really are.

In summary, the carbon-14 method, when corrected for the effects of the Flood, can give useful results, but needs to be applied carefully. It does not give dates of millions of years and when corrected properly fits well with the biblical Flood (Figure 3).

---

[6] Taylor, B.J., 1994. Carbon dioxide in the antediluvian atmosphere. *Creation Research Society Quarterly* **30**(4):193–197.

[7] Brown, R.H., 1992. Correlation of C-14 age with real time. *Creation Research Society Quarterly* **29**:45–47. Musk ox muscle was dated at 24,000 years, but hair was dated at 17,000 years. Corrected dates bring the difference in age approximately within the life span of a musk ox. With sloth cave dung, standard carbon dates of the lower layers suggested less than 2 pellets per year were produced by the sloths. Correcting the dates increased the number to a more realistic 1.4 per day.

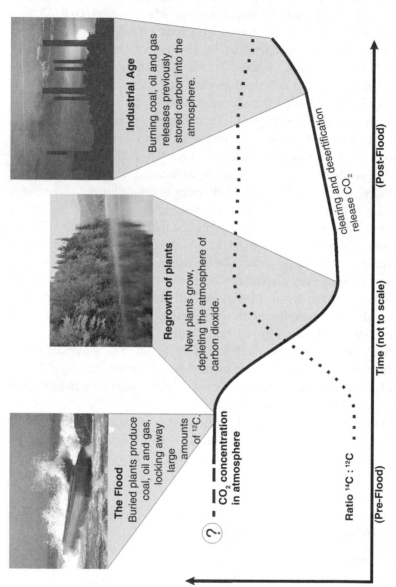

The Flood

Buried plants produce coal, oil and gas, locking away large amounts of ^{12}C.

Regrowth of plants

New plants grow, depleting the atmosphere of carbon dioxide.

Industrial Age

Burning coal, oil and gas releases previously stored carbon into the atmosphere.

clearing and desertification release CO_2

? — — CO$_2$ concentration in atmosphere

Ratio ^{14}C : ^{12}C

(Pre-Flood)   Time (not to scale)   (Post-Flood)

Figure 3. Likely effect of the Flood and man's activities on carbon isotopes, which affect carbon dating.

Other radiometric dating methods

There are various other radiometric dating methods used today to give ages of millions or billions of years for rocks. These techniques, unlike carbon dating, mostly use the relative concentrations of parent and daughter products in radioactive decay chains. For example, potassium-40 decays to argon-40, uranium-238 decays to lead-206 via other elements like radium, uranium-235 decays to lead-207, rubidium-87 decays to strontium-87, etc. These techniques are applied to igneous rocks, and are normally seen as giving the time since solidification.

The isotope concentrations can be measured very accurately, but isotope concentrations are not dates. To derive ages from such measurements, unprovable assumptions have to be made (see hourglass diagram below) such as,

1. The starting conditions are known (for example, that there was no daughter isotope present at the start, or that we know how much was there).

2. Decay rates have always been constant.

3. Systems were closed or isolated so that no parent or daughter isotopes were lost or added.

> **Isotope concentrations, or ratios, can be measured very accurately, but isotope concentrations, or ratios, are not dates.**

The hourglasses represent radiometric dating. It is assumed that we know the amount of parent and daughter elements in the original sample, the rate of decay is constant, and no parent or daughter material has been added or removed.

There are patterns in the isotope data

There is plenty of evidence that the radioisotope dating systems are not the infallible techniques many think, and that they are not measuring millions of years. However, there are still patterns to be explained. For example, deeper rocks often tend to give older 'ages'. Creationists agree that the deeper rocks are generally older, but not by millions of years. Geologist John Woodmorappe, in his devastating critique of radioactive dating,[8] points out that there are other large-scale trends in the rocks that have nothing to do with radioactive decay.

'Bad' dates?

When a 'date' differs from that expected, researchers readily invent excuses for rejecting the result. The common application of such posterior reasoning shows that radiometric dating has serious problems. Woodmorappe cites hundreds of examples of excuses used to explain 'bad' dates.[8]

For example, researchers applied posterior reasoning to the dating of *Australopithecus ramidus* fossils.[9] Most samples of basalt closest to the fossil-bearing strata gave dates of about 23 Ma (*Mega annum*, million years) by the argon-argon method. The authors decided that was 'too old', according to their beliefs about the place of the fossils in the evolutionary grand scheme of things. So they looked at some basalt further removed from the fossils and selected 17 of 26 samples to get an acceptable maximum age of 4.4 Ma. The other nine samples again gave much older dates but the authors decided they must be contaminated and discarded them. That is how radiometric dating works. It is very much driven by the existing long-age worldview that pervades academia today.

A similar story surrounds the dating of the primate skull known as KNM-ER 1470.[10,11] This started with an initial 212 to 230 Ma, which,

---

[8] Woodmorappe, J., 1999. *The Mythology of Modern Dating Methods,* Institute for Creation Research, San Diego, California.

[9] WoldeGabriel, G., *et al.,* 1994. Ecological and temporal placement of early Pliocene hominids at Aramis, Ethiopia. *Nature* **371**:330–333.

[10] Lubenow, M., 1995. The pigs took it all. *Creation* **17**(3):36–38.

[11] Lubenow, M., 1993. *Bones of Contention,* Baker Books, Grand Rapids, Michigan, pp. 247–266.

according to the fossils, was considered way off the mark (humans 'weren't around then'). Various other attempts were made to date the volcanic rocks in the area. Over the years an age of 2.9 Ma was settled upon because of the agreement between several different published studies (although the studies involved selection of 'good' from 'bad' results, just like *Australopithecus ramidus,* above).

However, preconceived notions about human evolution could not cope with a skull like 1470 being 'that old'. A study of pig fossils in Africa readily convinced most anthropologists that the 1470 skull was much younger. After this was widely accepted, further studies of the rocks brought the radiometric age down to about 1.9 Ma — again several studies 'confirmed' *this* date. Such is the dating game.

Are we suggesting that evolutionists are conspiring to massage the data to get the answers they want? No, not generally. It is simply that all observations must fit the prevailing paradigm. The paradigm, or belief system, of molecules-to-man evolution over eons of time, is so strongly entrenched it is not questioned — it is a 'fact'. So every observation *must* fit this paradigm. Unconsciously, the researchers, who are supposedly 'objective scientists' in the eyes of the public, select the observations to fit the basic belief system.

We must remember that the past is not open to the normal processes of experimental science, that is, repeatable experiments in the present. A scientist cannot do experiments on events that happened in the past. Scientists do not measure the age of rocks, they measure isotope concentrations, and these can be measured extremely accurately. However, the 'age' is calculated using assumptions about the past that cannot be proven

We should remember God's admonition to Job, *'Where were you when I laid the foundations of the earth?'* (Job 38:4).

Those involved with unrecorded history gather information in the present and construct stories about the past. The level of proof demanded for such stories seems to be much less than for studies in the empirical sciences, such as physics, chemistry, molecular biology, physiology, etc.

Williams, an expert in the environmental fate of radioactive elements, identified 17 flaws in the isotope dating reported in just three widely respected seminal papers that supposedly established the age of the earth at 4.6 billion years.[12] John Woodmorappe has produced an incisive critique of these dating methods.[8] He exposes hundreds of myths that have grown up around the techniques. He shows that the few 'good' dates left after the 'bad' dates are filtered out could easily be explained as fortunate coincidences.

What date would you like?

The forms issued by radioisotope laboratories for submission with samples to be dated commonly ask how old the sample is expected to be. Why? If the techniques were absolutely objective and reliable, such information should not be necessary. Presumably the laboratories know that anomalous dates are common, so they need some check on whether they have obtained a 'good' date.

Testing radiometric dating methods

If the long-age dating techniques were really objective means of finding the ages of rocks, they should work in situations where we know the age. Furthermore, different techniques should consistently agree with one another.

Methods should work reliably on things of known age

There are many examples where the dating methods give 'dates' that are wrong for rocks of known age. One example is K-Ar 'dating' of five historical andesite lava flows from Mt Ngauruhoe in New Zealand. Although one lava flow occurred in 1949, three in 1954, and one in 1975, the 'dates' ranged from less than 0.27 to 3.5 Ma.[13]

Again, using hindsight, it is argued that 'excess' argon from the magma (molten rock) was retained in the rock when it solidified. The secular scientific literature lists many examples of excess argon causing dates of millions of years in rocks of known historical age.[14] This excess appears to have come from the upper mantle, below the earth's

---

[12] Williams, A.R., 1992. Long-age isotope dating short on credibility. *CEN Technical Journal* **6**(1):2–5.

[13] Snelling, A.A., , 1998. The cause of anomalous potassium-argon 'ages' for recent andesite flows at Mt. Ngauruhoe, New Zealand, and the implications for potassium-argon 'dating'. *Proc. 4th ICC*, pp. 503–525.

[14] Ref. 13, lists many instances. For example, six cases were reported by Krummenacher, D., 1970. Isotopic composition of argon in modern surface

Lava flows of known age often give wrong radioisotope dates.

crust. This is consistent with a young world — the argon has had too little time to escape.[15] If excess argon can cause exaggerated dates for rocks of **known** age, then why should we trust the method for rocks of **unknown** age?

Other techniques, such as the use of isochrons,[16] make different assumptions about starting conditions, but there is a growing recognition that such 'fool-proof' techniques can also give 'bad' dates. So data are again selected according to what the researcher already believes about the age of the rock.

---

rocks. *Earth and Planetary Science Letters* **8**:109–117; five were reported by Dalrymple, G.B., 1969. $^{40}Ar/^{36}Ar$ analysis of historic lava flows. *Earth and Planetary Science Letters* **6**:47–55. A large excess was reported in Fisher, D.E., 1970. Excess rare gases in a subaerial basalt from Nigeria. *Nature* **232**:60–61.

[15] Ref. 13, p. 520.

[16] The isochron technique involves collecting a number of rock samples from different parts of the rock unit being dated. The concentration of a parent radioactive isotope, such as rubidium-87, is graphed against the concentration of a daughter isotope, such as strontium-87, for all the samples. A straight line is drawn through these points, representing the ratio of the parent:daughter, from which a 'date' is calculated. If the line is of good fit and the 'age' is acceptable it is considered a 'good' date. The method involves dividing both the parent and daughter concentrations by the concentration of a similar stable isotope — in this case, strontium-86. See pp. 79–80.

Geologist Dr Steve Austin sampled basalt from the base of the Grand Canyon strata and from lava that spilled over the edge of the canyon.[17] By evolutionary reckoning, the latter should be a billion years younger than the basalt from the bottom. Standard laboratories analysed the isotopes. The rubidium-strontium isochron technique suggested that the recent lava flow was 270 Ma *older* than the basalts beneath the Grand Canyon — an impossibility.

Different dating techniques should consistently agree

If the dating methods are an objective and reliable means of determining ages, they should agree. If a chemist were measuring the sugar content of blood, all valid methods for the determination would give the same answer (within the limits of experimental error). However, with radiometric dating, the different techniques often give quite different results.

In the study of Grand Canyon rocks by Austin,[17] different techniques gave different results (see Table below). Again all sorts of reasons can be suggested for the 'bad' dates, but this is again posterior reasoning. Techniques that give results that can be dismissed just because they don't agree with what we already believe cannot be considered objective.

Radiometric 'ages', using different methods, for basaltic rocks most geologists accept as only thousands of years old, from the Uinkaret Plateau of the Grand Canyon (Ma = millions of years).[17]

Method	'Age'
Six potassium-argon model ages	10,000 years to 117 Ma
Five rubidium-strontium ages	1,270–1,390 Ma
Rubidium-strontium isochron	1,340 Ma
Lead-lead isochron	2,600 Ma

In Australia, some wood found in Tertiary basalt was clearly buried in the lava flow that formed the basalt, as can be seen from the charring. The wood was 'dated' by radiocarbon (^{14}C) analysis at about 45,000 years old, but the basalt was 'dated' by the potassium-argon method

---

[17] Austin, S.A. (ed.) 1994. *Grand Canyon: Monument to Catastrophe.* Institute for Creation Research, Santee, California, pp. 120–131.

at 45 million years old![18]

Isotope ratios of uraninite crystals from the Koongarra uranium body in the Northern Territory of Australia gave lead-lead isochron ages of 841 ± 140 Ma.[19] This contrasts with an age of 1550–1650 Ma based on other isotope ratios,[20] and ages of 275, 61, 0, 0, and 0 Ma from thorium/lead (^{232}Th/^{208}Pb) ratios in five uraninite grains.[19] The latter figures are significant because thorium-derived dates should be the more reliable, since thorium is less mobile than the uranium minerals that are the parents of the lead isotopes in the lead-lead system.[19] The 'zero' ages in this case are consistent with the Bible.

More evidence something is wrong

^{14}C in fossils supposedly millions of years old

Carbon dating in many cases seriously embarrasses evolutionists by giving ages that are much younger than those expected from their model of Earth history. A specimen older than 50,000 years should have too little ^{14}C to measure.

Laboratories that measure ^{14}C would like a source of organic material with zero ^{14}C to use as a blank to check that their lab procedures do not add ^{14}C. Coal is an obvious candidate because the youngest coal is supposed to be millions of years old, and most of it is supposed to be 10s or 100s of millions of years old. Such old coal should be devoid of ^{14}C. It isn't. **No source of coal has been found that completely lacks ^{14}C.**

Fossil wood found in 'Upper Permian' rock that is supposedly 250 Ma old still contained ^{14}C.[21] Recently a sample of wood found in rock classed as 'middle Triassic', supposedly some 230 million years old, gave a ^{14}C date of 33,720 ± 430 years.[22] The accompanying checks showed that the ^{14}C date was not due to contamination and that the

---

[18] Snelling, A.A., 1998. Radiometric dating in conflict. *Creation* **20**(1):24–27.

[19] Snelling, A.A., 1995. The failure of U-Th-Pb 'dating' at Koongarra, Australia. *CEN Technical Journal* **9**(1):71–92.

[20] Maas, R., 1989. Nd-Sr isotope constraints on the age and origin of unconformity-type uranium deposits in the Alligator Rivers Uranium Field, Northern Territory, Australia. *Economic Geology* **84**:64–90.

[21] Snelling, A.A., 1998. Stumping old-age dogma. *Creation* **20**(4):48–50.

[22] Snelling, A.A., 1999. Dating dilemma. *Creation* **21**(3):39–41.

'date' was valid, within the standard (long ages) understanding of this dating system.

It is an unsolved mystery to evolutionists as to why coal has ^{14}C in it,[23] or wood supposedly many millions of years old still has ^{14}C present, but it makes perfect sense in a creationist worldview.

Many physical evidences contradict the 'billions of years'

Of the methods that have been used to estimate the age of the earth, 90 % point to an age far less than the billions of years asserted by evolutionists. A few of them:

● Evidence for rapid formation of geological strata, as in the biblical Flood. Some of the evidences are: lack of erosion between rock layers supposedly separated in age by many millions of years; lack of disturbance of rock strata by biological activity (worms, roots, etc.); lack of soil layers; polystrate fossils (which traverse several rock layers vertically — these could not have stood vertically for eons of time while they slowly got buried); thick layers of 'rock' bent without fracturing, indicating that the rock was all soft when bent; and more. For more, see Chapter 15 (pp. 179–182) and books by geologists Morris[24] and Austin.[17]

● Red blood cells and hemoglobin have been found in some

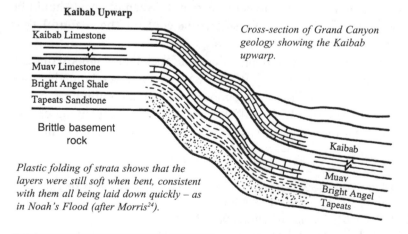

Kaibab Upwarp

Kaibab Limestone

Muav Limestone

Bright Angel Shale

Tapeats Sandstone

Brittle basement rock

Cross-section of Grand Canyon geology showing the Kaibab upwarp.

Kaibab

Muav

Bright Angel

Tapeats

Plastic folding of strata shows that the layers were still soft when bent, consistent with them all being laid down quickly – as in Noah's Flood (after Morris[24]).

---

[23] Lowe, D.C., 1989. Problems associated with the use of coal as a source of ^{14}C free background material. *Radiocarbon* **31**:117–120.

[24] Morris, J., 1994. *The Young Earth*. Creation-Life Publishers, Colorado Springs, Colorado.

(unfossilized!) dinosaur bone. But these could not last more than a few thousand years — certainly not the 65 Ma since the last dinosaurs lived, according to evolutionists.[25]

● The Earth's magnetic field has been decaying so fast that it looks like it is less than 10,000 years old. Rapid reversals during the Flood year and fluctuations shortly after would have caused the field energy to drop even faster.[26,27]

● Radioactive decay releases helium into the atmosphere, but not much is escaping. The total amount in the atmosphere is only 1/2000th of that expected if the atmosphere were really billions of years old. This helium originally escaped from rocks. This happens quite fast, yet so much helium is still in some rocks that it has not had time to escape — certainly not billions of years[28,29] (see also *Anomalies in deep rock crystals,* p. 81).

● A supernova is an explosion of a massive star — the explosion is so bright that it briefly outshines the rest of the galaxy. The supernova remnants (SNRs) should keep expanding for hundreds of thousands of years, according to the physical equations. Yet there are no very old, widely expanded (Stage 3) SNRs, and few moderately old (Stage 1) ones in our galaxy, the Milky Way, or in its satellite galaxies, the Magellanic Clouds. This is just what we would expect for 'young' galaxies that have not existed long enough for wide expansion.[30,31]

---

[25] Wieland, C., 1997. Sensational dinosaur blood report! *Creation* **19**(4):42–43, based on Schweitzer, M. and Staedter, T., 1997. The real Jurassic Park. *Earth,* June, pp. 55–57.

[26] Humphreys, D.R., 1986. Reversals of the earth's magnetic field during the Genesis Flood. *Proc. First ICC, Pittsburgh, PA* **2**:113–126

[27] Sarfati, J.D., 1998. The earth's magnetic field: evidence that the earth is young. *Creation* **20**(2):15–19.

[28] Vardiman, L., 1990. *The Age of the Earth's Atmosphere: A Study of the Helium Flux through the Atmosphere,* Institute for Creation Research, San Diego, CA.

[29] Sarfati, J.D., 1998. Blowing old-earth belief away: Helium gives evidence that the earth is young. *Creation* **20**(3):19–21.

[30] Davies, K., 1994. Distribution of supernova remnants in the galaxy. *Proc. Third ICC,* ed. R.E. Walsh, pp. 175–184.

[31] Sarfati, J.D., 1998. Exploding stars point to a young universe. *Creation* **19**(3):46–49.

● The moon is slowly receding from Earth at about 4 cm (1½ inches) per year, and this rate would have been greater in the past. But even if the moon had started receding from being in contact with the earth, it would have taken only 1.37 billion years to reach its present distance from the earth. This gives a **maximum** age of the moon, not the actual age. This is far too young for evolutionists who claim the moon is 4.6 billion years old. It is also much younger than the radiometric 'dates' assigned to moon rocks.[32,33]

● Salt is entering the sea much faster than it is escaping. The sea is not nearly salty enough for this to have been happening for billions of years. Even granting generous assumptions to evolutionists, the sea could not be more than 62 Ma old — far younger than the billions of years believed by evolutionists. Again, this indicates a maximum age, not the actual age.[34,35]

Dr Russell Humphreys gives other processes inconsistent with billions of years in the pamphlet *Evidence for a Young World.*

Creationists cannot prove the age of the earth using a particular scientific method, any more than evolutionists can. They realise that all science is tentative because we do not have all the data, especially when dealing with the past. This is true of both creationist and evolutionist scientific arguments — evolutionists have had to abandon many 'proofs' for evolution just as creationists have also had to modify their arguments. The atheistic evolutionist W.B. Provine admitted: 'Most of what I learned of the field [evolutionary biology] in graduate (1964–68) school is either wrong or significantly changed.'[36]

Creationists understand the limitations of dating methods better

---

[32] DeYoung, D., 1990. The Earth-Moon System. *Proc. Second ICC* **2**:79–84, Ed. Walsh R.E. and Brooks, C.L .

[33] Sarfati, J.D., 1998. The moon: the light that rules the night. *Creation* **20**(4):36–39.

[34] Austin S.A. and Humphreys, D.R., 1990. The sea's missing salt: a dilemma for evolutionists. *Proc. Second ICC* **2**:17–33.

[35] Sarfati, J.D., 1999. Salty seas: Evidence for a young earth. *Creation* **21**(1):16–17.

[36] A review of *Teaching about Evolution and the Nature of Science* (National Academy of Science USA, 1998) by Dr Will B. Provine, online at <http://fp.bio.utk.edu/darwin/NAS_guidebook/provine_1.html>, 18 Feb. 99.

than evolutionists who claim that they can use processes observed in the present to 'prove' that the earth is billions of years old. In reality, all dating methods, including those that point to a young Earth, rely on unprovable assumptions.

Creationists ultimately date the earth historically using the chronology of the Bible. This is because they believe that this is an accurate eyewitness account of world history, which bears the evidence within it that it is the Word of God, and therefore totally reliable and error-free (see Chapter 1 for some of the evidences).

What then do the radiometric 'dates' mean?

What then do the radiometric dates of millions of years mean, if they are not true ages? To answer this question, it is necessary to scrutinise further the experimental results from the various dating techniques, the interpretations made on the basis of the results and the assumptions underlying those interpretations.[37]

The isochron dating technique[16] was thought to be infallible because it supposedly covered the assumptions about starting conditions and closed systems.

Geologist Dr Andrew Snelling worked on 'dating' the Koongarra uranium deposits in the Northern Territory of Australia, primarily using the uranium-thorium-lead (U-Th-Pb) method. He found that even highly weathered soil samples from the area, which are definitely not closed systems, gave apparently valid 'isochron' lines with 'ages' of up to 1,445 Ma.

Such 'false isochrons' are so common that a whole terminology has grown up to describe them, such as apparent isochron, mantle isochron, pseudoisochron, secondary isochron, inherited isochron, erupted isochron, mixing line and mixing isochron. Zheng wrote:

'...some of the basic assumptions of the conventional Rb-Sr [rubidium-strontium] isochron method have to be modified and an observed isochron does not certainly define valid age information for a geological system, even if a goodness of fit of the experimental results is obtained in plotting $^{87}Sr/^{86}Sr$ against $^{87}Rb/^{86}Sr$. This problem cannot be overlooked, especially in evaluating the numerical time scale. Similar questions can also arise in applying

---

[37] See Woodmorappe, Ref. 8, for one such thorough evaluation.

Sm-Nd [samarium-neodymium] and U-Pb [uranium-lead] isochron methods.'[38]

Clearly, there are factors other than age responsible for the straight lines obtained from graphing isotope ratios. Again, the only way to know if an isochron is 'good' is by comparing the result with what is already believed.

Another currently popular dating method is the uranium-lead concordia technique. This effectively combines the two uranium-lead decay series into one diagram. Results that lie on the concordia curve have the same age according to the two lead series and are called 'concordant'. However, the results from zircons (a type of gemstone), for example, generally lie off the concordia curve — they are discordant. Numerous models, or stories, have been developed to explain such data.[39] However, such exercises in story-telling can hardly be considered as objective science that proves an old Earth. Again the stories are evaluated according to their success in agreeing with the existing long ages belief system.

Andrew Snelling has suggested that fractionation (sorting) of elements in the molten state in the earth's mantle could be a significant factor in explaining the ratios of isotope concentrations which are interpreted as ages.

As long ago as 1966, Nobel Prize nominee Melvin Cook, Professor of Metallurgy at the University of Utah, pointed out evidence that lead isotope ratios, for example, may involve alteration by important factors other than radioactive decay.[40] Cook noted that, in ores from the Katanga mine, for example, there was an abundance of lead-208, a stable isotope, but no Thorium-232 as a source of lead-208. Thorium has a long half-life (decays very slowly) and is not easily moved out of the rock, so if the lead-208 came from thorium decay, some thorium should still be there. The concentrations of lead-206, lead-207 and

---

[38] Zheng, Y.F., 1989. Influence of the nature of initial Rb-Sr system on isochron validity. *Chemical Geology* **80**:1–16 (p. 14).

[39] Gebauer, D. and Grunenfelder, M., 1979. U-Th-Pb dating of minerals. *In* Jager, E. and Hunziker, J.C. (eds). *Lectures in Isotope Geology,* Springer Verlag, New York, 105–131.

[40] Cook, M.A., 1966. *Prehistory and Earth Models,* Max Parrish, London, 353 pp.

lead-208 suggest that the lead-208 came about by neutron capture conversion of lead-206 to lead-207 to lead-208. **When the isotope concentrations are adjusted for such conversions, the ages calculated are reduced from some 600 Ma to recent.** Other ore bodies seemed to show similar evidence. Cook recognized that the current understanding of nuclear physics did not seem to allow for such a conversion under normal conditions, but he presents evidence that such did happen, and even suggests how it could happen.

Anomalies in deep rock crystals

Physicist Dr Robert Gentry has pointed out that the amount of helium and lead in zircons from deep bores is not consistent with an evolutionary age of 1,500 Ma for the granite rocks in which they are found.[41] The amount of lead may be consistent with current rates of decay over millions of years, but it would have diffused out of the crystals in that time.

Furthermore, the amount of helium in zircons from hot rock is also much more consistent with a young Earth (helium derives from the decay of radioactive elements).

The lead and helium results suggest that rates of radioactive decay may have been much higher in the recent past. Humphreys has suggested that this may have occurred during creation week and the Flood. This would make things look much older than they really are when current rates of decay are applied to dating. Whatever caused such elevated rates of decay may also have been responsible for the lead isotope conversions claimed by Cook (above).

Orphan radiohalos

Decaying radioactive particles in solid rock cause spherical zones of damage to the surrounding crystal structure. A speck of radioactive element such as Uranium-238, for example, will leave a sphere of discoloration of characteristically different radius for each element it produces in its decay chain to lead-206.[42] Viewed in cross-section with a microscope, these spheres appear as rings called radiohalos.

---

[41] Gentry, R.V., 1986. *Creation's Tiny Mystery*, Earth Science Associates, Knoxville, Tennessee.

[42] Only those that undergo alpha decay (releasing a helium nucleus).

Dr Gentry has reseached radiohalos for many years, and published his results in leading scientific journals.[41]

Some of the intermediate decay products — such as the polonium isotopes — have very short half-lives (they decay quickly). For example, ^{218}Po has a half-life of just 3 minutes. Curiously, rings created by polonium decay are often found embedded in crystals without the parent uranium halos. Now the polonium has to get into the rock before

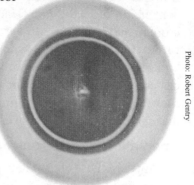

A concentric series of radiohalos

the rock solidifies, but it cannot derive from a uranium speck in the solid rock, otherwise there would be a uranium halo. **Either the polonium was created (primordial, not derived from uranium), or there have been radical changes in decay rates in the past**

Gentry has addressed all attempts to criticise his work.[41,43] There have been many attempts, because the orphan halos speak of conditions in the past, either at creation or after, perhaps even during the Flood, which do not fit with the uniformitarian view of the past, which is the basis of the radiometric dating systems. Whatever process was responsible for the halos could be a key also to understanding radiometric dating.[44]

Conclusions

There are many lines of evidence that the radiometric dates are not the objective evidence for an old Earth that many claim, and that the world is really only thousands of years old. We don't have all the answers, but we do have the sure testimony of the Word of God to the true history of the world.

---

[43] Wise, K.P., letter to the editor, and replies by Armitage, M., and Gentry, R.,1998. *CEN Technical Journal* **12**(3):285–90.

[44] An international team of creationist scientists is actively pursuing a creationist understanding of radioisotope dating. Known as the RATE (Radioisotopes and the Age of The Earth) group, it combines the skills of various physicists and geologists to enable a multi-disciplinary approach to the subject. Interesting insights are likely to come from such a group.

Chapter **5**

How can we see distant stars in a young universe?

If the universe is young and it takes millions of years for light to get to us from many stars, how can we see them? Did God create light in transit? Was the speed of light faster in the past? Does this have anything to do with the 'big bang'?

OME stars are many millions of light-years away. Since a light-year is the distance travelled by light in one year, does this mean that the universe is very old?

Despite all the biblical and scientific evidence for a young earth/universe, this has long been a problem. However, any scientific understanding of origins will always have opportunities for research — problems that need to be solved. We can never have complete knowledge and so there will always be things to learn.

One explanation used in the past was rather complex, involving light travelling along Riemannian surfaces (an abstract mathematical form of space). Apart from being hard to understand, it appears that such an explanation is not valid, since it would mean that we should see duplicates of everything.

Created light?

Perhaps the most commonly used explanation is that God created the light 'on its way', so that Adam could see the stars immediately without having to wait years for the light from even the closest ones to reach the earth. While we should not limit the power of God, this has some rather immense difficulties.

It would mean that whenever we look at the behaviour of a very distant object, what we see happening never happened at all. For instance, say we see an object a million light-years away which appears to be rotating; that is, the light we receive in our telescopes carries this information 'recording' this behaviour. However, according to this explanation, the light we are now receiving did not come from the star, but was created 'en route', so to speak.

This would mean, for a (say) 10,000-year-old universe, that anything we see happening beyond about 10,000 light-years away is actually part of a gigantic picture-show of things that have not actually happened, showing us objects which may not even exist.

To explain this problem further, consider an exploding star (supernova) at, say, an accurately measured 100,000 light-years away. Remember we are using this explanation in a 10,000-year-old universe. As the astronomer on Earth watches this exploding star, he is not just receiving a beam of light. If that were all, then it would be no problem at all to say that God could have created a whole chain of photons (light particles/waves) already on their way.

However, what the astronomer receives is also a particular, very specific pattern of variation within the light, showing him/her the changes that one would expect to accompany such an explosion — a predictable sequence of events involving neutrinos, visible light, X-rays and gamma-rays. The light carries information recording an apparently real event. The astronomer is perfectly justified in interpreting this 'message' as representing an actual reality — that there really was such an object, which exploded according to the laws of physics,

Photo by NASA

brightened, emitted X-rays, dimmed, and so on, all in accord with those same physical laws.

Everything he sees is consistent with this, including the spectral patterns in the light from the star giving us a 'chemical signature' of the elements contained in it. Yet the 'light created en route' explanation means that this recorded message of events, transmitted through space, had to be contained within the light beam from the moment of its creation, or planted into the light beam at a later date, without ever having originated from that distant point. (If it had started from the star — assuming that there really was such a star — it would still be 90,000 light-years away from Earth.)

To create such a detailed series of signals in light beams reaching Earth, signals which seem to have come from a series of real events but in fact did not, has no conceivable purpose. Worse, it is like saying that God created fossils in rocks to fool us, or even test our faith, and that they don't represent anything real (a real animal or plant that lived and died in the past). This would be a strange deception.

Did light always travel at the same speed?

An obvious solution would be a higher speed of light in the past, allowing the light to cover the same distance more quickly. This seemed at first glance a too-convenient *ad hoc* explanation. Then some years ago, Australian Barry Setterfield raised the possibility to a high profile by showing that there seemed to be a decreasing trend in the historical observations of the speed of light (**c**) over the past 300 years or so. Setterfield (and his later co-author, Trevor Norman) produced much evidence in favour of the theory.[1] They believed that it would have affected radiometric dating results, and even have caused the red-shifting of light from distant galaxies, although this idea was later overturned, and other modifications were made also.

Much debate has raged to and fro among equally capable people within creationist circles about whether the statistical evidence really supports **c** decay ('cdk') or not.

The biggest difficulty, however, is with certain physical consequences of the theory. If **c** has declined the way Setterfield

---

[1] Norman, T.G. and Setterfield, B., 1990. *The Atomic Constants, Light and Time,* Privately published, 88 pp.

proposed, these consequences should still be discernible in the light from distant galaxies but they are apparently not. In short, none of the theory's defenders has been able to answer all the problems raised.

A new creationist cosmology

Nevertheless, the c-decay theory stimulated much thinking about the issues. Creationist physicist Dr Russell Humphreys says that he spent a year on and off trying to get the declining c theory to work, but without success. However, in the process, he was inspired to develop a new creationist cosmology which appears to solve the problem of the apparent conflict with the Bible's clear, authoritative teaching of a recent creation.

This new cosmology is proposed as a creationist alternative to 'big bang' theory. It passed peer review, by qualified reviewers, for the 1994 Pittsburgh International Conference on Creationism.[2] Young-earth creationists have been cautious about the model,[3] which is not surprising with such an apparently radical departure from orthodoxy, but Humphreys has addressed the problems raised.[4] Believers in an old universe and the 'big bang' have vigorously opposed the new cosmology and claim to have found flaws in it.[5] However, Humphreys has been able to defend his model, as well as develop it further.[6,7] The debate will no doubt continue.

This sort of development, in which one creationist theory, c-decay, is overtaken by another, is a healthy aspect of science. The basic biblical framework is non-negotiable, as opposed to the changing views and models of fallible people seeking to understand the data within that framework (evolutionists also often change their ideas on exactly *how* things have made themselves, but never *whether* they did).

---

[2] Humphreys, D.R., 1994. Progress toward a young-earth relativistic cosmology. *Proceedings 3rd ICC, Pittsburgh, PA,* pp. 267–286.

[3] Byl, J., 1997. On time dilation in cosmology. *Creation Research Society Quarterly* **34**(1):26–32.

[4] Humphreys, D.R., 1997. It's just a matter of time. *Creation Research Society Quarterly* **34**(1):32–34.

[5] Conner, S.R. and Page, D.N., 1998. *Starlight and Time* is the Big Bang. *CEN Technical Journal* **12**(2):174–194.

[6] Humphreys, D.R., 1998. New vistas of space-time rebut the critics. *CEN Technical Journal* **12**(2):195–212.

[7] See further discussion in *CEN Technical Journal* **13**(1):49–62, 1999.

A clue

Let us briefly give a hint as to how the new cosmology seems to solve the starlight problem before explaining some preliminary items in a little more detail. Consider that the time taken for something to travel a given distance is the distance divided by the speed it is travelling. That is,

Time = Distance (divided by) Speed

When this is applied to light from distant stars, the time calculates out to be millions of years. Some have sought to challenge the distances, but this is a very unlikely answer.[8]

Astronomers use many different methods to measure the distances, and no informed creationist astronomer would claim that any errors would be so vast that billions of light years could be reduced to thousands, for example. There is good evidence that our own Milky Way galaxy is 100,000 light-years across!

If the speed of light (c) has not changed, the only thing left untouched in the equation is time itself. In fact, Einstein's relativity theories have been telling the world for decades that time is not a constant.

Two things are believed (with experimental support) to distort time in relativity theory — one is speed and the other is gravity. Einstein's general theory of relativity, the best theory of gravity we have at present, indicates that **gravity distorts time.**

This effect has been measured experimentally, many times. Clocks at the top of tall buildings, where gravity is slightly less, run faster than those at the bottom, just as predicted by the equations of general relativity (GR).[9]

When the concentration of matter is very large or dense enough, the gravitational distortion can be so immense that even light cannot escape.[10] The equations of GR show that at the invisible boundary surrounding such a concentration of matter (called the event horizon,

---

[8] Many billions of stars exist, many just like our own sun, according to the analysis of the light coming from them. Such numbers of stars have to be distributed through a huge volume of space, otherwise we would all be fried.

[9] The demonstrable usefulness of GR in physics can be separated from certain 'philosophical baggage' that some have illegitimately attached to it, and to which some Christians have objected.

[10] Such an object is called a 'black hole'.

the point at which light rays trying to escape the enormous pull of gravity bend back on themselves), time literally stands still.

Using different assumptions ...

Dr Humphreys' new creationist cosmology literally 'falls out' of the equations of GR, so long as one assumes that the universe has a boundary. In other words, that it has a centre and an edge — that if you were to travel off into space, you would eventually come to a place beyond which there was no more matter. In this cosmology, the earth is near the centre, as it appears to be as we look out into space.

This might sound like common sense, as indeed it is, but all modern secular ('big bang') cosmologies deny this. That is, they make the arbitrary assumption (without any scientific necessity) that the universe has no boundaries — no edge and no centre. In this assumed universe, every galaxy would be surrounded by galaxies spread evenly in all directions (on a large enough scale), and so therefore all the net gravitational forces cancel out.

However, if the universe has boundaries, then there is a net gravitational effect toward the centre. Clocks at the edge would be running at different rates to clocks on Earth. In other words, it is no longer enough to say God made the universe in six days. He certainly did, but six days measured by which clock? (If we say 'God's time' we miss the point that He created the flow of time as we now experience it; He is outside of time, seeing the end from the beginning.)[11]

There appears to be observational evidence that the universe has expanded in the past, supported by the many phrases God uses in the Bible to tell us that at creation he 'stretched out'[12] (other verses say 'spread out') the heavens.

If the universe is not much bigger than we can observe, and if it was only 50 times smaller in the past than it is now, then scientific deduction based on GR means it *has* to have expanded out of a previous state in which it was surrounded by an event horizon (a condition known technically as a 'white hole' — a black hole running in reverse, something permitted by the equations of GR).

---

[11] Gen. 1:1; Ecc. 3:11; Isa. 26:4; Rom. 1:20; 1 Tim. 1:17; Heb. 11:3. Interestingly, according to GR, time does not exist without matter, as was discussed in chapter 1.

[12] For example, Isa 42:5; Jer. 10:12; Zech. 12:1

As matter passed out of this event horizon, the horizon itself had to shrink — eventually to nothing. Therefore at one point this horizon would have been touching the earth. In that instant, time on the earth (relative to a point far away from it) would have been virtually frozen. An observer on Earth would not in any way 'feel different'. 'Billions of years' would be available (in the frame of reference within which it is travelling in deep space) for light to

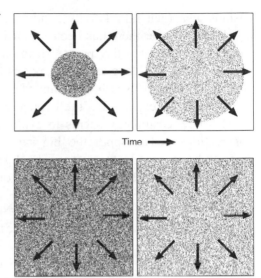

Time ⟶

Expansion of a bounded (top) and an unbounded (bottom) universe

reach the earth, for stars to age, etc. — while less than an ordinary day is passing on Earth. This massive gravitational time dilation would seem to be a scientific inevitability if a bounded universe has expanded significantly.

In one sense, if observers on Earth at that particular time could have looked out and 'seen' the speed with which light was moving toward them out in space, it would have appeared as if it were travelling many times faster than c. (Galaxies would also appear to be rotating faster) However, if an observer in deep space was out there measuring the speed of light, to him it would still only be travelling at c.

There is more detail of this new cosmology, at layman's level, in the book by Dr Humphreys, *Starlight and Time*, which also includes reprints of his technical papers showing the equations.[13]

It is fortunate that creationists did not invent such concepts as gravitational time dilation, black and white holes, event horizons and so on, or we would likely be accused of manipulating the data to solve this problem. The interesting thing about this cosmology is that it is based upon mathematics and physics totally accepted by all

[13] Humphreys, R., 1994. *Starlight and Time,* Master Books, Green Forest, AR.

cosmologists (general relativity), and it accepts (along with virtually all physicists) that there has been expansion in the past (though not from some imaginary tiny point). It requires no 'massaging' — the results 'fall out' so long as one abandons the arbitrary starting point which Big Bangers use (the unbounded cosmos idea, which could be called 'what the experts don't tell you about the "big bang"').

This new cosmology seems to explain in one swoop all of the observations used to support the 'big bang', including progressive redshift and the cosmic microwave background radiation, without compromising the data or the biblical record of a young Earth.

Caution

While this is exciting news, all theories of fallible men, no matter how well they seem to fit the data, are subject to revision or abandonment in the light of future discoveries. What we can say is that at this point a plausible mechanism has been demonstrated, with considerable observational and theoretical support.

What if no one had ever thought of the possibility of gravitational time dilation? Many might have felt forced to agree with those scientists (including some Christians) that there was **no** possible solution — the vast ages are fact, and the Bible must be 're-interpreted' (massaged) or increasingly rejected. Many have in fact been urging Christians to abandon the Bible's clear teaching of a recent creation because of these 'undeniable facts'. This re-interpretation also means having to accept that there were billions of years of death, disease, and bloodshed before Adam, thus eroding the Creation/Fall/Restoration framework within which the Gospel is presented in the Bible.

However, even without this new idea, such an approach would still have been wrong-headed. The authority of the Bible should never be compromised by mankind's 'scientific' proposals. One little previously unknown fact, or one change in a starting assumption, can drastically alter the whole picture so that what was 'fact' is no longer so.

This is worth remembering when dealing with those other areas of difficulty which, despite the substantial evidence for Genesis creation, still remain. Only God possesses infinite knowledge. By basing our scientific research on the assumption that His Word is true (instead of the assumption that it is wrong or irrelevant) our scientific theories are much more likely, in the long run, to come to accurately represent reality.

Chapter 6

How did bad things come about?

If God's original creation was 'very good', why is 'nature red in tooth and claw' now? Did God create animals with defence-attack structures? Or were they re-designed after the Fall? Wouldn't there be a population explosion if animals did not eat each other?

THE world before the Fall had no death, disease or suffering, as God proclaimed the finished creation 'very good' (Gen. 1:31). Consistent with this, God gave plants to the animals to eat (Gen. 1:29,30).

Nowadays, many creatures have equipment that seems designed for attacking, hurting, trapping, killing, or eating others, or defending themselves against such things — for example, the poison-injecting fangs of snakes, the great meat-eating cats, and the spider's web, to name just a few. So when and how did these things, which are suited to a fallen world but were unnecessary before the Fall, come to be?

Some creatures seem designed to kill and eat others.

There is no single position that would be agreed upon by all creationists in answer to this, so we will briefly look at the merits of a number of possibilities.

First, we need to look at the clear teachings of Scripture which bear on this question, remembering that the Bible gives us true, but not exhaustive, information. We may then try to fill in the gaps in our knowledge by reasoning, which will have to be somewhat speculative, using what we know about the living world. The Bible teaches:

● People and animals alike were given plants to eat in the beginning (Gen. 1:29–30). There was no meat eating before the Fall, whether by man or animal. The carnivorous part of the present 'food chain' did not exist. And God appropriately described His creation as 'very good' (Gen.1:31).

● The Bible makes a clear distinction between the status of plants and animals. People and animals are described in Genesis as having, or being, *nephesh* (Hebrew) — see Genesis 1:20,21,24 where *nephesh chayyah* is translated 'living creatures', and Genesis 2:7 where Adam became a 'living soul' (*nephesh chayyah*). *Nephesh* conveys the basic idea of a 'breathing creature'. It is also used widely in the Old Testament, in combination with other words, to convey ideas of emotions, feelings, etc. Perhaps *nephesh* refers to life with a certain level of consciousness. Plants do not have such *nephesh,* and so Adam eating a carrot did not involve death in the biblical sense.

● The world will one day be restored (Acts 3:21) to a state in which, once again, there will be no violence and death involving animals. Whether Isaiah 11:6–9 is taken to refer to a millennial kingdom or a new Earth, the point is the same. Lambs, wolves, leopards, children, bears, calves and snakes will all dwell together peacefully. Lions will once again be plant-eaters. Clearly, this vision of future bliss reflects the former paradise lost through sin.

● Clearly there was no disease, suffering or death of animals (*nephesh* creatures) before the Fall. This raises the question of just what is a *nephesh* animal. Do one-celled organisms like bacteria and yeast, or invertebrates like worms, insects and prawns have *nephesh* life? Scripture gives us some clues. It tells us that *'the life* (nephesh) *of the flesh is in the blood'* (Lev. 17:11. See also Gen. 9:4). If we use this to classify organisms into those with or without such '*nephesh* life', it is helpful up to a point — this would exclude microorganisms from having *nephesh*-life. But there are still difficulties as to what counts as blood. For example, insects and crustaceans have a form of blood, although it is somewhat different from the blood of animals with backbones. The presence of hemoglobin cannot be definitive, as it is found even in some plants.

Adam's naming of the land animals in Genesis 2 may give us further clues. Adam named 'each *living creature* (nephesh chayyah)' (Gen.2:19). What did he name? *'Adam gave names to all the cattle, and to the birds of the air, and to every animal of the field'* (Gen. 2:20).[1] It may be significant at this point that the *remes,* the 'creeping things' of Gen. 1.24, were not included, as Leupold, the respected theologian, noted. If 'creeping things' included insects and worms, for example, then maybe they are not *nephesh* life. However, Scripture is not clear on this, so we should not be dogmatic.

It can be safely said, however, that there was no violent death, especially that involving bloodshed. In other words, creatures we would normally call 'animals' in everyday speech, were not fighting, killing, shedding the blood of others, and eating one another, as many do today.

● Man was permitted to eat meat only after the Flood (Gen. 9:3). This may have been due to the extinction, in the Flood, of many plant species that formerly were able to provide all the protein and vitamin requirements for humans. To be well nourished by a totally vegetarian diet today is difficult, though not impossible. Of course, people may have eaten animals anyway, even before God gave permission. If that did happen, then it was probably not widespread, because Scripture implies that the animals had minimal fear of man before the Flood (Gen. 9:2).

Man and the animals were originally vegetarian.

---

[1] For a discussion of what Adam named, see Grigg, R., 1996. Naming the animals: All in a day's work for Adam. *Creation* **18**(4):46–49.

Animals today have certain biological equipment, which they use either to attack others, or to defend themselves. Let's group these together and call them 'defence-attack structures' (DAS). The first question is, 'Are these created structures — designed to do harm, for instance?'

The next, related, question is, 'When did they come about?' DAS would seem to have been quite out of place in a pre-Fall world.

The following are some of the possible answers, along with a discussion of some of the difficulties.

Position No. 1

Those things that are now used as DAS were not designed for this purpose, and had a different function, pre-Fall. They reached their present function by degeneration — for example, through mutations.

One can point to the fact that some creatures today have sharp teeth that look as if they would be used to rip meat, but we know they don't use them for that. The fruit bat is a prime example. Some species in the piranha group of fish use their jaws and teeth entirely for plants. So, the argument goes, could not the lion's teeth have been used to chew fruit before the Fall? Viruses that today inject harmful genes into their hosts may have had a useful pre-Fall role.[3]

Different species of bats differ in what they eat, but their teeth are similar.[2]

[2] Weston, P., 1998. Bats: sophistication in miniature. *Creation* **21**(1):29–31.
[3] Viruses, for instance, could have had a pre-Fall role in transferring genetic information to maintain/increase genetic diversity. It would not take any informational leap upwards in complexity to enable them to cause disease instead. Genes could have been acquired from hosts, even being modified by mutations to make the enzymes less specific (note this is a loss of information due to mutation), thus enabling disease-causing actions. Many disease-causing organisms are even degenerate from their own point of view — they quickly kill their host, thus destroying themselves. Also, the host might have degenerated and lost resistance. See Bergman, J., 1999. Did God make

Perhaps other harmful structures had a different pre-Fall function, which has been lost or modified, either by choice[4] or (the explanation usually given) by degenerate muta-tions.

The giant panda has sharp teeth and claws, and yet uses them to rip off and eat mainly plant (bamboo) material. Occas-ionally they have been seen to eat small animals. If, by the time man first observed them, most pandas ate animals, we would find it hard to imagine that their teeth and claws originally were for the purpose of eating plants.

Pandas have sharp teeth and claws and eat mainly bamboo.

Immune systems basically distinguish 'self' from 'non-self', which would be important for maintaining bodily integrity even in the pre-Fall world. Of course such systems became even more important in the post-Fall world, to protect against disease-causing organisms.

Position No. 1 avoids the problem of a good God designing harmful structures.[5] However, difficulties arise if this position is used to explain

---

pathogenic viruses? *CEN Technical Journal* **13**(1):115–125.

[4] This raises another problem: how much does an animal choose its way of life, as opposed to having programmed instinct? The only indirect scriptural support for this seems to be Genesis 6:7, 11–13, which has been understood by some to mean that violence in the animal kingdom was one reason for the eradication of the land animals outside the Ark. However, this does not necessarily mean that God attributes any moral responsibility to the animals. Perhaps He was grieved because man's sin opened the door to the whole post-Fall reign of death and bloodshed.

[5] This raises an old and interesting theological question. Would God, being omnipotent, be any less responsible for DAS by allowing them to happen 'naturally' rather than by actively designing them? An analogy is a doctor who, knowing that he could save a patient with the oxygen in his possession, fails to administer it. Is he less responsible than if he had actively killed the patient with cyanide? Some have pointed out that God is frequently actively involved in judgment without there being any ethical/theological dilemma; for instance, the sending of the great Flood that brought death and destruction to millions.

all occurrences of DAS. Virtually all creatures have some form of DAS, even if only a highly sensitive nervous system for warning of attack. They certainly give every indication of being designed to cope in a fallen world. Most of these DAS show great evidence of complex and specific design.

In fact, most, if not all, of the examples used by creationists to show design in living things involve DAS. If we say that DAS, or at least some aspects of their present function, arose by chance mutations, then we may have seriously undermined the main argument from design. It would mean saying that millions of different, complex and intricate patterns came about by chance (mutations and natural selection). Think of the sophisticated chemistry behind spider silk and the engineering marvel of spiders' webs, some of which are used to trap birds. All the complex machinery to make these webs is coupled with programmed instincts (programming of which involves coded information) to tell the spiders where to build them for best hunting results, and when and how to move in for the kill of the trapped prey. In literally millions of examples, since we would maintain that complex, purposive design means intelligent, purposive creation, there is *prima facie* evidence of God having purposely designed the DAS as well.

The other problem with this argument is that in each case of an

Charcoal by Robert Smith

The design adaptations for meat eating in the great cats are more than just sharp teeth

observed DAS, the true (pre-Fall) function was something different. It may be argued that our ignorance of the pre-Fall function does not mean that there wasn't one. This is true, of course, but if used for each and every one of the millions of DAS, it risks stretching credulity to the limit. One should also not overlook the full extent of what is involved in any particular defence-attack mechanism. For instance, discussions on the shape of teeth and claws may overlook the fact that the design features for meat eating in the great cats are more than just sharp teeth. A lion has finely-programmed hunting instincts, and immense muscular power capable of breaking a wildebeest's neck with one blow. Its digestive system is attuned to a diet of fresh meat (though lions can cope with vegetables in a crisis and, since meat is easier to digest, degenerative changes could be responsible for dependence on meat). All this makes it overwhelmingly appear to be a highly designed hunting and killing machine.

Such qualities are very common. Before the Fall, what was the function of the cheetah's blinding speed?[6] What did the bombardier beetle use its highly complex twin cannons for (useful now to blast attackers)? If we could think of a purpose, it would still leave open the question of how and when the programmed instincts to fire at beetle-eaters arose.

---

[6] Perhaps it was created to reveal God's glory by running fast (just as an eagle soars at high altitude or a dolphin rides waves, apparently for 'recreation'). Also, many of God's designs have inspired human inventions — e.g., the iris diaphragm in cameras and Velcro®. This could be part of the providence of God.

The idea that the snake's fangs may have been used to inject a fruit-softening substance pre-Fall has the same problem. That is, why, how and when (if not by direct creation) did snakes change not only their diet but their behaviour, which appears to be programmed in their genetic code and not a matter of conscious choice?[7]

In any case, snake venom contains complex chemicals that appear to be designed for purposes far removed from fruit eating. One of these chemicals is highly specific in its attack on the central nervous system to arrest breathing; another specifically blocks the clotting mechanism so that the prey bleeds to death internally.

Despite the above problems, this may still be the correct explanation in at least some, if not many, instances. The female mosquito draws blood, as it needs hemoglobin to reproduce. However, the male mosquito only sucks sap from plants. Perhaps both sexes drew sap from plants before the Fall, and with the eventual extinction of some plant species they could no longer get hemoglobin from plants as easily (as already mentioned, some living plants have hemoglobin).

Position No. 2

This essentially looks at complex design as requiring the direct hand of the Designer, whether for DAS or not. There are different possibilities within this, however. For example,

1. *There were no creatures with DAS pre-Fall — these creatures were all created afterwards.*

This would mean that most creatures alive today would not have had a pre-Fall representative. The Bible makes no mention of such a new creation, and Exodus 20:11 directly contradicts the idea. Not

---

[7] Based on the premise that the pre-Flood world had no desert or cold environments, some have queried the design features in many animals that are only useful in such conditions — e.g. the anti-dehydration equipment of a camel, or the special insulating features of a polar bear's fur. However, the Bible nowhere says that there were no deserts or cold areas before the Flood. In any case, such adaptive design features could have been present in the genes of more generalized created kinds of these creatures. For example, polar bears, which have special adaptations for the cold and are almost exclusively carnivorous, hybridize with brown bears, which do not have special cold adaptations and are mainly vegetarian (75%), suggesting that both derived from an original created bear kind.

surprisingly, this view is not widely held.

2. *The design information for DAS was already present before the Fall, perhaps in latent or masked form.*

This implies that the Fall was foreknown by God, which of course reflects His omniscience, and also is clearly stated in various Bible passages which speak of such things as God choosing us *'in him before the foundation of the world'* (Eph. 1:4). This information was allowed to become expressed, either through direct unmasking at the Fall, or through the natural processes of recombination and selection. If the latter were the case, this would again involve the foreknowledge of God, this time that there would be only a short time between creation and the Fall. Otherwise, these DAS would have come to the fore in Eden eventually.

However, it is not easy to imagine genetically how such self-activation could take place for such a vast number of creatures which must also interact ecologically (the appearance of a defence structure must take place very smartly after one's enemy has a new weapon).

3. *No new creatures were created, but many existing ones were 'redesigned' after the Fall, with the addition of new design information into their DNA.*

This position has some indirect Scriptural support. The Curse placed upon the creation at the Fall involved biological changes to people — they would now die (Gen. 3:19) and pain in childbirth would increase (Gen. 3:16). The ground was also cursed such that thorns and thistles would spring forth (Gen. 3:18) — suggesting that biological changes occurred in plants. And the serpent, at least, appears to have been radically and permanently redesigned by God with the Curse (Gen. 3:14). So changes occurred in man, animals, plants and the soil because of the Fall. The sense suggests that these things resulted from a sovereign directive as a result of Adam's sin; they did not result from something just being 'let go.'[8] This understanding agrees with

---

[8] In the future restoration, to get meat-eating lions (ML) to become grass-eating lions (GL) would seem to require supernatural rearranging of the DNA so as to make the change permanent for all future generations. Since ML→ GL requires this, and since this is a 're'-storation (i.e. a reversal of the results of the Fall), perhaps this indicates that GL→ML happened by the same route (supernatural DNA reprogramming), only in reverse.

Scriptures such as Romans 8 where the *'whole creation'* is described as subject to the Curse and awaiting redemption from the consequences of sin.

Conclusion

Scripture simply does not provide enough information for Christians to insist dogmatically that one or other of these possible explanations is totally right or wrong. Several of them may apply together.

As fallen creatures in a fallen world, we have difficulty imagining what a pre-Fall world was really like. We are also finite creatures lacking all the information. We therefore need to be particularly careful about arguing from the present to the past.

What is clear from God's Word is that the present 'reign of tooth and claw', of violent death, cruelty, and bloodshed, had no place in the world before Adam sinned, and will have no place in the restored creation.

APPENDIX

Population Explosion?

We see in today's post-Fall world that death, and animals eating others, is a useful way of avoiding overcrowding of the earth by any one type. Some, therefore, ask how, if there had been no Fall, such overcrowding could have been avoided without death and bloodshed.

This may be a non-question, since Scripture indicates that Adam's rebellion (and thus the need for the shed blood of God's Lamb, Jesus Christ) was foreknown before creation. Even if this were not so, it is surely presumptuous to suggest that the all-powerful Creator would have been unable to devise other means of avoiding such a problem. God gave the command to reproduce to 'fill the earth' (Gen. 1:22,28), and once that was completed, the command would no longer apply and the filling would stop.

One natural mechanism already exists for limiting population growth, and is well known. Some animals, when subjected to overcrowding, drastically reduce their reproductive rate, only to increase it again if the population density should drop once more.

Chapter **7**

What about similarities and other such arguments for evolution?

Do similarities between creatures prove that they had a common ancestor (evolved)? Is human and chimp DNA very similar? Do human embryos go through animal stages as they develop? Do we have useless left-over bits of animals in us? What about 'ape-men'?

Similarities?[1,2]

WE are similar in many respects to animals, especially the apes, and evolutionists argue that therefore we are related to them; we must have a common ancestor with them.

What does the Bible say? In Genesis 1 we are told that God made mankind, a man and a woman, specially:

And God said, Let us make man in our image, after our likeness: and let them have dominion over the fish of the sea, and over the fowl of the air, and over the cattle, and over all the earth, and over every creeping thing that creeps on the earth. (Gen. 1:26)

God created mankind in *His* image, not in the image of animals. Furthermore, man was to rule, have dominion, over the animals.

In Genesis 2, we are given more details of the creation process and we find that Adam was created from *'the dust of the ground'* (Gen. 2:7), not from an ape. When God pronounced judgment on Adam, He affirmed that Adam came from the ground:

In the sweat of your face you shall eat bread until you return to the ground, for out of it you were taken. For dust you are, *and to dust you shall return.* (Gen. 3:19)

Some wish to allegorize the Genesis account of man's creation to

---

[1] See Chapter 1 for some evidences for creation.
[2] Known technically as homologies.

make it conform to the current evolutionary fashion that man evolved from the apes. They are countered right here: if the dust Adam was made from represents the ape that he evolved from, then Adam must have turned back into an ape because of his sin! Of course not; the Bible is clear that man is a special creation.

Indeed, various kinds of animals and plants were created individually, not just humans. Plants were to produce seed *'after their kind'* meaning that bean plants were to produce bean seeds; and cattle would give birth to cattle, etc. (Gen. 1:11,12,21,24,25). So there is no hint in Scripture of any kind of an evolutionary process where one kind of organism would change into another kind.

Evolutionists believe not only that mankind evolved from an ape-like creature, but that ultimately everything evolved from a single-celled organism which happened to arise from non-living matter. They claim that the similarities between living things are proof that they evolved from common ancestors. They cite such things as the similarity between human and chimp DNA, similarities between embryos, claimed vestigial organs, and claimed transitional fossils between different kinds — such as supposed ape-men.

Human / chimp DNA similarity — evidence for evolutionary relationship?

The idea that human beings and chimps have close to 100 % similarity in their DNA is often claimed to prove that humans evolved from apes. The figures quoted vary: 97 %, 98 %, or even 99 % similarity, depending on who is telling the story. What is the basis for these claims, and do the data mean that there really is not much difference between chimps and people? Are we are just (slightly) evolved apes?

Firstly, similarity is not necessarily evidence for common ancestry (evolution) but may be due to a common designer (creation). Think about a Porsche and a Volkswagen 'Beetle' car. They both have air-cooled, flat, horizontally-opposed, 4-cylinder engines in the rear, independent rear suspension, two doors, boot (trunk) in the front, and many other similarities. Why do these two very different cars have so many similarities? Because they had the same designer! Whether similarity is morphological (shape, form) or biochemical is of no consequence to the lack of logic in this argument for evolution.

If humans were entirely different to all other living things, or indeed every living thing was entirely different, would this reveal the Creator to us? No! We could logically think that there must have been many creators rather than one. The unity of the creation is testimony to the One True God who made it all (Romans 1:20).

If humans were entirely different to all other living things, then what would we eat? If we are to eat food to gain nutrients and energy to live, what would we eat if every other organism on Earth were fundamentally different biochemically? How could we digest them and how could we use the amino acids, sugars, etc., if they were different from the ones we have in our bodies? Biochemical similarity is necessary for us to eat! Even in an unfallen world where animals and people ate only plants, **if animals and humans did not share similar biochemistry, there would have to be separate plant kingdoms for animals and humans to eat.**

We know that DNA in cells contains much of the information necessary for the development of an organism. In other words, if two organisms look similar, we would expect there to be some similarity also in their DNA. The DNA of a cow and a whale, two mammals, should be more alike than the DNA of a cow and a bacterium. If it were not so, then the whole idea of DNA being the information carrier in living things would have to be questioned. Likewise, humans and apes have many morphological similarities, so we would expect similarities in their DNA. Of all the animals, chimps are most like humans, so we would expect that their DNA would be most like human DNA, but not totally like human DNA.

Certain biochemical capacities are common to all living things, so there is even a degree of similarity between the DNA of yeast, for example, and that of human beings. Because human cells can do many of the things that yeast can do, we share similarities in the DNA sequences that code for the enzymes and proteins that do these same jobs in both types of cells. Some of the sequences, for example those that code for the histone proteins, are almost identical.

What of the 97 % similarity claimed between humans and chimps? The figures quoted do not mean quite what is claimed in the popular publications (and even some science journals). DNA contains its information in the sequence of four chemical compounds known as *nucleotides*, abbreviated C,G,A,T. Complex translation machinery in the cell 'reads' a series of three-letter 'words' of these chemical 'letters' and translates these into the sequences of the 20 different amino acids in proteins (a typical protein has hundreds of amino acids). The human DNA has over 3 billion nucleotides. Neither the human nor the chimp DNA has been anywhere near fully sequenced to allow a proper comparison.[3]   It may be a while before such a comparison can be made because it may be 2005 before we have the full sequence of human DNA, and chimp DNA sequencing has a much lower priority.

Where then did the '97 % similarity' come from? It was inferred from a fairly crude technique called *DNA hybridization,* where small parts of human DNA are split into single strands and allowed to re-form double strands (duplex) with chimp DNA.[4]   However, there are various reasons why DNA does or does not hybridize, only one of which is degree of similarity. Consequently, those working in the field of molecular homology do not use this somewhat arbitrary figure; other figures derived from the shape of the 'melting curve' are used instead.[5] Why has the 97 % figure been popularized then? Perhaps it served the purpose of indoctrinating the scientifically illiterate with evolution — like the imaginative 'ape-men' reconstructions in many museums.

Interestingly, the original papers did not contain the basic data and the reader had to accept the interpretation of the data 'on faith'. Sarich and co-workers[5] obtained the original data and used them in their discussion of which parameters should be used in homology studies.[6]

---

[3] This would take a lot of computer time — imagine comparing two sets of 1,000 large books, sentence by sentence, for similarities and differences!

[4] Sibley, C.G. and Ahlquist, J.E., 1987. DNA hybridization evidence of hominoid phylogeny: results from an expanded data set. *Journal of Molecular Evolution* **26**:99–121.   The resulting hybrid duplex material is then separated from the single-strand DNA remaining and heated in 2 to 3 degree increments from 55 to 95 °C. The amount of DNA separating at each temperature is measured and totalled, comparing it with human-human DNA re-formed as duplex. This gives the 'melting curve'. If 90 % of the human DNA is recovered with heating from the human-chimp hybrid, compared with the human-human DNA, then there is said to be 90 % normalized percentage hybridization.

[5] Sarich, V.M., Schmid, C.W. and Marks, J., 1989. DNA hybridization as a guide to phylogenies: a critical analysis. *Cladistics* **5**:3–32.

[6] Molecular homology studies could be quite useful to creationists in determining what were the original created 'kinds' and what has happened

Sarich *et al.,* discovered considerable sloppiness in the way Sibley and Ahlquist generated their data as well as their statistical analysis. Even if everything else were above criticism, the 97 % figure came from making a very basic statistical error — averaging two figures without taking into account differences in the number of observations contributing to each figure. When a proper mean is calculated it is 96.2 %, not 97 %. However, the work lacked true replication, so no real meaning can be attached to the figures published by Sibley and Ahlquist.

What if human and chimp DNA were even 96 % similar? What would that mean? Would it mean that humans could have 'evolved' from a common ancestor with chimps? Not at all! The amount of information in the 3 billion base pairs in the DNA in every human cell has been estimated to be equivalent to that in 1,000 books of 500 pages each.[7] If humans were 'only' 4 % different this still amounts to 120 million base pairs, equivalent to about 12 million words, or 40 large books of information. This is an impossible barrier for mutations (random changes) to cross.

Does a high degree of similarity mean that two DNA sequences have the same meaning or function? No, not necessarily. Compare the following sentences:

There are many scientists today who question the evolutionary paradigm and its atheistic philosophical implications.

There are **not** many scientists today who question the evolutionary paradigm and its atheistic philosophical implications.

These sentences have 97 % homology and yet have opposite meanings! There is a strong analogy here to the way in which large DNA sequences can be turned on or off by relatively small control sequences.

---

since to generate new species within each kind. For example, the varieties / species of finch on the Galápagos Islands obviously derived from an original small number that migrated to the islands. Recombination of the genes in the original migrants, and natural selection, could account for the varieties of finch on the islands today — just as all the breeds of dogs in the world today were artificially bred from an original wild dog kind not long ago. It is notable that molecular homology studies have been most consistent when applied within what are probably biblical kinds, but such studies often contradict the major predictions of evolution regarding the relationships between the major groups such as phyla and classes (see Ref. 7 regarding the latter).

[7] Denton, M., 1985, *Evolution: Theory in Crisis,* Burnett Books, London.

In summary, the methods used to generate the figures so often quoted (and misquoted!) are very clumsy. They do not legitimize the claim that people and chimps are related in an evolutionary sense. The more we learn of the complexities of the biochemical systems in our cells, the more marvellous they become. Furthermore, even if we accept the data as legitimate, there is no way that mutations could bridge the gap between chimps and humans. Chimps are just animals. We are made in the image of God (no chimps will be reading this).

Similarities between embryos

Most people have heard of the idea that the human embryo, during its early development in the womb, goes through various evolutionary stages, such as having gill slits like a fish, a tail like a monkey, etc. Abortion clinics have used the idea to soothe the consciences of clients, saying, for example, 'We're only taking a fish from your body.'

This concept was pretentiously called the 'biogenetic law', which the German evolutionist Ernst Haeckel popularized in the late 1860s. It is also known as 'embryonic recapitulation' or 'ontogeny recapitulates phylogeny', meaning that during an organism's early development it supposedly re-traces its evolutionary history. So, a human embryo is supposed to pass through a fish stage, an amphibian stage, a reptile stage, and so on.

Within months of the popular publication of Haeckel's work in 1868, L. Rütimeyer, professor of zoology and comparative anatomy at the University of Basel, showed it to be fraudulent. William His Sr, professor of anatomy at the University of Leipzig, and a famous comparative embryologist, corroborated Rütimeyer's criticisms.[8] These scientists showed that Haeckel fraudulently modified his drawings of embryos to make them look more alike. Haeckel even printed the same woodcut several times, to make the embryos look absolutely identical, and then claimed they were embryos of different species! Despite this exposure, Haeckel's woodcuts appeared in textbooks for many years.[9]

Has the 'biogenetic law' any merit? In 1965, evolutionist

---

[8] Rusch, W.H. Sr, 1969. Ontogeny recapitulates phylogeny. *Creation Research Quarterly* **6**(1):27–34.
[9] Grigg, R., 1996, Ernst Haeckel: evangelist for evolution and apostle of deceit. *Creation* **18**(2):33–36.

George Gaylord Simpson said, 'It is now firmly established that ontogeny does not repeat phylogeny.'[10] Prof. Keith Thompson (biology, Yale) said,[11]

'Surely the biogenetic law is as dead as a doornail. It was finally exorcised from biology textbooks in the fifties. As a topic of serious theoretical inquiry, it was extinct in the twenties.'

However, even textbooks in the 1990s were still using Haeckel's fraudulent drawings, including a textbook used in introductory biology courses in many universities, which said,[12]

'In many cases the evolutionary history of an organism can be seen to unfold during its development, with the embryo exhibiting characteristics of the embryos of its ancestors. For example, early in their development, human embryos possess gill slits like a fish ...'

Despite the fraudulent basis of the idea and its debunking by many high-profile scientists, the idea persists.

Scientists who should have known better have promoted the myth of embryonic recapitulation in the 1990s. For example, science popularizer, the late Carl Sagan, in a popular article titled 'Is it possible to be pro-life and pro-choice?'[13] described the development of the human embryo as follows:

'By the third week ... it looks a little like a segmented worm. ... By the end of the fourth week, ... something like the gill-arches of a fish or an amphibian have become conspicuous ... It looks something like a newt or a tadpole. ... By the sixth week ... reptilian face ... By the end of the seventh week ... the face is mammalian, but somewhat pig-like. ... By the end of the eighth week, the face resembles a primate, but is still not quite human.'

This is straight from Haeckel. A human embryo never looks reptilian or pig-like. A human embryo is always a human embryo, from the moment of conception; it is never anything else, contrary to what Sagan implies! It does not **become** human sometime after eight

---

[10] Simpson and Beck, 1965. *An Introduction to Biology*, p. 241.

[11] Thompson, K., 1988. Ontogeny and phylogeny recapitulated. *American Scientist* **76**:273.

[12] Raven, P.H. and Johnson, G.B., 1992. *Biology (3rd edition)*, Mosby–Year Book, St. Louis, p.396.

[13] *Parade Magazine*, 22 April, 1990

weeks. This is just what the Bible says — the unborn baby is a tiny human child (Gen. 25:21–22, Psalm 139:13–16, Jer. 1:5, Luke 1:41–44), so abortion takes an innocent human life.

Gill slits — something fishy?

The university textbook referred to above[12] claims that 'human embryos possess gill slits like a fish', although it has been known for many decades that humans embryos *never* have 'gill slits'. There are markings on a human embryo which superficially look like the 'gill slits' on a fish embryo. These 'pharyngeal clefts', as they are more properly called, or 'throat pouches', never have any breathing function, and are never 'slits' or openings. They develop into the thymus gland, parathyroid glands and middle ear canals — none of which has anything to do with breathing, under water or above water!

Specialist embryology textbooks acknowledge that human embryos do not have gill slits. For example, Langman said,[14]

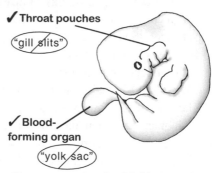

'Since the human embryo never has gills — branchia — the term pharyngeal arches and clefts has been adopted in this book.'

However, most evolutionists still use the term 'gill slits', especially in public presentations and when teaching students. The term prevails in school and university textbooks.

Wrong terms are used to label human embryos, indoctrinating students in evolutionary belief.

More revelations about Haeckel's fraud!

While the popularisers of evolution, when pressed, will admit that human embryos do not have gill slits and that Haeckel's drawings were to some extent fraudulent, they still believe that similarities between embryos are evidence for evolution (common ancestry). But this confidence rests, consciously or unconsciously, on the woodcuts published by Haeckel and reproduced, in whole or in part, in many

---

[14] Langman, J., 1975. *Medical Embryology* (3rd edition), p. 262.

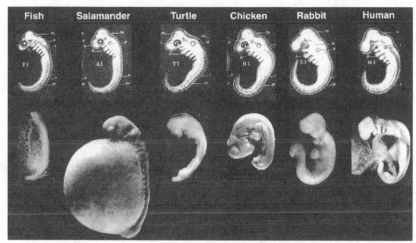

Haeckel's fraudulent drawings (top row) and photographs of the actual embryos (bottom row). After Richardson et al.[16] Used with permission.

textbooks since.[15] These drawings are widely believed to bear some resemblance to reality. But apparently no one had bothered to check.

Now it comes to light that Haeckel's fraud was far worse than anyone realised. An embryologist, Dr Michael Richardson, with the co-operation of biologists around the world, collected and photographed the types of embryos Haeckel supposedly drew.[16] Dr Richardson found that Haeckel's drawings bore little resemblance to the embryos.[17] Haeckel's drawings could only have come from his imagination, which was harnessed to produce 'evidence' to promote the acceptance of evolution.

Haeckel's drawings should no longer be used to support the evolutionists' claim that embryos are similar and that this supports evolution.

Are some similarities in early embryos inevitable?

To construct anything, you begin with something without shape, or with a basic form and then build upon that. An illustration from

---

[15] For example, Gilbert, S., 1997. *Developmental Biology* (5th edition), Sinauer Associates, Ma, pp. 254, 900. Gilbert wrongly credits the drawings to 'Romanes, 1901'.

[16] Richardson, M., *et al.,* 1997. There is no highly conserved stage in the vertebrates: implications for current theories of evolution and development. *Anatomy and Embryology* **196**(2):91–106.

[17] Grigg, R., 1998. Fraud rediscovered. *Creation* **20**(2):49–51.

pottery may help. A potter starts with a lump of clay. For a goblet or a slender vase, the potter would shape it initially into a cylinder. At this stage both the goblet and the vase look similar — they have the same basic plan. Further work results in the goblet and vase looking more and more different. The analogy with embryos breaks down in that the potter could change his mind and make *either* a vase or goblet at the completion of the basic plan. A fish embryo, however, could never become a human embryo (or *vice versa*) because a fish embryo has the coded instructions only for making a fish.

Some principles known as *von Baer's Laws* express this concept in regard to embryo development. Namely, the general features of a large group of animals appear earlier in the embryo than the specialised features. Less general characters are developed from the more general, and so forth, until finally the most specialised appear. Each embryo of a given species, instead of passing through the stages of other animals, departs more and more from them as it develops.

Von Baer's laws indicate that the younger the embryonic stage, the more closely organisms tend to resemble each other because they share the more generalised features, which appear first. Development can be likened to the radial spokes on a wheel. The spokes start at the hub and diverge outward, getting further and further apart.

Anomalies point to creation!

There are interesting exceptions to von Baer's laws. If we compare vertebrate embryos at the pharyngula stage (i.e. the stage showing the pharyngeal clefts), they look somewhat similar, but at *earlier* stages they are quite different! Ballard said,[18]

'... from very different eggs the embryos of vertebrates pass through cleavage stages of very different appearance, and then through a period of morphogenetic movements showing patterns of migration and temporary structures unique to each class. All then arrive at a pharyngula stage, which is remarkably uniform throughout the subphylum, consisting of similar organ rudiments similarly arranged (though in some respects deformed in respect to habitat and food supply).'

After 'converging' together, the embryos then diverge away from

---

[18] Ballard, W.W., 1976. Problems of gastrulation: real and verbal. *Bioscience* **26**(1):36–39.

each other in the classic von Baer pattern. How can this be explained through evolution? ReMine[19] argues that it points to an intelligent designer who designed living things. God made things similar to show that there is *one* creator (similarity at the pharyngula stage), but with a pattern of similarity that could not result from common ancestry (the earlier stages of embryo development differ). The differences at the earlier stages give no support to a naturalistic explanation for similarities at the later pharyngeal stage being due to common descent.

Likewise, with the mode of development of amphibian and mammal foot bones in the embryo. They can end up looking very similar, but the amphibian's toes develop from a bony plate by the dissolving of bone between the toes, whereas the mammal's toes develop by growth from buds outwards. Thus the similarities we see in amphibians and mammals are due to common design, not common ancestry.

Sir Gavin de Beer, embryologist and past Director of the British Museum of Natural History, addressed the problem of the lack of a genetic or embryological basis for homology more than 25 years ago in a monograph titled *Homology, an Unsolved Problem* (1971, Oxford Biology Reader, Oxford University Press). Although De Beer believed in evolution, he showed that similarity is often only apparent and is not consistent with common ancestry.

Patterns of embryo development point to creation, not evolution! We are indeed *'fearfully and wonderfully made'* (Psalm 139:14).[20]

Useless organs?

Evolutionists often argue that such things as flightless birds' small wings, pigs' toes, male nipples, legless lizards, the rabbit's digestive system, the human appendix, and hip bones and teeth in whales are useless and have no function. They claim these features are 'leftovers of evolution' and evidence for evolution.

The 'vestigial' organ argument for evolution is an old chestnut, but it is not valid.

---

[19] ReMine, W.J., 1993. *The Biotic Message: Evolution versus Message Theory,* St Paul Science, St Paul, Minn., USA, p. 370.

[20] For more information on embryos: Parker, G., 1994, *Creation: Facts of Life,* Master Books, Green Forest, AR; Vetter, J., 1991, Hands and feet — uniquely human, right from the start! *Creation* 13(1):16–17; Glover, W. and Ham, K., 1992. A surgeon looks at creation. *Creation* 14(3):46–49.

First, it is impossible to prove that an organ is useless. The function may simply be unknown and its use may be discovered in future. This has happened with more than 100 formerly alleged useless vestigial organs in humans that are now known to be essential.

Second, even if the alleged vestigial organ were no longer needed, it would prove 'devolution' not evolution. The creation model allows for deterioration of a perfect creation since the Fall. However, the particles-to-people evolution model needs to find examples of *nascent* organs, i.e. those which are *increasing* in complexity.

Wings on birds that do not fly?

There are at least two possibilities as to why flightless birds such as ostriches and emus have wings:

The emu's wings are not useless.

1. The wings are indeed 'useless' and derived from birds that once could fly. This is possible in the creationist model. Loss of features is relatively easy by natural processes, whereas acquisition of new characters, requiring specific new DNA information, is impossible. Loss of wings most probably occurred in a beetle species that colonised a windy island. Again, this is *loss* of genetic information, so it is not evidence for microbe-to-man evolution, which requires masses of new genetic information.[21]

2. The wings have a function. Some possible functions, depending on the species of flightless bird, are: balance while running, cooling in hot weather, warmth in cold weather, protection of the rib-cage in falls, mating rituals, scaring predators (emus will run at perceived enemies of their chicks, mouth open and wings flapping), sheltering of chicks, etc. If the wings are useless, why are the muscles functional, allowing these birds to move their wings?

Pigs with two toes that do not reach the ground?

Does this mean that the shorter toes have no function? Not at all. Pigs spend a lot of time in water and muddy conditions for cooling

---

[21] Wieland, C., 1997. Beetle bloopers: even a defect can be an advantage sometimes. *Creation* **19**(3):30.

purposes. The extra toes probably make it easier to walk in mud (a bit like the rider wheels on some long trucks that only touch the road when the truck is heavily loaded). Perhaps the muscles attached to the extra toes give strength to the 'ankle' of the pig.

Why do males have nipples?

Males have nipples because of the common plan followed during early embryo development. Embryos start out producing features common to male and female — again an example of 'design economy'. Nipples are a part of this design economy. However, as Bergman and Howe[22] point out, the claim that they are useless is debatable.

What is the evolutionist's explanation for male nipples? Did males evolve (devolve) from females? Or did ancestral males suckle the young? No evolutionist would propose this. Male nipples are neither evidence for evolution nor evidence against creation.

Why do rabbits have digestive systems that function 'so poorly that they must eat their own feces'?

This is an incredible proposition. One of the most successful species on Earth would have to be the rabbit! The rabbit's mode of existence is obviously very efficient (what about the saying 'to breed like rabbits'?) Just because eating feces may be abhorrent to humans, it does not mean it is inefficient for the rabbit! Rabbits have a special pouch called the *caecum*, containing bacteria, at the beginning of the large intestine. These bacteria aid digestion, just as bacteria in the rumen of cattle and sheep aid digestion. Indeed, rabbits 'chew the cud' in a manner that parallels sheep and cattle.

The rabbit produces two types of fecal pellet, a hard one and a special soft one coming from the caecum. It is only the latter that is eaten to enrich the diet with the nutrients produced by the bacteria

Sceptics have claimed that rabbits are poorly designed, yet they are one of the most successful animals, in terms of reproduction.

[22] Bergman J. and Howe, G., 1990. *'Vestigial Organs' are Fully Functional,* Creation Research Society Monograph No. **4**, Creation Research Society Books, Terre Haute, Indiana.

in the caecum. In other words, this ability of rabbits is a design feature; it is not something they have learned to do because they have 'digestive systems that function so poorly'. It is part of the variety of design, which speaks of creation, not evolution.

Sceptics have claimed the Bible is in error in saying that the rabbit 'chews the cud' (Lev. 11:6). The Hebrew literally reads, 'raises up what has been swallowed'. The rabbit does re-eat what has been swallowed — its partly digested fecal pellets. The sceptics are wrong.

Legless lizards

It is quite likely that legless lizards could have arisen through loss of genetic information from an original created kind, and the structures are consistent with this. 'Loss' of a structure is of no comfort to evolutionists, as they have to find a mechanism for creating new structures, not losing them. Loss of information cannot explain how evolution 'from ameba to man' could occur. Genesis 3:14 suggests that snakes may have once had legs.[23]

Adaptation and natural selection are biological facts; ameba-to-man evolution is not. Natural selection can only work on the genetic information present in a population of organisms — it cannot create new information. For example, since no known reptiles have genes for feathers, no amount of selection will produce a feathered reptile. Mutations in genes can only modify or eliminate existing structures, not create new ones. If in a certain environment a lizard survives better with smaller legs, or no legs, then varieties with this trait will be selected for. This might more accurately be called **devolution**, not **evolution**.

Rapid minor changes in limb length can occur in lizards, as demonstrated on Bahamian islands by Losos *et al.*[24] The changes occurred much faster than evolutionists thought they could. Such changes do not involve new genetic information and so give no support to microbe-to-man evolution. They do illustrate how quickly animals could have adapted to different environments after the Flood.

---

[23] Brown, C., 1989. The origin of the snake (letter). *Creation Research Society Quarterly* **26**:54. Brown suggests that monitor lizards may have been the precursors of snakes.

[24] Losos, J.B., Warheit, K.I. and Schoener, T.W., 1997. Adaptive differentiation following experimental island colonization in anolis lizards. *Nature* **387**:70–73. See comment by Case, T.J., *Nature* **387**:15–16, and *Creation* **19**(4):9.

The human appendix

It is now known that the human appendix contains lymphatic tissue and helps control bacteria entering the intestines. It functions in a similar way to the tonsils at the upper end of the alimentary canal, which are known to fight throat infections. Tonsils also were once thought to be useless organs.[25,26]

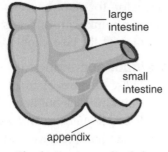

The human appendix helps protect the small intestine from microbes in the large intestine.

Hip bones in whales

Some evolutionists claim that these bones show that whales evolved from land animals. However, Bergman and Howe[22] point out that they are different in male and female whales. They are not useless at all, but help with reproduction (copulation).[27]

Teeth in embryonic baleen whales

Evolutionists claim that these teeth show that baleen whales evolved from toothed whales. However they have not provided an adequate mechanism for scrapping one perfectly good system (teeth) and replacing it with a very different system (baleen or whalebone). Also, the teeth in the embryo function as guides for the correct formation of the massive jaws.

As Scadding, an evolutionist, said, '...vestigial organs provide no evidence for evolutionary theory.'[28]

Ape-men?

Is there really evidence that man descended from the apes? Many people believe that the ancestry of mankind has been mapped faithfully and nearly completely. They have heard about 'missing links', and regard them as scientific proof of man's evolution. However, no

[25] Ham, K. and Wieland, C., 1997. Your appendix ... it's there for a reason. *Creation* **20**(1):41–43.

[26] Glover, J.W., 1988. The human vermiform appendix — a general surgeon's reflections, *CEN Technical Journal* **3**:31–38.

[27] See Wieland, C., 1998. The strange tale of the leg on a whale. *Creation* **20**(3):10–13.

[28] Scadding, S.R., 1981. Do vestigial organs provide evidence for evolution? *Evolutionary Theory* **5**:173–176.

ancestor for man has ever been convincingly documented. The 'missing links' are still missing. Here is a summary of facts relating to some of the best known fossils.[29,30]

Defunct ape-men

These are ones claimed at various times as intermediates between apes and humans but now rejected by evolutionists themselves.

• **Homo sapiens neanderthalensis (Neandertal man)** — 150 years ago Neandertal reconstructions were stooped, very much like an 'ape-man'. Many now admit that the stooped posture was due to disease (such as rickets) and that Neandertals were human, fully able to speak, artistic and religious.[31]

• **Ramapithecus** — once widely regarded as the ancestor of humans, it has now been recognised as merely an extinct type of orangutan (an ape).

• **Eoanthropus** (Piltdown man) — a hoax based on a human skull cap and an orangutan's jaw. It was widely publicised as the missing link for 40 years, and it was not even a competent forgery.

• **Hesperopithecus** (Nebraska man) — based on a single tooth of a type of pig now living only in Paraguay.

• **Pithecanthropus** (Java man) — now regarded as human and called *Homo erectus* (see below).

• **Australopithecus africanus** — this was at one time promoted as the missing link. It is very ape-like and evolutionists no longer consider it to be transitional.

• **Sinanthropus** (Peking man) — has now been reclassified as *Homo erectus,* of the human kind (see below).

Currently fashionable 'ape-men'

These 'ape-men' adorn the evolutionary trees today that supposedly trace how *Homo sapiens* evolved from a chimp-like creature.

• **Australopithecus** — various species of these have been proclaimed

---

[29] For details, see Lubenow, M., 1994, *Bones of Contention: A Creationist Assessment of the Human Fossils,* Baker Books, Grand Rapids, Michigan.

[30] For a documentary video on so-called 'ape-men', see *The Image of God,* Keziah Films.

[31] Lubenow, M.L., 1998, Recovery of Neandertal mtDNA: an evaluation. *CEN Technical Journal* **12**(1):87–97.

at times as human ancestors. One remains: *Australopithecus afarensis*, popularly known by the fossil 'Lucy'. However, detailed studies of the inner ear, skulls and bones indicate that 'Lucy' and her like are not part-human transitions. For example, they may have walked differently to most apes, but not in the human manner. *Australopithecus afarensis* is very similar to the pygmy chimpanzee, or bonobo.

• ***Homo habilis*** — there is a growing consensus among most palaeoanthropologists that this is a 'junk' category. It actually includes bits and pieces of various other types — such as *Australopithecus* and *Homo erectus*. It is therefore an 'invalid taxon'. Such a creature never existed. This was formerly claimed as *the* 'clear link' between apes and humans, but it is no longer valid.

• ***Homo erectus*** — many remains of this type have been found around the world. This classification now includes Java man *(Pithecan-thropus)* and Peking man *(Sinanthropus)*, which were once promoted as 'missing links'. Their skulls have prominent brow ridges, similar to Neandertals; their bodies were just like those of people today, only more robust. The brain size is within the range of people today and studies of the middle ear have shown that *Homo erectus* walked just like us. Both morphology and associated archaeological/cultural findings in association suggest that *Homo erectus* was fully human. Some evolutionists now agree that *erectus* is fully human and should be included in *Homo sapiens*.[32]

Homo erectus, a variant of the human kind, was once promoted as 'the missing link'.

There is no clear fossil evidence that man evolved from apes. The whole chain of missing links is still missing because they simply never existed. The Bible clearly states, *'then the LORD God formed man of the dust of the ground, and breathed into his nostrils the breath of life; and man became a living soul.'* (Gen. 2:7). Considering the history of defunct 'ape-men', all new claims should be treated sceptically.

---

[32] For example, Milford Wolpoff — see Ref. 29, pp. 134–143.

Other transitional fossils

If the evolutionary story about the origin of living things were true there should be millions of fossils showing the transitions from one kind of organism to another. After all, they say there have been hundreds of millions of years of mutations and natural selection, and the rock layers recorded this 'natural history' as fossils. Yet there are precious few, and even evolutionists cannot agree on their significance. Claimed evidence of fossils linking different kinds of organisms does not stand scrutiny.[33]

The lack of transitional fossils even drove evolutionists to propose a new mode of evolution in the late 1970s so they could go on believing in evolution without the need to find transitional fossils. This idea — *punctuated equilibrium* — basically says that the evolutionary changes occurred so quickly, geologically speaking, that no fossils were preserved to show them.[34]

Conclusion

The supposed evidence for evolution does not withstand critical examination.[35] The evidence is better understood in the context of God creating different basic kinds of organisms. These were capable of adapting to different environments by sorting the original created genetic information (re-shuffled by sexual reproduction), via natural selection. Some variation has been generated by mutations, but these are degenerate changes involving loss of genetic information, or at best horizontal changes where information is not lost or gained.

The probability of natural processes generating new genetic information is so low that evolution could not possibly account for the origin of the vast amounts of complex coded information in living things.[36] Creation is the explanation consistent with the evidence.

---

[33] Gish, D.T., 1995. *Evolution: The Fossils Still Say No!* Institute for Creation Research, El Cajon, CA, 391 pp.

[34] Batten, D., 1994. Punctuated equilibrium: come of age? *CEN Technical Journal* **8**(2):131–137.

[35] For further reading on the supposed evidence for evolution: Wieland, C., 1994. *Stones and Bones,* Answers in Genesis, Acacia Ridge, Qld, Australia, Parker, G., 1994. *Creation: Facts of Life,* Master Books, Green Forest, AR, and Sarfati, J., 1999. *Refuting Evolution*, Master Books, Green Forest, AR. For in depth reading see Ref. 19.

[36] Spetner, L.M., 1998. *Not by Chance,* Judaica Press, New York.

Chapter 8

Cain's wife — who was she?

It is not lawful to marry your sister, so who did Cain marry? Were there other people on the earth? Who lived in the land of Nod? Does this have any relevance to the Gospel?

WE don't even know her name, yet she was discussed at the Scopes Trial, mentioned in the play and movie *Inherit the Wind*[1-3] and the book and movie *Contact*,[4] and has been talked about in countries all over the world. Is she the most-talked-about wife in history?

Sceptics have used Cain's wife time and again to try to discredit the book of Genesis as a true historical record. Sadly, most Christians have not been able to give an adequate answer to this question. As a result, the world thinks Christians cannot defend the authority of Scripture and thus the Christian faith.

For instance, at the historic Scopes Trial in Tennessee in 1925, William Jennings Bryan, the prosecutor who stood for the Christian faith, failed to answer the question about Cain's wife posed by the outspokenly anti-Christian ACLU[5] lawyer, Clarence Darrow.[6]

---

[1] A 'Hollywood' version of the famous Scopes Trial. The play claimed not to be based on the real Scopes, but it was clearly intended to be seen as a representation of the Scopes Trial. See footnote 3.

[2] Ham, K., 1996. The Wrong Way Round! *Creation* **18**(3):38–41.

[3] Menton, D., 1997. 'Inherit the Wind': an historical analysis. *Creation* **19**(1):35–8. Menton documents the gross distortion and anti-Christian bigotry of the play.

[4] *Contact*. Released July 11, 1997. A Robert Zemeckis Film. Warner Bros. Based upon *Contact* by Carl Sagan, 1985, Pocket Books, New York.

[5] American Civil Liberties Union — an organisation at the forefront of attempts to remove all vestiges of Christianity from public life in the United States.

[6] *The World's Most Famous Court Trial, The Tennessee Evolution Case* (A word-for-word report), 1990. Bryan College (reprinted original edition), p. 302.

The world's press was focused on this trial, and what they heard has affected Christianity to this day — Christians are seen as unable to defend the biblical record. And sceptics then make the logically fallacious jump of concluding that the biblical record is indefensible!

The atheist Carl Sagan used this same question in his book *Contact*[4] (which was on *The New York Times* bestseller list), and the movie *Contact*, which was based on Sagan's book, also used it.

In the book, the fictional character Ellie could not get answers about Cain's wife, and other questions, from a minister's wife, who was the leader of a church discussion group.[7]

Sagan cleverly used common questions — such as, 'Who was Cain's wife?' — questions that are often directed at Christians in an attempt to 'prove' the Bible cannot be defended.

Sadly, most Christians probably could not answer these questions! And yet, there *are* answers. But, since most churches are lacking in the teaching of apologetics,[8] particularly in regard to the book of Genesis, most believers in the church are not *'ready always to give an answer to everyone who asks you a reason for the hope in you'* (1 Peter 3:15).

Cain's wife? A question many Christians cannot answer.

Why is it important?

Many sceptics have claimed that, for Cain to find a wife, there must have been other 'races' of people on the earth who were not descendants of Adam and Eve. To many people, this question is a stumbling block to accepting the Creation account in Genesis and its

---

[7] Sagan, C., 1985. *Contact,* Pocket Books, New York, pp. 19–20.

[8] Apologetics — from the Greek word, *apologia,* meaning to give a defence. Christian apologetics provides a defence of our faith in Jesus Christ and our hope in Him for our salvation (1 Peter 3:15). This requires a thorough knowledge of Scripture, including the doctrines of Creation, Original Sin, Curse, Flood, Virginal Conception, life and ministry of Jesus of Nazareth, the Cross, Crucifixion, Resurrection, Ascension, the Second Coming, and the New Heaven and New Earth. It involves explaining these doctrines logically, so as to justify one's faith and hope in Jesus Christ. Finally, one needs to be able to defend these doctrines, and the Bible in general, from attacks by unbelievers.

record of only one man and woman at the beginning of history — a record on which many Old and New Testament doctrines depend.

Defenders of the Gospel must be able to show that all human beings are descendants of one man and one woman (Adam and Eve) — as only those people who are descendants of Adam and Eve can be saved. Thus, believers need to be able to account for Cain's wife and show clearly that she was a descendant of Adam and Eve. (The relevant Bible passage is Genesis 4:1–5:5.)

Before we answer this question, we will first show how important it is to the meaning of the Gospel.

The first man

Therefore, even as through one man sin entered into the world, and death by sin, and so death passed on all men inasmuch as all sinned. (Rom. 5:12)

We read in 1 Corinthians 15:45 that Adam was 'the first man'. God did not start by making a whole group of men.

The Bible makes it clear that *only* the descendants of Adam can be saved. Romans 5 teaches that we sin because Adam sinned. The death penalty, which Adam received as judgment for his sin of rebellion, also passed on to all his descendants.

Since Adam was the head of the human race when he 'fell', we who were in the loins of Adam 'fell' also. Thus, we are all separated from God. The final consequence of sin would be separation from God in our sinful state forever. However, the good news is that there is a way for us to return to God!

Because a man brought sin and death into the world, all the descendants of Adam need a sinless Man to pay the penalty for sin and the resulting judgment of death. However, the Bible teaches that *'all have sinned'* (Romans 3:23). What is the solution?

The last Adam

God provided the solution — a way to deliver man from his wretched state. Paul explains in 1 Corinthians 15 that God provided another Adam! The Son of God took on human nature in addition to His full divinity, becoming a perfect God-Man — Jesus Christ. In His humanity He was a descendant of Adam (through Noah, Abraham and David) — He thus became our relation! He is called *'the last Adam'* (1 Cor. 15:45), because he took the place of the first Adam.

He became the new head and, because He was sinless, He was able to pay the penalty for sin:

> *For since by a man* came *death, by a man* came *also the resurrection of the dead. For as in Adam all die, even so in Christ shall all be made alive. (1 Corinthians 15:21,22)* [9]

Christ suffered death (the penalty for sin) on the Cross, shedding His blood (*'without shedding of blood is no remission'* — Heb. 9:22) so that those who repent of their sin of rebellion and put their trust in His work on the Cross can be reconciled to God.

Since the Bible describes **all** human beings as sinners, except the God-man Jesus, and we are **all** related (Acts 17:26 — *'And He has made all nations of men of one blood to dwell on all the face of the earth*), the Gospel makes sense only on the basis that all humans alive and all who have ever lived are descendants of the first man Adam. [10] If this were not so, then the Gospel could not be explained or defended.

The book of Hebrews amplifies how Jesus took upon himself the nature of a man to save mankind (Heb. 2:11–18).

Thus, only descendants of the first man Adam can be saved.

All related

Thus, there was only *one* man at the beginning — made from the dust of the earth (Gen. 2:7).

This also means that Cain's wife was a descendant of Adam. She could not have come from another 'race' of people and must be one of Adam's descendants.

The first woman

In Genesis 3:20 we read, *'And Adam called his wife's name Eve; because she was the mother of all living.'* [11] In other words, all people are descendants of Adam and Eve — she was the first woman.

Eve was made from Adam's rib (or side) (Gen. 2:21–24) — this was a unique event. Jesus (Mat. 19:4–6) and Paul (Eph. 5:31) use this historical and one-time event as the doctrinal foundation for the marriage of one man to one woman.

---

[9] In this passage, the Greek word for 'man' is in the singular ('**a** man').

[10] Eve, in a sense, was a 'descendant' of Adam in that she was made from his flesh and thus had a biological connection to him (Gen. 2:21–23).

[11] The Hebrew literally means 'she was to be the mother of all living'.

Also, in Genesis 2:20, we are told that when Adam looked at the animals, he could not find a mate — there was no one of his kind.

All this makes it obvious that there was only *one* woman, Adam's wife, at the beginning. There were never any other women around who were not Eve's descendants.

If Christians cannot defend that all humans (including Cain's wife) can trace their ancestry ultimately to Adam and Eve, then how can they understand and explain the Gospel? How can they justify sending missionaries to every tribe and nation? Therefore, one needs to be able to answer the question about Cain's wife, to illustrate that Christians *can* defend the Gospel and all that it teaches.

Cain's brothers and sisters

Cain was the first child of Adam and Eve recorded in Scripture (Gen. 4:1). He and his brothers, Abel (Gen. 4:2) and Seth (Gen. 4:25), were part of the *first* generation of children ever born on this Earth.

Even though only these three males are mentioned by name, Adam and Eve had other children. In Genesis 5:4 a statement sums up the life of Adam and Eve — *'And the days of Adam after he had fathered Seth were eight hundred years. And he fathered sons and daughters.'* This does not say *when* they were born. Many could have been born in the 130 years (Gen. 5:3) before Seth was born.

During their lives, Adam and Eve had a number of male and female children. The Jewish historian Josephus wrote that, 'The number of Adam's children, as says the old tradition, was thirty-three sons and twenty-three daughters.'[12]

The Bible does not tell us how many children were born to Adam and Eve. However, considering their long life spans (Adam lived for 930 years — Gen. 5:5), it would seem reasonable to suggest there were many! Remember, they were commanded to *'Be fruitful, and multiply'* (Gen. 1:28).

The wife

If we now work totally from Scripture, without any personal prejudices or other extra-biblical ideas, then back at the beginning, when there was only the first generation, brothers would have had to

---

[12] Josephus, Flavius, (translated by William Whiston, A.M.) 1981. *The Complete Works of Josephus,* Kregel Publications, Grand Rapids, Michigan, p. 27.

have married sisters or there would have been no more generations!

We are not told when Cain married or any of the details of other marriages and children, but we can say for certain that some brothers had to marry their sisters at the beginning of human history.

Objections

God's laws

Many people immediately reject the conclusion that Adam and Eve's sons and daughters married each other by appealing to the law against brother-sister intermarriage. Some say that you cannot marry your relation. Actually, if you don't marry your relation, you don't marry a human! A wife is related to her husband even before they marry because *all* people are descendants of Adam and Eve — all are of 'one blood'. The law forbidding marriage between close relatives was not given until the time of Moses (Lev. 18–20). Provided marriage was one man to one woman for life (based on Gen. 1 and 2), there was no disobedience to God's law originally when close relatives (even brothers and sisters) married each other.

Remember that Abraham married his half-sister (Gen. 20:12). God blessed this union to produce the Hebrew people through Isaac and Jacob. It was not until some 400 years later that God gave Moses laws that forbade such marriages.

Biological deformities

Today, brothers and sisters (and half-brothers and half-sisters, etc.) are not permitted by law to marry because their children have an unacceptably high risk of being deformed. The more closely the parents are related, the more likely it is that any offspring will be deformed.

There is a very sound genetic reason for such laws that is easy to understand. Every person has two sets of genes, there being some 130,000 pairs that specify how a person is put together and functions. Each person inherits one gene of each pair from each parent. Unfortunately, genes today contain many mistakes (because of sin and the Curse), and these mistakes show up in a variety of ways. For instance, some people let their hair grow over their ears to hide the fact that one ear is lower than the other — or perhaps someone's nose is not quite in the middle of his or her face, or someone's jaw is a little out of shape — and so on. Let's face it, the main reason we call each other normal is because of our common agreement to do so!

The more distantly related parents are, the more likely it is that they will each have ***different*** mistakes in their genes. Children, inheriting one set of genes from each parent, are likely to end up with pairs of genes containing a maximum of one bad gene in each pair. The good gene in a pair tends to override the bad so that a deformity (a serious one, anyway) does not occur. Instead of having totally deformed ears, for instance, a person may have only crooked ones! (Overall, though, the human race is slowly degenerating as mistakes accumulate generation after generation.)

However, the more closely related two people are, the more likely it is that they will have similar mistakes in their genes, since these have been inherited from the same parents. Therefore, a brother and a sister are likely to have similar mistakes in their genes. A child of a union between such siblings could inherit the same bad gene on the same gene pair from both, resulting in two bad copies of the gene and serious defects.

However, Adam and Eve did not have accumulated genetic mistakes. When the first two people were created, they were physically perfect. Everything God made was *'very good'* (Gen. 1:31), so their genes were perfect — no mistakes! But, when sin entered the world (because of Adam — Gen. 3:6ff, Rom. 5:12), God cursed the world so that the perfect creation then began to degenerate, that is, suffer death and decay (Rom. 8:22). Over thousands of years, this degeneration has produced all sorts of genetic mistakes in living things.

Cain was in the first generation of children ever born. He (as well as his brothers and sisters) would have received virtually no imperfect

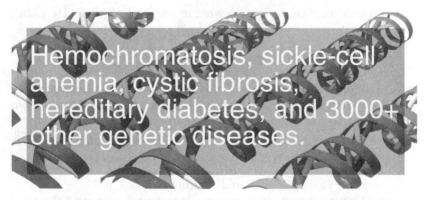

Hemochromatosis, sickle-cell anemia, cystic fibrosis, hereditary diabetes, and 3000+ other genetic diseases.

Mutations have accumulated since the Fall, causing many human diseases.

genes from Adam or Eve, since the effects of sin and the Curse would have been minimal to start with (it takes time for these copying errors to accumulate). In that situation, brother and sister could have married with God's approval, without any potential to produce deformed offspring.

By the time of Moses (a few thousand years later), degenerative mistakes would have built up in the human race to such an extent that it was necessary for God to forbid brother-sister (and close relative) marriage (Lev. 18–20).[13] (Also, there were plenty of people on the earth by now, and there was no reason for close relations to marry.)

Cain and the land of Nod

Some claim that the passage in Genesis 4:16–17 means that Cain went to the land of Nod and found a wife. Thus, they conclude there must have been another race of people on the earth, who were not descendants of Adam, who produced Cain's wife.

And Cain went out from the presence of the LORD, and dwelt in the land of Nod, on the east of Eden. And Cain knew his wife; and she conceived, and bore Enoch: and he built a city, and called the name of the city, after the name of his son, Enoch.

From what has been stated previously, it is clear that *all* humans, Cain's wife included, are descendants of Adam. However, this passage does *not* say that Cain went to the land of Nod and found a wife. John Calvin, commenting on these verses, states:

'From the context we may gather that Cain, before he slew his brother, had married a wife; otherwise Moses would now have related something respecting his marriage.'[14]

Cain was married *before* he went to the land of Nod. He didn't find a wife there, but 'knew' (had sexual relations with) his wife.[15]

---

[13] Some have claimed this means God changed his mind by changing the laws. But God did not change his mind — because of the changes that sin brought, and because God never changes, He introduced new laws for our sake. Also, there is in the Bible a progressive revealing of the Messianic program which was in the mind of God from eternity. See Grigg, R., 1998. Unfolding the Plan. *Creation* **20**(3):22–24.

[14] Calvin, John, 1979. *Commentaries on The First Book of Moses Called Genesis,* Baker House, Grand Rapids, Michigan, Vol. 1, p. 215.

[15] Even if Calvin's suggestion concerning this matter is not correct, there was

Others have argued that because Cain built a 'city' in the land of Nod, there must have been a lot of people there. However, the Hebrew word translated as 'city' need not mean what we might imagine from the connotations of 'city' today. The word meant 'a walled town', or a protected encampment.[16] Even a hundred people would be plenty for such a 'city'. Nevertheless, there could have been many descendants of Adam on the earth by the time of Abel's death (see below).

Who was Cain fearful of? (Genesis 4:14)

Some claim that there had to be lots of people on Earth other than Adam and Eve's descendants, otherwise Cain would not have been fearful of people wanting to slay him for killing Abel.

First of all, in the days before civil government was instituted to punish murderers (Gen. 9:6), someone would want to harm Cain for killing Abel only if they were closely related to Abel! Strangers could hardly have cared. So the people Cain was afraid of could not have been another race of people.

Secondly, Cain and Abel were born quite some time before Abel's death. Genesis 4:3 states:

And in the course of time it came to pass, that Cain brought of the fruit of the ground an offering unto the LORD.

Note the phrase *'in the course of time'*. We know Seth was born when Adam was 130 years old (Gen. 5:3), and Eve saw him as a 'replacement' for Abel (Gen. 4:25). Therefore, the period from Cain's birth to Abel's death may have been 100 years or more — allowing plenty of time for other children of Adam and Eve to marry and have children and grandchildren. By the time Abel was killed, there could well have been a considerable number of descendants of Adam and Eve, involving several generations.

Where did the technology come from?

Some claim that for Cain to go to the land of Nod and build a city he would have required a lot of technology that must have already been in that land, presumably developed by other 'races'.

---

still plenty of time for numerous descendants of Adam and Eve to move out and settle areas such as the land of Nod.

[16] *Strong's Concordance*: 'city, town, a place guarded by waking or a watch in the widest sense (even of a mere encampment or post).'

However, Adam and Eve's descendants were very intelligent people. Jubal made musical instruments such as the harp and organ (Gen. 4:21), and Tubal-Cain worked with brass and iron (Gen. 4:22).

Because of intense evolutionary indoctrination, many people today think that our generation is the most intelligent that has ever lived on this planet. But just because we have jet airplanes and computers, it does not mean we are the most intelligent. Modern technology results from the accumulation of knowledge. We stand on the shoulders of those who have gone before us.

Our brains have suffered from 6,000 years (since Adam) of the Curse. We are greatly degenerated compared with people many generations ago. We may be nowhere near as intelligent or inventive as Adam and Eve's children. Scripture gives us a glimpse of what appears to be great inventiveness from the beginning.[17]

Conclusion

Many Christians cannot answer the question about Cain's wife because they focus on today's world (and the problems associated with close relations marrying), and do not understand the clear historical record God has given to us.

They try to interpret Genesis from our present situation, rather than understand the true biblical history of the world and the changes that have occurred because of sin. Because they are not building their worldview on Scripture, but taking a secular way of thinking to the Bible, they are blinded to the simple answers.

Genesis is the record of the God who was there as history happened. It is the Word of One who knows everything, and Who is a reliable Witness from the past. Thus, when we use Genesis as a basis for understanding history, we can make sense of questions that would otherwise be a mystery.

---

[17] See Chittick, D., 1997. *The Puzzle of Ancient Man,* Creation Compass, Newberg, OR, USA.

Chapter 9

Were the 'sons of God' and/or the *nephilim* extra-terrestrials?[1]

Has Earth been visited by extra-terrestrials? Could life exist 'out there'? What about UFOs and government cover-ups?

FOR decades, speculation about extra-terrestrial life has been boosted by tales of flying saucers and encounters with aliens. Some have even claimed that the 'sons of God' and/or the *nephilim* of Genesis 6:4 were aliens (see later).

In 1996 this was fuelled from another source. NASA researchers claimed to have found evidence for simple life forms in a meteorite, allegedly from Mars, found in Antarctica.

Since then, this 'proof' of life in the 'Mars rock' has very much lost favour among the scientific community.[2-4] The supposed 'nanofossils' were probably no more than magnetite whiskers plus artefacts of the experimental process.[5]

Photo by NASA

Despite this, the 2 kg rock has ignited a new surge of 'Mars fever'. In the next 20 years, the Americans, Europeans, Japanese and Russians plan around 20 projects to explore our neighbouring planet, which is some 78 million kilometres away at its closest approach to us.

Meanwhile, belief in extra-terrestrial intelligences continues to grow with an almost religious fervour.

The meteorite that was falsely claimed to show that life was once on Mars.

[1] Much of this chapter is based on an article by Dr Werner Gitt published in *Creation* **19**(4):46–48, 1997.

[2] Sarfati, J.D., 1996. Life on Mars? *Creation* **19**(1):18–20.

[3] Sarfati, J.D., 1996. Life from Mars? *CEN Technical Journal* **10**(3):293–296.

[4] Holmes, Bob, 1996. Death knell for Martian life. *New Scientist* **152**(2061/2):4.

[5] See Anon., 1998. Another blow to Mars 'life' claim. *Creation* **20**(2):8.

The UFO wave

Harvard University psychiatry professor John E. Mack recently attracted world-wide attention with his collection of cases of people claiming they were 'abducted by aliens'.

There was also the release of a film of an alleged autopsy on an alien from a crash in New Mexico close to the U.S. Air Force Base at Roswell. The blurry footage, which most have dismissed as an obvious and crude forgery, was nevertheless the main attraction at the 1995 UFO World Congress in Düsseldorf, Germany.

Then of course, there was the 'alien invasion' film *Independence Day,* which grossed more in its opening week than any previous film.

A recent poll in Germany revealed that 17 % of the population believe in visits by alien craft, while 31 % believe there is intelligent life in other galaxies.

What should Christians think about UFO accounts?

What does the Bible say?

(a) Scripture does not mention 'ET' visits.

The Bible, the revealed written Word of God, teaches that life is only possible through a process of creation. Even if there were other galaxies with planets very similar to Earth, life could only be there if the Creator had fashioned it. If God had done that, and if these beings were going to visit us one day, then He would surely not have left us unenlightened about this.

God *has* given us rather specific details of the future — for example, the return of Jesus, and some details about the end of the world. The universe will, at some future point, be rolled up like a scroll (Isa. 34:4, Rev. 6:14). If God had created living beings elsewhere, this would automatically destroy their dwelling place as well. Adam's sin caused all of creation to be affected by the curse, so why would a race of beings, not of Adam's (sinful) seed, have their part of creation affected by the Curse, and then be part of the restoration brought about by Christ, the last Adam? All of this would seem exceedingly strange.[6]

---

[6] Furthermore, Jesus dying for alien beings makes no sense, since Jesus took on **human** nature, and remains the God-man forever as our Saviour. If he were to atone for Vulcans, say, he would need to become a Vulcan. The whole purpose of creation is focused on the race on Earth, of which some will be Christ's

Some have claimed that the *nephilim,* or the 'sons of God', both mentioned in Genesis 6:2–4, were aliens. This is a wild extension of a common view that the 'sons of God' who married the 'daughters of men' were fallen angels, and that the *nephilim* were products of those 'marriages'.

'Sons of God' is clearly used of angels in Job 38:7. The Septuagint (LXX) here translates 'sons of God' as 'angels of God'. This need not mean that evil angels, or demons, actually cohabited with women — Jesus made it clear that angels do not engage in sexual activities, at least not angels in Heaven (Matt. 22:30). Nevertheless, evil angels on Earth could have used the bodies of ungodly men, by demonic possession, to achieve their evil purpose of producing an evil generation of people (Gen. 6:12).[7]

There are other reasonable suggestions as to the identity of the 'sons of God' and the *nephilim.* Interestingly, the word *nephilim* is only used here and in Numbers 13:33, where it clearly refers to the descendants of Anak, who were big people, but still people. Furthermore, 'sons of God' is not used exclusively of angels — the children of Israel are called *'the sons of the living God'* in Hosea 1:10 (see also Psalm 73:15; 80:17).

Bible scholars such as H.C. Leupold believe that the 'sons of God' were descendants of Seth, the godly line who are detailed in the preceding chapter (Gen. 4:25–5:32). Leupold wrote, 'But who were these "sons of God"? Without a shadow of a doubt, the Sethites …'. [8] In this view, the descendants of Seth became wayward and married the 'daughters of men' indis-criminately, basing their choice only on appearance, without concern for godliness, and the *nephilim* were their offspring.

Rulers of old were often called 'gods'.

Rulers in ancient Egypt and Mesopotamia

'bride' throughout eternity. Christ will not have multiple 'brides'.

[7] Morris, H.M., 1976. *The Genesis Record,* Baker Book House, Grand Rapids, MI, p. 169.

[8] Leupold, H.C., 1942. *Exposition of Genesis, Vol. 1,* Wartburg Press, Ann Arbor, MI, p. 250.

often proclaimed themselves as 'sons of God' to enhance their power and prestige. So, another view with much support is that the 'sons of God' were power-hungry rulers and despots, who, in their hunger for power and influence, took many wives in polygamy. They, and their offspring, through tyranny, became 'mighty men' (Nimrod was described as such a 'mighty one', Gen. 10:8).

So, there is no need to resort to fanciful suggestions involving aliens to understand this passage of Scripture.

(b) The purpose of the stars

The reasons stars were made are given to us in several places in the Bible, not only in the well-known Psalm 19 but especially in the Creation account. In Genesis 1:14 we read: *'And God said, Let there be lights in the expanse of the heavens to divide between the day and the night. And let them be for signs, and for seasons, and for days and years.'*

Thus God made the stars for mankind on Earth, not for another alien race 'out there'. Add to this the sequence of creation (on the first day the earth, and only on the fourth day the stars), and it is easy to see the thrust of the biblical testimony, that the purpose of creation is uniquely centred on this Earth.

Science

1. Never a single contact with an 'extra-terrestrial'

In 1900, the French Academy of Science offered a prize of 100,000 francs for the first person to make contact with an alien civilisation — so long as the alien was not from Mars, because the Academy was convinced that Martian civilisation was an established fact!

Since then, not a trace of 'little green men', or indeed any life, has been found on any of the planets that our probes have explored, including Mars.

Despite this, a great number of astronomers think that, since life supposedly evolved here on Earth, it must have evolved near one of the many stars out there. Around the world SETI (Search for Extra Terrestrial Intelligence) researchers have scanned the sky, looking in vain for signals from intelligent beings. Despite all the listening, on thousands of frequencies over many years, nothing indicating intelligent alien life has ever been heard.

2. Conditions must be 'just right'.

Life on any planet can only survive provided a great number of very stringent requirements are met. For example, the planet must be at the right distance from its sun, so as to be neither too hot nor too cold. In particular, it must be in a very narrow temperature range so that liquid water exists.

Even if planets around other stars are confirmed, it is extremely improbable that any of them would fulfil all the require-

'Is it true that not one of your experiments has shown signs of intelligence?'

ments needed for life. Just having liquid water is completely insufficient, despite the excitement created when such was possibly detected on the surface of Jupiter's moon, Europa (the fluid is now thought to be sulfuric acid).

3. Life cannot form spontaneously anyway.

Without intelligent, creative input, lifeless chemicals cannot form themselves into living things.[9] This is the theory of spontaneous generation, disproved by the great creationist founder of microbiology, Louis Pasteur. Without unfounded evolutionary speculation, UFOlogy would not have its present grip on the public imagination.

4. Vast distances

Even if we assumed life existed somewhere else in the universe, a visit by extra-terrestrials to Earth, such as is claimed in UFO reports, seems completely impracticable, if not impossible. The distances (and therefore the likely travel times) are unimaginably vast.

---

[9] Some recent creationist critiques of evolutionary origin of life theories are: Aw, S.E., 1996. The origin of life: a critique of current scientific models. *CEN Technical Journal* **10**(3):300–314; Sarfati, J.D., 1997. Self-replicating enzymes. *CEN Technical Journal* **11**(1):4–6; Thaxton, C.B., Bradley, W.L. and Olsen, R.L., 1984. *The Mystery of Life's Origin*, Philosophical Library Inc., New York.

The *closest* star to Earth, Proxima Centauri (α-Centauri C) is 40.7 million million kilometres (c. 25 million million miles) away. The Apollo flights took three days to get to the moon. At the same speed, one would need 870,000 years to get to this nearest star. Of course, one could accelerate (particularly unmanned) probes to a greater speed.

At the incredible speed of one-tenth of the speed of light, the trip, *one way*, would still take 43 years. However, one would need enormous amounts of energy for such an acceleration, roughly equivalent to the electricity consumption of the entire world's population for one month (see the Appendix, p. 136).

Furthermore, in every cubic kilometre of space, there are an estimated 100,000 dust particles (made up of silicates and ice) weighing only a tenth of a gram. At such a velocity, colliding with even one of these tiny objects could destroy a spaceship.[10]

So what about UFOs?

How, then, should one understand the UFO phenomena and all the associated hype? In the German magazine *Focus,* it was recently stated '90 % of UFO reports turn out to be humbug, but there is a residual 10 % which are not easy to dismiss.'[11]

The article quoted sociologist Gerald Eberlein as saying:

'research has shown that people who are not affiliated with any church, but who claim that they are religious, are particularly susceptible to the possible existence of extra-terrestrials. For them, UFOlogy is a substitute religion.'[12]

The Bible goes somewhat deeper in this matter, identifying a supplementary cause and effect:

whose coming is according to the working of Satan with all power and signs and lying wonders, and with all deceit of unrighteousness in those who perish, because they did not receive the love of the truth, so that they might be saved. And for this cause God shall send them strong delusion, that they should believe a lie. (2 Thess. 2:9–11)

---

[10] This means there is a very small chance of hitting one in each linear kilometre travelled, but over such vast distances, a hit is almost certain. The appendix (p. 136) gives calculations of the damaging effects of dust at such high speeds.

[11] Erdling, Hallo, 1995. Ufologie. *Focus* **45**:254.

[12] Ref. 11, p. 252.

The Bible gives a description of reality concerning all living things. The living God reveals himself as the Triune One — Father, Son and Holy Spirit. In heaven there are the angels, powerful created beings who also serve mankind on the earth.

There is another kingdom — that of the devil and the demons.[13] Ephesians 2:2 talks about the 'prince of the power of the air', whose reign is on Earth.

The devil has his own repertoire of deception in the form of various occult practices and a multitude of religious rites. It could be that behind those unexplainable UFO reports there is the work of the arch-deceiver.[14] UFO reports, by definition, remain nebulous and not identifiable. People who do not know Christ are easily fascinated by all sorts of phenomena that are difficult to explain. For Christians there is Jesus' warning in Matthew 24:4 to *'Take heed that no man deceive you.'* What is the best antidote to deception? Paul exhorts us, in 2 Timothy 2:15, to *'study'* the Scripture, so we might *'accurately handle the word of truth'.*

Secret bases? ... government cover-ups? ...

Many UFO enthusiasts spread the 'urban myth' of secret U.S. Government experiments on aliens, etc. — an idea reinforced by the movie *Independence Day.* However, does a cover up make sense when, under the inspiration of atheists like the late Carl Sagan, the U.S. government has spent millions of taxpayers' dollars listening 'out there' for signs of intelligent ET life? Many other evolutionary humanists, like Sagan, passionately believe that intelligent life has evolved 'out there' in addition to Earth, and would pounce on any hard evidence for this idea. Consider the media frenzy about the 'life in Mars rock' fiasco. To imagine that a much more exciting discovery would be kept secret for decades defies credibility.

---

[13] The devil and his evil angels are fallen created beings. Satan's kingdom will exist only as long as God permits.

[14] William Alnor, cult expert and award-winning journalist, has studied the UFO phenomenon for many years. His book, *UFOs in the New Age* (Baker Book House), 1992, documents his investigations that lead to the conclusion that some UFO phenomena have an occult source.

Appendix: feasibility of inter-stellar travel

The following calculations are given for the benefit of the more technically-minded.

1. For a spacecraft to acquire a speed of $c/10$, the kinetic energy needed is given accurately enough by the non-relativistic formula of $\frac{1}{2}mv^2$. For a very small unmanned spacecraft of 10 kg, this is $\frac{1}{2}$ x 10 kg x $(3 \times 10^7 \text{ m/s})^2 = 4.5 \times 10^{15}$ J, or approximately the whole world's electricity production for a month.

For a manned spacecraft weighing several tonnes, the energy requirements would greatly exceed the world's annual electricity consumption. For the city-sized spacecraft in *Independence Day,* the energy requirements would be staggering. And when the spacecraft slowed again, it would need to use up almost this amount of energy in braking.

If the spacecraft had to accelerate to $c/10$, slow down and speed up many times, the energy needed would be many times greater.

It would probably be impossible for enough fuel to be carried without some sort of antimatter drive. If perfect annihilation — complete conversion of matter to energy ($E = mc^2$) — were possible, 1 tonne of antimatter could annihilate 1 tonne of ordinary matter to produce: 2000 kg x $(3 \times 10^8 \text{ m/s})^2$, or 1.8×10^{20} J. And this is the absolute maximum amount of energy that could be produced from a given mass of fuel. A real spacecraft could be nowhere near this efficient.

2. The kinetic energy of a speck of dust with a mass of just 0.1 gram impacting at a tenth of the speed of light, calculated from the spacecraft's reference frame, is $\frac{1}{2}mv^2$, or

$\frac{1}{2}$ x 10^{-4} kg x $(3 \times 10^7 \text{ m/s})^2 = 4.5 \times 10^{10}$ J.

The combustion energy of TNT is 4,520 kJ/kg, or 4.52×10^9 J/tonne. So 4.5×10^{10} J is equivalent to 9.95 tonnes of TNT. Therefore the impact energy of a 0.1 g object hitting a spacecraft travelling at $c/10$ would be the equivalent to an explosion of about 10 tonnes of TNT.

10

Was the Flood global?

Does it matter? Does the Bible say that Noah's Flood covered the whole earth? Is there any evidence outside the Bible for such a Flood?

MANY Christians today claim that the Flood of Noah's time was only a *local* flood. They claim it was confined to somewhere around the Mesopotamian region and never really covered the whole earth. The discovery of a layer of mud by archaeologists in the Middle East and more recently the finding of evidence for a local flood in the Black Sea have both been claimed as evidence for a (local) biblical flood.

People generally want a local flood because they have accepted the widely believed evolutionary history of the earth, which interprets the fossils under our feet as the history of the sequential appearance of life over eons of time.

Scientists once understood the fossils (which are buried in water-carried sediments of mud and sand) to be mostly the result of the great Flood. Those who now accept the evolutionary billions of years of gradual accumulation of fossils have, in their way of thinking, explained away the evidence for the Flood — hence their belief in a local flood, or none at all. If they would think from a biblical perspective, they would see the abundant evidence for the Flood. As someone quipped, 'I wouldn't have seen it if I hadn't believed it.'

Those who accept the eons of time with its fossil accumulation also, perhaps unwittingly, rob the Fall of its serious consequences. They put the fossils, which testify of disease, suffering and death before mankind appeared; before Adam and Eve sinned and brought death and suffering into the world. In doing this they also undermine the meaning of the death and resurrection of Christ. Such a scenario also robs God's description of His finished creation as 'very good' of all meaning (see Chapter 2).

Some preachers will say they believe in a 'universal' or 'world-wide' flood, but really they do not believe that the flood covered the whole earth. They side-step the clear teaching of the Bible, while giving the appearance of believing it, by cleverly re-defining words. They mean 'universal' and 'world-wide' only in terms of an imagined limited extent of human habitation at the time. They imagine that people lived only (say) in a valley in Mesopotamia and so the flood could kill all the people without being global in extent.

Biblical evidence for the global Flood

The local flood idea is totally inconsistent with the Bible, as the following points demonstrate:

The need for the Ark

If the Flood were local, why did Noah have to build an Ark? He could have walked to the other side of the mountains and escaped. Travelling just 20 km per day, Noah and his family could have travelled over 3,000 km in six months. God could have simply warned Noah to flee, as He did for Lot in Sodom.

The size of the Ark

If the Flood were local, why was the Ark big enough to hold all the different kinds of land vertebrate animals in the world? If only Mesopotamian animals were aboard, or only domestic animals, the Ark could have been much smaller.[1]

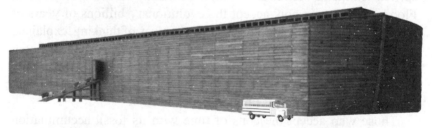

The size of the Ark makes sense only if the Flood were global.

The need for animals to be on the Ark

If the Flood were local, why did God send the animals to the Ark to escape death? There would have been other animals to reproduce those kinds even if they had all died in the local area. Or He could have sent them to a non-flooded region.

---

[1] See Chapter 13, p. 167.

The need for birds to be on the Ark

If the Flood were local, why would *birds* have been sent on board? These could simply have winged across to a nearby mountain range. Birds can fly several hundred kilometres in one day.

The judgment was universal

If the Flood were local, people who did not happen to be living in the vicinity would not have been affected by it. They would have escaped God's judgment on sin. It boggles the mind to believe that, after all those centuries since creation, no one had migrated to other parts — or that people living on the periphery of such a local flood would not have moved to the adjoining high ground rather than be drowned. Jesus believed that the Flood killed everyone not on the Ark (Matt. 24:37–39).

Of course those who want to believe in a local flood generally say that the world is old and that people were here for many tens of thousands of years before the Flood. If this were the case, it is inconceivable that all the people could have fitted in a localised valley in Mesopotamia, for example, or that they had not migrated further afield as the population grew.

The Flood was a type of the judgment to come

What did Christ mean when He likened the coming world judgment to the judgment of 'all' men (Matt. 24:37–39) in the days of Noah? In 2 Peter 3, the coming judgment by fire is likened to the former judgment by water in Noah's Flood. A partial judgment in Noah's day would mean a partial judgment to come.

The waters were above the mountains

If the Flood were local, how could the waters rise to 15 cubits (8 metres) *above* the mountains (Gen. 7:20)? Water seeks its own level. It could not rise to cover the local mountains while leaving the rest of the world untouched.[2]

---

[2] Mt Everest has marine fossils at its peak. There is enough water in the oceans so that, if all the surface features of the earth were evened out, including the ocean basins, water would cover the earth to a depth of 2.7 km. This is not enough to cover mountains the height of Everest now, but it shows that the pre-Flood mountains could have been quite high and still been covered. See Chapter 11 for more details about how this could have occurred.

The duration of the Flood

Noah and company were on the Ark for one year and 10 days (Gen. 7:11, 8:14) — surely an excessive amount of time for any local flood? It was more than seven months before the tops of any mountains became visible. How could they drift around in a local flood for that long without seeing any mountains?

God's promise broken?

If the Flood were local, God would have repeatedly broken His promise never to send such a Flood again. There have been huge 'local' floods in recent times: in Bangladesh, for example, where 80 % of that country has been inundated.

All people are descendants of Noah and his family

The genealogies of Adam (Gen. 4:17–26, 5:1–31) and Noah (Gen. 10:1–32) are exclusive — they tell us that all the pre-Flood people came from Adam and all the post-Flood people came from Noah. The descendants of Noah were all living together at Babel and refusing to 'fill the earth', as they had been commanded (Gen. 9:1). So God confused their one language into many and scattered them (Gen. 11:1–9).

There is striking evidence that all peoples on Earth have come from Noah, found in the Flood stories from many cultures around the world — North and South America, South Sea Islands, Australia, Papua New Guinea, Japan, China, India, the Middle East, Europe and Africa. Hundreds of such stories have been gathered.[3] The stories closest to the area of dispersion from Babel are nearest in detail to the biblical account — for example, the Gilgamesh epic.

---

[3] Frazer, J.G. 1918. *Folk-lore in the Old Testament: studies in comparative religion, Vol. 1,* Macmillan, London, pp. 105–361.

The Hebrew terminology of Genesis 6-9[4]

● *'The earth'* (Heb. *erets*), is used 46 times in the Flood account in Genesis 6–9, as well as in Genesis 1. The explicit link to the big picture of creation, especially in Genesis 6:6–7, clearly implies a universal Flood. Furthermore, the judgment of God is pronounced not just on *all flesh*, but on *the earth:*

> *And God said to Noah, The end of all flesh has come before me, for the earth is filled with violence through them. And, behold, I will destroy them* **with the earth***.* (Gen. 6:13)

● *'Upon the face of all the earth'* (Gen. 7:3, 8:9) clearly connects with the same phrase in the creation account where Adam and Eve are given the plants on Earth to eat (Gen. 1:29). Clearly, in God's decree the mandate is universal — the whole earth is their domain. God uses the phrase in Genesis also of the dispersal of people at the Tower of Babel (Gen. 11:8,9) — again, the context is the whole land surface of the globe. The exact phrase is used nowhere else in Genesis.

● *'Face of the ground'*, used five times in the Flood account, also connects back to the universal context of creation (Gen. 2:6), again emphasising the universality of the Flood.

● *'All flesh'* (Heb. *kol-basar*) is used 12 times in the Flood account and nowhere else in Genesis. God said he would destroy *'all flesh'*, apart from those on the Ark (Gen. 6:13,17),[5] and He did (Gen. 7:21–22). In the context of the Flood, 'all flesh' clearly includes all nostril-breathing land animals as well as mankind — see Genesis 7:21–23. 'All flesh' could not have been confined to a Mesopotamian valley.

● *'Every living thing'* (Heb. *kol chai*), is again used in the Flood account (Gen. 6:19, 8:1,17) and in the creation account (Gen. 1:28). In the creation account the phrase is used in the context of Adam and Eve's dominion over the animals. God said (Gen. 7:4) that He would destroy *'every living thing'* He had made and this happened — *only* Noah and those with him on the Ark survived (Gen. 7:23).

---

[4] Davidson, R.M., 1995. Biblical evidence for the universality of the Genesis Flood. *Origins* **22**(2):58–73.

[5] Some translations wrongly render 'all flesh' in Gen. 6:13 as 'all people' (e.g. NIV, whereas KJV and NASB are correct). This is clearly not the meaning of 'all flesh', as revealed by its use in Genesis 7:21 (where the NIV renders 'all flesh' correctly as 'every living thing').

● *'Under the whole heaven'* (Gen. 7:19) is used six times outside of the Flood account in the Old Testament, and always with a universal meaning (Deut. 2:25, 4:19, Job 28:24, 37:3, 41:11, Daniel 9:12). For example, *'Whatever is under the whole heaven is mine'* said the LORD (Job 41:11).

● *'All the fountains of the great deep'.* The fountains of the great deep are mentioned only in the Flood account (Gen. 7:11, 8:2) and Proverbs 8:28. *'The deep'* (Heb. *tehom*) relates back to creation (Gen. 1:2) where it refers to the one ocean covering the whole world before the land was formed. And it was not just *'the fountains of the great deep'* but *'**all** the fountains of the great deep'* which broke open.

● A special Hebrew word was reserved for the Flood or Deluge: *Mabbul.* In every one of the 13 occasions this word is used, it refers to Noah's Flood. Its one use outside of Genesis, Psalm 29:10, refers to the universal sovereignty of God in presiding over the Deluge. The New Testament also has a special word reserved for the Flood, *cataclysmos,* from which we derive our English word 'cataclysm'.

The decrees in Genesis 9 parallel those in Genesis 1

In Genesis 9:1 God gives man the exact same commission as in Genesis 1:28 — *'Be fruitful and multiply and fill the earth'.* He also gives man dominion over *'every beast of the earth'* (Gen. 9:2, cf. 1:28) and man is instructed as to what he can and cannot eat (Gen. 9:4–5), which parallels Genesis 1:29–30. These decrees in Genesis 1 are universal in extent, and clearly they are also here, after the Flood. If Adam and his descendants were to rule the whole earth, so were Noah and his descendants. If 'earth' in Genesis 9:1 is the whole earth, as all would agree it is, then surely it is also the whole earth in the context of the Flood in Genesis 8:13!

The New Testament speaks of the Flood as global[4]

New Testament passages which speak of the Flood use universal language: *'the flood came and took them **all** away'* (Jesus, Matt. 24:39); *'the flood came and destroyed them **all**'* (Jesus, in Luke 17:27); *'did not spare the ancient **world** [Greek:* kosmos*], but preserved Noah, a preacher of righteousness, and seven others, bringing in the flood upon the **world** of the ungodly'* (2 Peter 2:5); *'a **few**, that is eight people, were saved through the water'* (1 Peter 3:20); Noah *'condemned the **world'*** through his faith in God (Heb. 11:7); *'the **world** that then was, being flooded by water, perished'* (2 Pet 3:6). All these statements presuppose a global Flood, not some localised event.

Objections to a global Flood

Objection 1: 'All' does not always mean 'all'[6]

Some have argued that since 'all' does not always mean 'each and every' (e.g. Mark 1:5) that the use of 'all' in the Flood account does not necessarily mean the Flood was universal. That is, they claim that this use of 'all' allows for a local flood.

However, the meaning of a word is decided by the context. From the context of 'all' in Luke 2:1, for example, we can see that 'all the world' meant all the Roman Empire. So, it is the context that tells us that 'all' here does not mean every bit of the whole land surface of the globe.

However, to determine the meaning of 'all' in Genesis 6–9, we must consider the context, not just transfer the inferred meaning from somewhere else.

The word 'all' (Heb. *kol*) is used 72 times in the 85 verses of Genesis 6–9, 21% of all the times it is used in all 50 chapters of Genesis.

In Genesis 7:19 we read that *'all* (Heb. *kol*) *the high mountains under all* (Heb. *kol*) *the heavens were covered'.* Note the double use of 'all'. In Hebrew this gives emphasis so as to eliminate any possibility of ambiguity.' This could be accurately translated as 'all the high mountains under the *entire* heavens', to reflect the emphasis in the Hebrew. Leupold, in his authoritative commentary on Genesis, said of this, '... the text disposes of the question of the universality of the Flood'.[7]

Objection 2: The post-Flood geography is the same as the pre-Flood

Because the Tigris and Euphrates rivers were mentioned in the description of the Garden of Eden, and we have the Tigris and Euphrates rivers now, some have argued that the Flood could not have altered the topography of the world, and therefore it must have been local.[8]

---

[6] For a full treatment, see Kruger, M., 1996. Genesis 6–9: Does 'all' always mean all? *CEN Technical Journal* 10(2):214–218.

[7] Leupold, H.C., 1942. *Exposition of Genesis,* Baker Book House, Grand Rapids, MI, USA, vol. 1, pp. 301–302.

[8] For example, Young, D.A., 1977. *Creation and the Flood: an alternative to*

However, there are major differences in the topography described for the Garden of Eden and the world now. There was one river flowing from Eden which separated into four rivers (Gen. 2:10–14), two of which were called the Tigris and the Euphrates. So the rivers had a common source before the Flood, which is very different from today. The other two rivers were the Pishon and the Gihon. The Pishon is not mentioned post-Flood and Gihon is used of the locality of a spring near Jerusalem in the times of Kings David, Solomon and Hezekiah.[9]

The post-Flood world is not the same as the pre-Flood world. Someone may ask, 'Then why do we have a Tigris and Euphrates today?' Answer: the same reason there is a Liverpool and Newcastle in Australia; and London, Oxford and Cambridge in North America, although they were originally place names in England. Features in the post-Flood world were given names familiar to those who survived the Flood.

Objection 3: There is no evidence for such a Flood in the geologic record

What evidence would one expect from a global watery cataclysm that drowned the animals, birds and people not on the Ark? All around the world, in rock layer after rock layer, we find billions of dead things that have been buried in water-carried mud and sand. Their state of preservation frequently tells of rapid burial and fossilization, just like one would expect in such a flood.

There is abundant evidence that many of the rock strata were laid down quickly, one after the other, without significant time breaks between them. Preservation of animal tracks, ripple marks and even raindrop marks, testifies to rapid covering of these features to enable their preservation. Polystrate fossils (ones which traverse many strata) speak of very quick deposition of the strata. The scarcity of erosion, soil formation, animal burrows and roots between layers also shows

---

Flood geology and theistic evolution, Baker Book House, Grand Rapids, MI, USA, p.210. Sadly, Dr Young has drifted more and more towards full-blown theistic evolution since he wrote this book, where he compromised the Bible by advocating 'progressive creationist' views.

[9] The Gihon spring of 1 Kings 1:33,38,45 and 2 Chron. 32:30; 33:14 clearly has nothing to do with the Tigris-Euphrates river system of today, or the four-way split river system described in Eden.

Fossil 'graveyards' around the world, where the bones of many animals were washed together, buried and fossilised, are evidence for a watery cataclysm like the Flood.

they must have been deposited in quick succession. The radical deformation of thick layers of sediment without evidence of cracking or melting also shows how all the layers must have been still soft when they were bent. Dykes (walls) and pipes (cylinders) of sandstone which connect with the same mat-erial many layers beneath show that the layers beneath must have been still soft, and contained much water. That the sandstone could be squeezed up through cracks above to form the 'clastic' dykes and pipes, again shows rapid deposition of many strata.

Preservation of ripple marks requires rapid burial, as in the Flood (lower Triassic rock, England).

The world-wide distribution of many geological features and rock types is also consistent with a global Flood. The Morrison Formation is a layer of sedimentary rock that extends from Texas to Canada, clearly showing the fallacy of the still popular belief that 'the present is the key to the past' — there are no

Folding of sedimentary rock without cracking or heating, such as at Eastern Beach, Auckland, New Zealand, suggests the folding occurred before the sand and mud had time to turn into stone, consistent with rapid deposition during the Flood (note people for scale).

processes occurring on Earth today that are laying down such large areas of sedimentary layers. In reality, God's revelation about the past is the key to understanding the present.

The limited geographic extent of unconformities (clear breaks in the sequence of deposition with different tilting of layers, etc.), is also consistent with the reality of the global Flood. And there are many other evidences for the Flood.[10,11]

The problem is not the evidence but the mind-set of those looking at the evidence. One geologist testified how he never saw any evidence for the Flood — until, as a Christian, he was convinced from the Bible that the Flood must have been a global cataclysm. Now he sees the evidence everywhere. It's a case of 'I would not have seen it if I had not believed it!' The Bible talks about people being corrupted in their thinking after turning their backs on God (Romans 1:18ff.) and of people being so spiritually blind that they cannot see the obvious (Acts 28:25–27).

See chapters 11–15 for other questions about the Flood and Noah's Ark.

Conclusion

A universal **world-wide, globe-covering,** Flood is clearly taught by the Bible. The only reasons for thinking the Flood was otherwise come from outside the Bible. When we use the framework provided by the Bible we find that the physical evidence from the rocks and fossils beautifully fits what the Bible says.

Furthermore, the realisation of the reality of God's judgment by the Flood in the past should warn us of the reality of the judgment to come — a judgment by fire — and stimulate us to be ready for that judgment (2 Peter 3:3–13). Those who are not 'in Christ' will suffer the wrath of God (John 3:36).

---

[10] Morris, J.D. 1994. *The Young Earth,* Master Books, Colorado Springs.
[11] Austin, S. (Ed.), 1994. *Grand Canyon: Monument to Catastrophe,* Institute for Creation Research, Santee, CA, USA.

Chapter 11

What about continental drift?

Have the continents really moved apart? How could this relate to the Bible's account of history? Could it have had something to do with the Flood?

BEFORE the 1960s, most geologists were adamant that the continents were stationary. A handful promoted the notion that the continents had moved (continental drift), but they were accused by the majority of indulging in pseudo-scientific fantasy. Today, that opinion has reversed — plate tectonics, incorporating continental drift, is the ruling theory. (Interestingly, it was a creationist, Antonio Snider, who in 1859 first proposed horizontal movement of continents catastrophically during the Genesis Flood.[1] The statements in Genesis 1:9,10 about the gathering together of the seas in one place, which implies there was one landmass, influenced his thinking.)

Geologists put forward several lines of evidence that the continents were once joined together and have moved apart, including:

● The fit of the continents (taking into account the continental shelves).

● Correlation of fossil types across ocean basins.

● A zebra-striped pattern of magnetic reversals parallel to mid-ocean floor rifts, in the volcanic rock formed along the rifts, implying sea-floor spreading along the rifts.

● Seismic observations interpreted as slabs of former ocean floor now located inside the earth.

The current theory that incorporates sea-floor spreading and continental drift is known as 'plate tectonics'.[2]

---

[1] Snider, A., 1859. *Le Création et ses Mystères Devoilés*, Franck and Dentu, Paris.

[2] Some geologists are still sceptical of various aspects of plate tectonics.

Plate tectonics

The general principles of plate tectonic theory may be stated as follows.[3] The earth's surface consists of a mosaic of rigid plates, each moving relative to adjacent plates. Deformation occurs at the edges of the plates by three types of horizontal motion: extension (or rifting, moving apart), transform faulting (horizontal slipping along a fault line), and compression, mostly by subduction (one plate plunging beneath another).

Extension occurs as the sea floor pulls apart at rifts, or splits.

Transform faulting occurs where one plate slips horizontally past another (e.g., the San Andreas Fault of California).

Compressional deformation occurs when one plate subducts beneath another, e.g., the Pacific Plate beneath Japan and the Cocos Plate beneath South America, or when two continental plates collide to produce a mountain range, e.g., the Indian-Australian Plate colliding with the Eurasian Plate to form the Himalayan Mountains. Volcanoes often occur in regions of subduction.

Sea-floor spreading

One argument advanced for plate tectonics is sea-floor spreading. In the ocean basins, along mid-ocean ridges (e.g., the Mid-Atlantic Ridge and East Pacific Rise), observations are interpreted to indicate that plates are diverging, with molten material from the mantle[4] rising up in the gap between the plates and cooling to form new crust under the ocean. The youngest crust is at the ridge axis, with progressively older rocks away from the axis. World-wide, it is estimated that currently about 20 cubic kilometres of molten magma rises each year to create new oceanic crust.[5]

At the time of cooling, some of the rocks' minerals acquire magnetism from the earth's magnetic field, recording the field's direction at the time. Evidence indicates that the earth's magnetic field has

---

[3] Nevins, S.E. [Austin, S.A.], 1978. Continental drift, plate tectonics, and the Bible. In: *Up with Creation!* D.R. Gish, and D.H. Rohrer (eds.), Creation-Life Publishers, San Diego, pp. 173–180. See also *Longman Illustrated Dictionary of Geology,* Longman Group, Essex, UK, 1982, pp. 137–172.

[4] The zone within the earth that extends from below the crust down to the core — i.e. to a depth of about 2,900 km.

[5] Cann, J., 1998. Subtle minds and mid-ocean ridges. *Nature* **393**:625,627.

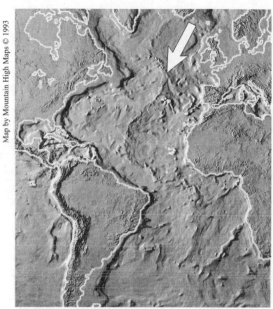

The mid-Atlantic Ridge (arrow), clearly visible by satellite imaging.

reversed many times in the past. So, during the cooling, some of the oceanic crust was magnetized in a reverse direction. If sea-floor spreading is continuous, the ocean floor should possess a smooth magnetic 'tape-recording' of reversals.

Indeed, the zebra stripe pattern of linear 'magnetic anomalies' parallel to the mid-ocean ridge crest has been recorded in many areas.[6]

Problems for 'slow-and-gradual' plate tectonics

While the zebra-stripe pattern has been confirmed, drilling through the basalt adjacent to the ridges has shown that the neat pattern recorded by dragging a magnetometer above the ridge is not present when the rock is actually sampled. The magnetic polarity changes in patches down the holes, with no consistent pattern with depth.[7] This would be expected with rapid formation of the basalt, combined with rapid field reversals, not the slow-and-gradual formation with slow reversals assumed by uniformitarians.

Physicist Dr Russell Humphreys predicted that evidence for rapid field reversals would be found in lava flows thin enough to cool in a few weeks.[8] He suggested that such rapid reversals could have

---

[6] Cox, A. (ed.), 1973. *Plate Tectonics and Geomagnetic Reversals,* W.H. Freeman and Co., San Francisco, pp. 138–220.

[7] Hall, J.M. and Robinson, P.T., 1979. Deep crustal drilling in the North Atlantic Ocean. *Science* **204**:573–586.

[8] Humphreys, D.R. 1986. Reversals of the earth's magnetic field during the Genesis Flood. *Proc. First ICC,* Pittsburgh, PA **2**:113–126.

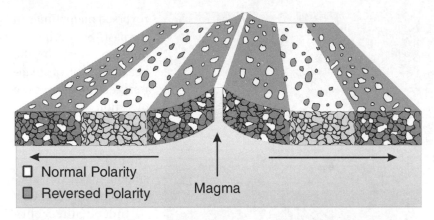

The magnetic pattern in the volcanic rock formed on the sea-floor at the mid-ocean ridges suggests very rapid processes, not millions of years. The patchwork patterns of polarity are evidence for rapid formation of the rock.

happened during Noah's Flood. Such evidence for rapid reversals was later found by the respected researchers, Coe and Prévot.[9,10] Their later work[11] confirmed these findings and showed that the magnetic reversals were 'astonishingly rapid'.

A biblical view

Evidence indicates that the continents have moved apart in the past, but can today's supposed drift rates of 2 – 15 cm per year be extrapolated far back into the past? Is the present really the key to the past, as uniformitarians earnestly proclaim? Such extrapolation would mean that an ocean basin or mountain range would take about 100 million years to form.

The Bible does not speak directly about continental drift and plate tectonics, but if the continents were once together, as Genesis 1:9–10

---

[9] Coe, R.S. and Prévot, M., 1989. Evidence suggesting extremely rapid field variation during a geomagnetic reversal. *Earth and Planetary Science Letters* **92**:292–298.

[10] For details, see Snelling, A.A., 1991. 'Fossil' magnetism reveals rapid reversals of the earth's magnetic field. *Creation* **13**(3):46–50.

[11] Coe, R.S., Prévot, M. and Camps, P., 1995. New evidence for extraordinary rapid change of the geomagnetic field during a reversal. *Nature* **374**:687–692. For comment see Snelling, A.A., 1995. The 'Principle of Least Astonishment'! *CEN Technical Journal* **9**(2):138–139.

suggests, and are now apart, how does that fit into a biblical view of geology with a time line of only thousands of years?[12]

Dr John Baumgardner, working at the Los Alamos National Laboratory (USA), has used supercomputers to model processes in the earth's mantle to show that tectonic plate movement could have occurred very rapidly, and 'spontaneously'.[13–17] This concept is known as *catastrophic plate tectonics*. At the time of writing, Baumgardner, a creationist scientist, is acknowledged as having developed the world's best 3-D super-computer model of plate tectonics.[16]

Catastrophic plate tectonics

The model proposed by Baumgardner begins with a pre-Flood super-continent (*'Let the waters . . . be gathered together into one place'*, Genesis 1:9) and dense ocean floor rocks. The process starts with the cold and dense ocean floor beginning to sink into the softer, less dense mantle beneath. The friction from this movement generates heat, especially around the edges, which softens the adjacent mantle material, making it less resistant to the sinking of the ocean floor.[17] The edges sink faster, dragging the rest of the ocean floor along, in

---

[12] Some have suggested that the continents (with their loads of Flood-deposited, fossil-bearing strata) separated to their present position, for example, at the time of the Tower of Babel, because Genesis 10:25 says *'the earth was divided'* in the days of Peleg. However, the Hebrew translated 'the earth' can as easily refer to the people (nations) divided because of Babel. Also, the short time involved would lead to enormous difficulties in accounting for the heat energy to be dissipated, not to mention the destruction at the earth's surface that would result from rapid continent-wide motion. This would be a global catastrophe as devastating as the Noachian Flood itself.

[13] Baumgardner, J.R., 1986. Numerical simulation of the large-scale tectonic changes accompanying the Flood. *Proc. First ICC* **2**:17–30.

[14] Baumgardner, J.R., 1990. 3-D finite element simulation of the global tectonic changes accompanying Noah's Flood. *Proc. Second ICC* **2**:35–45.

[15] Baumgardner, J.R., 1994. Computer modeling of the large-scale tectonics associated with the Genesis Flood. *Proc. Third ICC*, pp. 49–62.

[16] Beard, J., 1993. How a supercontinent went to pieces. *New Scientist* **137**:19, Jan. 16.

[17] Baumgardner, J.R., 1994. Runaway subduction as the driving mechanism for the Genesis Flood. *Proc. Third ICC*, Pittsburgh, pp. 63–75.

conveyor-belt fashion. Faster movement creates more friction and heat in the surrounding mantle, reducing its resistance further and so the ocean floor moves even faster, and so on. At its peak, this thermal runaway instability would have allowed for subduction at rates of metres-per-second. This key concept is called runaway subduction.

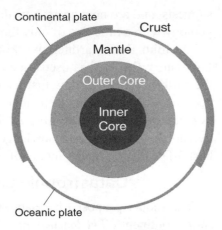

Earth's current structure.

The sinking ocean floor would displace mantle material, starting large-scale movement throughout the entire mantle. However, as the ocean-floor sank and rapidly subducted adjacent to the pre-Flood super-continent's margins, elsewhere the earth's crust would be under such tensional stress that it would be torn apart (rifted), breaking up both the pre-Flood super-continent and the ocean floor.

Thus, crustal spreading zones would rapidly extend along cracks in the ocean floor for some 10,000 km where the splitting was occurring. Hot mantle material displaced by the subducting slabs would well up, rising to the surface along these spreading zones. On the ocean floor, this hot mantle material would vaporize copious amounts of ocean water, producing a linear geyser of superheated steam along the whole length of the spreading centres (perhaps the *'fountains of the great deep'?* Gen. 7:11; 8:2). This steam would disperse, condensing in the atmosphere to fall as intense global rain (*'and the flood-gates of heaven were opened'?* Gen. 7:11). This could account for the rain persisting for 40 days and 40 nights (Gen. 7:12).

Baumgardner's catastrophic plate tectonics global Flood model for Earth history[18] is able to explain more geological data than the conventional plate tectonics model with its many millions of years. For example, rapid subduction of the pre-Flood ocean floor into the mantle results in new ocean floor that is dramatically hotter, especially

---

[18] Austin, S.A., Baumgardner, J.R., Humphreys, D.R., Snelling, A.A., Vardiman, L. and Wise, K.P., 1994. Catastrophic plate tectonics: a global Flood model of earth history. *Proc. Third ICC*, Pittsburgh, pp. 609–621.

in its upper 100 km, not just at spreading ridges, but everywhere. Being hotter, the new ocean floor is of lower density and therefore rises 1,000 to 2,000 metres higher than before and implies a dramatic rise in global sea level.

This higher sea level floods the continental surfaces and makes possible the deposition of large areas of sedimentary deposits on top of the normally high-standing continents. The Grand Canyon provides a spectacular window into the amazing layer-cake character of these sediment deposits that in many cases continue uninterrupted for more than 1,000 km.[19] Uniformitarian ('slow and gradual') plate tectonics simply cannot account for such thick continental sediment sequences of such vast horizontal extent.

Moreover, the rapid subduction of the cooler pre-Flood ocean floor into the mantle would have resulted in increased circulation of viscous fluid (note: plastic, not molten) rock within the mantle. This mantle-flow (i.e. 'stirring' within the mantle) suddenly altered the temperatures at the core-mantle boundary, as the mantle near the core would now be significantly cooler than the adjacent core, and thus convection and heat loss from the core would be greatly accelerated. The model suggests that under these conditions of accelerated convection in the core, rapid geomagnetic reversals would have occurred. These in turn would be expressed on the earth's surface and recorded in the so-

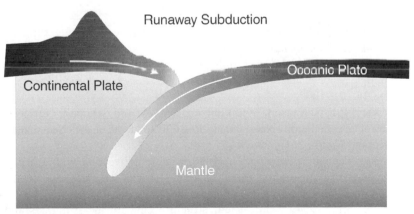

The movement of Earth's crustal plates during 'runaway subduction'.

[19] Austin, S.A. (ed.), 1994. *Grand Canyon: Monument to Catastrophe,* Institute for Creation Research, Santee, California.

called magnetic stripes.[20] However, these would be erratic and locally patchy, laterally and at depth, just as the data indicate,[7] even according to the uniformitarian scientists cited earlier.

This model provides a mechanism that explains how the plates could move relatively quickly (in a matter of months) over the mantle and subduct. And it predicts that little or no movement would be measurable between plates today, because the movement would have come almost to a standstill when the entire pre-Flood ocean floor was subducted. From this we would also expect the trenches adjacent to subduction zones today to be filled with undisturbed late-Flood and post-Flood sediments, just as we observe.

Aspects of Baumgardner's mantle modelling have been independently duplicated and thus verified by others.[21-23] Furthermore, Baumgardner's modelling predicts that because this thermal runaway subduction of cold ocean floor crustal slabs occurred relatively recently, during the Flood (about 5,000 or so years ago), then those slabs would not have had sufficient time since to be fully assimilated into the surrounding mantle. So evidence of the slabs above the mantle-core boundary (to which they sank) should still be found today. Indeed, evidence for such unassimilated relatively cold slabs has been found in seismic studies.[24-26]

The model also provides a mechanism for retreat of the Flood

---

[20] Humphreys, D.R., 1988. Has the earth's magnetic field ever flipped? *Creation Research Society Quarterly* **25**(3):130–137.

[21] Weinstein, S.A., 1993. Catastrophic overturn of the earth's mantle driven by multiple phase changes and internal heat generation. *Geophysical Research Letters* **20**:101–104.

[22] Tackley, P.J., Stevenson, D.J., Glatzmaier, G.A. and Schubert, G., 1993. Effects of an endothermic phase transition at 670 km depth on spherical mantle convection. *Nature* **361**: 699–704.

[23] Moresi, L., and Solomatov, V., 1998. Mantle convection with a brittle lithosphere: thoughts on the global tectonic styles of the earth and Venus. *Geophysical Journal International* **133**:669–682.

[24] Grand, S.P., 1994. Mantle shear structure beneath the Americas and surrounding oceans. *Journal of Geophysical Research* **99**:11591–11621.

[25] Vidale, J.E., 1994. A snapshot of whole mantle flow. *Nature* **370**:16–17.

[26] Vogel, S., 1995. Anti-matters. *Earth: The Science of Our Planet*, August 1995, pp. 43–49.

waters. Psalm 104:6–7 describes the abating of the waters which had stood above the mountains. Verse 8 most naturally translates as, *'The mountains rose up; the valleys sank down,'* [27] implying that vertical earth movements were the dominant tectonic forces operating at the close of the Flood, in contrast to the horizontal forces dominant during the spreading phase.

Plate collisions would have pushed up mountains, while cooling of the new ocean floor would have increased its density, causing it to sink and thus deepen the new ocean basins to receive the retreating Flood waters. It may be significant, therefore, that the *'mountains of Ararat'* (Genesis 8:4), the resting place of the Ark after the 150th day of the Flood, are in a tectonically active region at what is believed to be the junction of three crustal plates.[28]

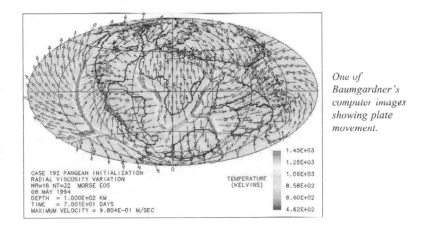

One of Baumgardner's computer images showing plate movement.

---

[27] Many English translations, following the KJV, have *'the waters'* in verse 6 the subject of the verbs *'go up'* and *'go down'* in verse 8. According to linguist Dr Charles Taylor, the more natural and literal reading is to have the *'mountains'* in verse 8 going up and the *'valleys'* (verse 8) going down. The Septuagint (LXX), a Greek translation done about 250 BC, Luther's German translation, which pre-dates the KJV, and French and Italian translations all agree. English translations that convey this meaning include the ASV, RSV and NASB. See Taylor, C.V., 1998. Did the mountains really rise according to Psalm 104:8? *CEN Technical Journal* **12**(3):312–313.

[28] Dewey, J.F., Pitman, W.C., Ryan, W.B.F. and Bonnin, J., 1973. Plate tectonics and the evolution of the Alpine System. *Geological Society of America Bulletin* **84**:3137–3180.

If a centimetre or two per year of inferred movement today is extrapolated back into the past as uniformitarians do, then their conventional plate tectonics model has limited explanatory power. For example, even at a rate of 10 cm/yr, it is questionable whether the forces of the collision between the Indian-Australian and Eurasian Plates could have been sufficient to push up the Himalayas. On the other hand, catastrophic plate tectonics in the context of the Flood can explain how the plates overcame the viscous drag of the earth's mantle for a short time due to the enormous catastrophic forces at work, followed by a rapid slowing down to present rates.

Continental separation solves apparent geological enigmas. For instance, it explains the amazing similarities of sedimentary layers in the north-eastern United States to those in Britain. It also explains the absence of those same layers in the intervening North Atlantic ocean basin, as well as the similarities in the geology of parts of Australia with South Africa, India, and Antarctica.

Conclusion

Early scepticism about plate tectonics has largely evaporated because the framework has such great explanatory power. The catastrophic plate tectonics model for the Flood not only includes these explanatory elements, but also accounts for widespread evidences of massive flooding and catastrophic geological processes on the continents. Future refinement of the model may also help to explain the order and distribution of fossils observed in the fossil record in the context of the Genesis Flood (see Chapter 15).

The Bible is silent about plate tectonics. Many creationists believe the concept is helpful in explaining Earth's history. Some are still cautious. The idea is quite new, and radical, and much work has yet to be done to flesh out the details. There may even be major modifications to the theory that increase its explanatory power, or future discoveries could cause the model to be abandoned. Such is the nature of scientific progress. Scientific models come and go, *'But the word of the Lord endures forever'* (1 Peter 1:25).

Chapter 12

Noah's Flood — what about all that water?

Where did all the water come from for the Flood? Was there a water vapour canopy? How was Mt Everest covered with water? Where did the water go after the Flood? How could this have happened?

IN telling us about the globe-covering Flood in the days of Noah, the Bible gives us information about where the waters came from and where they went.

The sources of the water are given in Genesis 7:11 as *'the fountains of the great deep'* and the *'windows of heaven'*.

The fountains of the great deep

The *'fountains of the great deep'* are mentioned before the *'windows of heaven'*, indicating either relative importance or the order of events.

What are the *'fountains of the great deep'*? This phrase is used only in Genesis 7:11. *'Fountains of the deep'* is used in Genesis 8:2, where it clearly refers to the same thing, and Proverbs 8:28, where the precise meaning is not clear. *'The great deep'* is used three other times: Isaiah 51:10, where it clearly refers to the ocean, Amos 7:4, where God's fire of judgment is said to dry up the great deep, probably the oceans, and Psalm 36:6 where it is used metaphorically of the depth of God's justice/judgment. *'The deep'* is used more often, and usually refers to the oceans (e.g. Gen. 1:2, Job 38:30, 41:32, Psalm 42:7, 104:6, Isa. 51:10, 63:13, Eze. 26:19, Jon. 2:3), but sometimes to subterranean sources of waters (Eze. 31:4,15). The Hebrew word (*mayan*) translated 'fountains' means 'fountain, spring, well' (Strong's Concordance).

So, the *'fountains of the great deep'* are probably oceanic or possibly subterranean sources of water. In the context of the Flood account, it could mean both.

If the fountains of the great deep were the major source of the waters, then they must have been a huge source of water. Some have suggested that when God made the dry land appear from under the waters on the third day of creation, some of the water that covered the earth became trapped underneath and within the dry land.[1]

Genesis 7:11 says that on the day the Flood began, there was a 'breaking up' of the fountains, which implies a release of the water, possibly through large fissures in the ground or in the sea floor. The waters that had been held back burst forth with catastrophic consequences.

There are many volcanic rocks interspersed between the fossil layers in the rock record — layers that were obviously deposited during Noah's Flood. So it is quite plausible that these fountains of the great deep involved a series of volcanic eruptions with prodigious amounts of water bursting up through the ground. It is interesting that up to 70 % or more of what comes out of volcanoes today is water, often in the form of steam.

In their catastrophic plate tectonics model for the Flood (see Chapter 11), Austin *et al.*[2] have proposed that at the onset of the Flood, the ocean floor rapidly lifted up to 2,000 metres (6,500 feet) due to an increase in temperature as horizontal movement of the tectonic plates accelerated. This would spill the seawater onto the land and cause massive flooding — perhaps what is aptly described as the breaking up of the *'fountains of the great deep'*.

The windows of heaven

The other source of the waters for Noah's Flood was *'the windows of heaven'*. Genesis 7:12 says that it rained for 40 days and 40 nights continuously.

---

[1] Evidence is mounting that there is still a huge amount of water stored deep in the earth in the crystal lattices of minerals, which is possible because of the immense pressure. See Bergeron, L., 1997. Deep waters. *New Scientist* **155**(2097):22–26: 'You have oceans and oceans of water stored in the transition zone. It's sopping wet.'

[2] Austin, S.A., Baumgardner, J.R., Humphreys, D.R., Snelling, A.A., Vardiman, L. and Wise, K.P., 1994. Catastrophic plate tectonics: A global Flood model of Earth history. *Proc. Third ICC*, pp. 609–621.

A lot of volcanic activity would be expected with such a cataclysm as the Flood.

Genesis 2:5 tells us that there was no rain before man was created. Some have suggested that there was no rainfall anywhere on the earth until the time of the Flood. However, the Bible does not actually say this, so we should not be dogmatic.[3]

Some have argued that God's use of the rainbow as the sign of His covenant with Noah (Gen. 9:12–17) suggests that there were no rainbows, and therefore no clouds or rain, before the Flood. However, if rainbows (and clouds) existed before the Flood, this would not be the only time God used an existing thing as a special 'new' sign of a covenant (e.g., bread and wine in the Lord's Supper).

It is difficult to envisage a pre-Flood water cycle without clouds and rain, as the sun's heat, even in that era, must have evaporated large volumes of surface waters which would have to eventually condense back into liquid water. And droplets of liquid water form clouds from which we get rain.

---

[3] Some have claimed that because the people scoffed at Noah's warnings of a coming flood, that they must not have seen rain. But people today have seen lots of rain and floods, and many still scoff at the global Flood. Gen. 2:5 says there was no rain *yet* upon the earth, but whether or not it rained after that in the pre-Flood world is not stated.

The expression 'windows of heaven' is used twice in reference to the Flood (Gen. 7:11, 8:2). It is used only three times elsewhere in the Old Testament: twice in 2 Kings 7:2,19, referring to God's miraculous intervention in sending rain, and once in Malachi 3:10, where the phrase is used again of God intervening to pour out abundant blessings on his people. Clearly, in Genesis the expression suggests the extraordinary nature of the rainfall attending the Flood. It is not a term applied to ordinary rainfall.

What about 'the waters above'?

We are told in Genesis 1:6–8 that on the second day of creation God divided the waters that were on the earth from the waters that He placed above the earth when He made a *'firmament'* (Hebrew, *raqiya,* meaning 'expanse') between those waters.[4] Many have concluded that this *'expanse'* was the atmosphere, because God placed the birds in the expanse, suggesting that the expanse includes the atmosphere where the birds fly. This would put these waters above the atmosphere.

---

[4] In trying to disparage the Bible, some sceptics claim that *raqiya* describes a solid dome and that the ancient Hebrews believed in a flat Earth with a slotted dome over it. Such ideas are not in the Bible or *raqiya*. See Holding, J.P., 1999. Is the *raqiya* ' ('firmament') a solid dome? Equivocal language in the cosmology of Genesis 1 and the Old Testament: a response to Paul H. Seely. *CEN Technical Journal* **13**(2):44–51.

However, Gen. 1:20, speaking of the creation of the birds says (literally) *'let birds fly above the ground* **across the face of** *the expanse of the heavens.'*[5] This at least allows that 'the expanse' may include the space beyond the atmosphere.

Dr Russell Humphreys[6] has argued that since Genesis 1:17 tells us that God put the sun, moon and stars also *'in the expanse of the heaven'* then the expanse must at least include interstellar space, and thus the waters above the expanse of Genesis 1:7 would be beyond the stars at the edge of the universe.[7]

However, prepositions (in, under, above, etc.) are somewhat flexible in Hebrew, as well as English. A submarine can be spoken of as both *under* the sea and *in* the sea. Likewise, the waters could be *above* the expanse and *in* the expanse, so we should perhaps be careful not to draw too much from these expressions.

So what were these *'waters above'*? Some have said that they are simply the clouds. Others thought of them as a 'water vapour canopy', implying a blanket of water vapour surrounding the earth.

A water vapour canopy?

Dr Joseph Dillow did much research into the idea of a blanket of water vapour surrounding the earth before the Flood.[8] In a modification of the canopy theory, Dr Larry Vardiman[9] suggested that much of the *'waters above'* could have been stored in small ice particles distributed in equatorial rings around the earth similar to those around Venus.

The Genesis 7:11 reference to the windows of heaven being opened has been interpreted as the collapse of such a water vapour canopy, which somehow became unstable and fell as rain. Volcanic eruptions associated with the breaking up of the fountains of the great deep could have thrown dust into the water vapour canopy, causing the water vapour to nucleate on the dust particles and make rain.

---

[5] Leupold, H.C., 1942. *Exposition of Genesis,* Vol. 1, Baker Book House, Grand Rapids, Michigan, p.78.

[6] Humphreys, D.R., 1994. A biblical basis for creationist cosmology. *Proc. Third ICC,* Pittsburgh, PA, pp. 255–266).

[7] This could help explain the background microwave radiation seen in the Universe. See Chapter 5 and Humphreys, Ref. 6.

[8] Dillow, J.C., 1981. *The Waters Above,* Moody Press, Chicago.

[9] Vardiman, L., 1986. The sky has fallen. *Proc. First ICC* 1:113–119.

Dillow, Vardiman and others have suggested that the vapour canopy caused a greenhouse effect before the Flood with a pleasant subtropical-to-temperate climate all around the globe, even at the poles where today there is ice. This would have caused the growth of lush vegetation on the land all around the globe. The discovery of coal seams in Antarctica containing vegetation that is not now found growing at the poles, but which obviously grew under warmer conditions, was taken as support for these ideas.[10]

A vapour canopy would also affect the global wind systems. Also, the mountains were almost certainly not as high before the Flood as they are today (see later). In today's world, the major winds and high mountain ranges are a very important part of the water cycle that brings rain to the continents. Before the Flood, however, these factors would have caused the weather systems to be different.

Those interested in studying this further should consult Dillow's and Vardiman's works.

A major problem with the canopy theory

Vardiman[11] recognized a major difficulty with the canopy theory. The best canopy model still gives an intolerably high temperature at the surface of the earth.

Rush and Vardiman have attempted a solution,[12] but found that they had to drastically reduce the amount of water vapour in the canopy from a rain equivalent of 12 m (40 ft) to only 0.5 m (20 in.). Further modelling suggested that a maximum of 2 m of water could be held in such a canopy, even if all relevant factors were adjusted to the best possible values to maximize the amount of water stored.[13] Such a reduced canopy would not significantly contribute to the 40 days and nights of rain at the beginning of the Flood.

Many creationist scientists are now either abandoning the water

---

[10] Movement of tectonic plates could also explain the polar occurrence of such warm-climate plant remains (see Chapter 11, p. 147).

[11] Vardiman, Ref. 9, pp. 116,119.

[12] Rush, D.E. and Vardiman, L., 1990. Pre-Flood vapor canopy radiative temperature profiles. *Proc. Second ICC*, Pittsburgh, PA **2**:231–245.

[13] Vardiman, L. and Bousselot, K., 1998. Sensitivity studies on vapor canopy temperature profiles. *Proc. Fourth ICC*, pp. 607–618.

vapour canopy model[14] or no longer see any need for such a concept, particularly if other reasonable mechanisms could have supplied the rain.[15] In the catastrophic plate tectonics model for the Flood (see Chapter 11),[16] volcanic activity associated with the breaking up of the pre-Flood ocean floor would have created a linear geyser (like a wall) of superheated steam from the ocean, causing intense global rain.

Nevertheless, whatever the source or mechanism, the scriptural statement about the windows of heaven opening is an apt description of global torrential rain.

A vapour canopy holding more than two metres (7 feet) of rain would cause the earth's surface to be intolerably hot, so a vapour canopy could not have been a significant source of the Flood waters.

Where did the waters go?

The whole earth was covered with the Flood waters (see Chapter 10, *Was the Flood global?*), and the world that then existed was destroyed by the very waters out of which the land had originally emerged at God's command (Gen. 1:9, 2 Pet. 3:5–6). But where did those waters go after the Flood?

There are a number of Scripture passages that identify the Flood waters with the present-day seas (Amos 9:6 and Job 38:8–11, note 'waves'). If the waters are still here, why are the highest mountains not still covered with water, as they were in Noah's day? Psalm 104 suggests an answer. After the waters covered the mountains (verse 6), God rebuked them and they fled (verse 7); the mountains rose, the valleys sank down (verse 8) and God set a boundary so that they will never again cover the earth (verse 9).[17] They are the same waters!

---

[14] Psalm 148:4 seems to speak against the canopy theory. Written after the Flood, this refers to *'waters above the heavens'* still existing, so this cannot mean a vapour canopy that collapsed at the Flood. Calvin, Leupold and Keil and Delitzsch all wrote of *'the waters above'* as merely being the clouds.

[15] Of course we may never arrive at a correct understanding of exactly how the Flood occurred, but that does not change the fact that it did occur.

[16] Austin *et al.,* Ref. 2.

[17] The most natural translation of Psalm 104:8a is *'The mountains rose up; the valleys sank down'.* See Chapter 11, footnote 27, p. 155.

Isaiah gives this same statement that the waters of Noah would never again cover the earth (Isa. 54:9). Clearly, what the Bible is telling us is that God altered the earth's topography. New continental land-masses bearing new mountain chains of folded rock strata were uplifted from below the globe-encircling waters that had eroded and levelled the pre-Flood topography, while large deep ocean basins were formed to receive and accommodate the Flood waters that then drained off the emerging continents.

That is why the oceans are so deep, and why there are folded mountain ranges. Indeed, if the entire earth's surface were levelled by smoothing out the topography of not only the land surface but also the rock surface on the ocean floor, the waters of the ocean would cover the earth's surface to a depth of 2.7 kilometres (1.7 miles). We need to remember that about 70 % of the earth's surface is still covered by water. Quite clearly, then, the waters of Noah's Flood are in today's ocean basins.

Without mountains or seabasins, water would cover the whole earth to a depth of 2.7 km, or 1.7 miles (not to scale).

A mechanism?

The catastrophic plate tectonics model (Chapter 11) gives a mechanism for the deepening of the oceans and the rising of mountains at the end of the Flood.

As the new ocean floors cooled, they would have become denser and sunk, allowing water to flow off the continents. Movement of the water off the continents and into the oceans would have weighed down the ocean floor and lightened the continents, resulting in the further sinking of the ocean floor, as well as upward movement of the continents.[18] The deepening of the ocean basins and the rising of the continents would have resulted in more water running off the land.

---

[18] The geological principle involved is *isostasy*, where the plates are 'floating' on the mantle. The ocean basins are composed of denser rock than the continents, so the ocean basins sit lower in the mantle than the less dense continents with their mountains.

Even the high mountains of today have fossils of sea creatures near their peaks.

The collision of the tectonic plates would have pushed up mountain ranges also, especially towards the end of the Flood.

Could the water have covered Mount Everest?

Mt Everest is more than 8 km (5 miles) high. How, then, could the Flood have covered *'all the high hills under the whole heaven'*?

The Bible refers only to 'high hills', and the mountains today were formed only towards the end of, and **after**, the Flood by collision of the tectonic plates and the associated upthrusting. In support of this, the layers that form the uppermost parts of Mt Everest are themselves composed of fossil-bearing, water-deposited layers.

This uplift of the new continental land masses from under the Flood waters would have meant that, as the mountains rose and the valleys sank, the waters would have rapidly drained off the newly emerging land surfaces. The collapse of natural dams holding back the floodwaters on the land would also have caused catastrophic flooding. Such rapid movement of large volumes of water would have caused extensive erosion and shaped the basic features of today's Earth surface.

Thus it is not hard to envisage the rapid carving of the landscape features that we see on the earth today, including places such as the Grand Canyon of the USA. The present shape of Uluru (Ayers Rock), a sandstone monolith in central Australia, is the result of erosion, following tilting and uplift, of previously horizontal beds of water-laid sand. The feldspar-rich sand that makes up Uluru must have been deposited very quickly and recently. Long-distance transport of the sand would have caused the grains to be rounded and sorted, whereas they are jagged and unsorted. If they had sat accumulating slowly in a lake bed drying in the sun over eons of time, which is the story told in the geological display at the park centre, the feldspar would have weathered into clay. Likewise, if Uluru had sat in the once-humid area of central Australia for millions of years, it would have weathered to clay.[19] Similarly, the nearby Kata Tjuta (The Olgas) are composed of an unsorted mixture of large boulders, sand and mud, indicating that the material must have been transported and deposited very rapidly.

Kata Tjuta in central Australia is composed of material which must have been deposited very quickly by water.

Photo by Kevin Walmsley

The erosion caused by receding floodwaters is the reason that river valleys are far larger than the rivers now flowing in them could have carved. The water flow that carved out the river valleys must have been far greater than the volume of water we see flowing in the rivers today. This is consistent with voluminous Flood waters draining off the emerging land surfaces at the close of Noah's Flood, and flowing into the rapidly sinking, newly prepared, deep ocean basins.

Our understanding of how the Flood could have occurred is continually developing. Ideas come and go, but the fact of the Flood remains. Genesis clearly testifies to it, Jesus and the Apostles confirmed it, and there is abundant global geological evidence for a global watery cataclysm.

---

[19] Snelling, A.A., 1998. Uluru and Kata Tjuta: Testimony to the Flood. *Creation* **20**(2):36–40.

Chapter 13

How did the animals fit on Noah's Ark?

What animals did Noah take onto the Ark? Where did they store all the food? How could the Ark be big enough? What about all the animal wastes?

MANY sceptics assert that the Bible must be wrong, because they claim that the Ark could not possibly have carried all the different types of animals. This has persuaded some Christians to deny the Genesis Flood, or believe that it was only a local flood involving comparatively few animals.

Usually such doubters have not thought it through. On the other hand, the classic creationist book *The Genesis Flood* contained a detailed analysis as far back as 1961.[1] A more comprehensive and updated technical study of this and many other related questions is John Woodmorappe's book *Noah's Ark: a Feasibility Study*.[2] This chapter is based on material in these books plus some independent calculations. There are two questions to ask:

● How many types of animals did Noah need to take?
● Was the Ark's volume large enough to carry all the necessary types?

---

[1] Whitcomb, J.C. and Morris, H.M., 1961. *The Genesis Flood*, Presbyterian and Reformed Publishing Co., Phillipsburg, NJ, USA.

[2] Woodmorappe, J., 1997. *Noah's Ark: A Feasibility Study.* Institute for Creation Research, El Cajon, CA, USA. Woodmorappe has devoted seven years to this scholarly, systematic answer to virtually all the anti-Ark arguments, alleged difficulties with the biblical account, and other relevant questions. Nothing else like this has been written before — a powerful vindication of the Genesis Ark account.

How many types of animals did Noah need to take?

Relevant passages are:

And you shall bring into the ark two of every kind *of every living thing of all flesh, to keep them alive with you. They shall be male and female. Two of every kind shall come to you to keep* them *alive; of birds after their kind, and of beasts after their kind, of every creeping thing of the earth after its kind.* (Gen. 6:19–20)

You shall take with you every clean animal by sevens, the male and female. And take two of the animals that are *not clean, the male and female. Also take of the birds of the air by sevens, the male and the female, to keep seed alive upon the face of all the earth.* (Gen. 7:2–3)

In the original Hebrew, the word variously translated as 'beast' or 'cattle' in these passages is the same: *behemah*, and it refers to land vertebrate animals in general. The word for 'creeping things' is *remes*, which has a number of different meanings in Scripture, but here it probably refers to reptiles.[3] Noah did not need to take sea creatures[4] because they would not necessarily be threatened with extinction by a flood. However, turbulent water carrying sediment would cause massive carnage, as seen in the fossil record, and many oceanic species probably did become extinct because of the Flood. However, if God in His wisdom decided not to preserve some ocean creatures, this was none of Noah's business.

Noah did not need to take plants either — many could have survived as seeds, and others could have survived on floating mats of tangled vegetation, as seen today after severe storms. Many insects and other invertebrates were small enough to have survived on these mats as well. According to Genesis 7:22, the Flood wiped out all land animals that breathed *through nostrils* except those on the Ark. Insects do not breathe through nostrils but through tiny pores ('tracheae') in their exterior skeleton ('shell').

---

[3] Jones, A.J., 1973. How many animals on the Ark? *Creation Research Society Quarterly* **10**(2):16–18.

[4] It is high time that certain atheistic sceptics showed some intellectual integrity and actually read the Bible. Then they would stop making ridiculous comments about whales flopping up gangplanks and fish-tanks on the Ark.

God brought to Noah all kinds of air-breathing land animals to be saved from the Flood.

Clean animals: Bible commentators are evenly divided about whether the Hebrew means 'seven' or 'seven pairs' of each type of clean animal. Woodmorappe takes the latter meaning just to concede as much to the sceptics as possible. But the vast majority of animals are not clean, and were represented by only two specimens each. The term 'clean animal' is not defined in Scripture until the Mosaic Law. But since Moses was also the writer / compiler of Genesis, if we follow the principle that 'Scripture interprets Scripture', the Mosaic Law definitions can be applied to Noah's situation. Actually, Leviticus 11 and Deuteronomy 14 list very few 'clean' land animals.

What is a 'kind'?

God created a number of different types of animals with much capacity for variation within limits.[5] The descendants of each of these different kinds, apart from humans, would today mostly be represented

---

[5] One common fallacy brought up by evolutionists is that variation within a kind somehow proves particles-to-people evolution. Examples cited, such as antibiotic resistance in bacteria, are indeed examples of *natural selection*. But this is *not* evolution. Evolution requires the creation of *new* genetic information, which is not possible by natural processes, such as mutations and natural selection. See Chapter 1, pp. 9–10, 13–15.

by a larger grouping than what is called a *species*. In many cases, those species descended from a particular original kind would be grouped today within what modern taxonomists (biologists who classify living things) call a *genus* (plural *genera*).

One common definition of a species is a group of organisms which can interbreed, producing fertile offspring, and do not mate with other species. However, most of the so-called species within a particular genus or family have not been tested to see what they can or cannot mate with. Obviously the extinct ones cannot be tested. In fact, not only are there known crosses between so-called species, but there are many instances of mating between genera, so the 'kind' may in some cases be as high as the family. Identifying the 'kind' with the genus is also consistent with Scripture, which spoke of kinds in a way that the Israelites could easily recognize without the need for tests of reproductive isolation.

For example, horses, zebras and donkeys are probably descended from an equine (horse-like) kind, since they can interbreed, although the offspring are largely sterile. Dogs, wolves, coyotes and jackals are probably from a common canine (dog-like) kind. All different types of domestic cattle (which are clean animals) are

Zebras, donkeys and horses — probably one biblical kind.

descended from the aurochs,[6] so there were probably at most seven (or possibly 14) domestic cattle aboard. The aurochs itself may have been descended from a cattle kind that also gave rise to bison and water buffaloes. We know that tigers and lions can produce hybrids called tigons and ligers, so it is likely that they are descended from the same original kind.

Woodmorappe tallied up about 8,000 genera, including extinct genera. Thus about 16,000 individual animals had to be aboard. With extinct genera, there is a tendency among some paleontologists to give each of their new finds a new genus name. But this is arbitrary, so the number of extinct genera is probably highly overstated.

---

[6] Wieland, C., 1992. Re-creating the extinct aurochs? *Creation* **14**(2):25–28.

Consider the sauropods, which were the largest dinosaurs — the huge plant-eaters like *Brachiosaurus*, *Diplodocus*, *Apatosaurus*, etc. There are 87 sauropod genera commonly cited, but only 12 are 'firmly established' and another 12 are considered 'fairly well established'.[7]

Dinosaurs?

One commonly raised problem is 'How could Noah fit all those huge dinosaurs on the Ark?' First, of the 668 supposed dinosaur genera, only 106 weighed more than ten tonnes when fully grown. Second, the Bible does not say that the animals had to be fully-grown. The largest animals were probably represented by 'teenage' or even younger specimens. It may seem surprising, but the median size of all animals on the Ark would most likely have been that of a small rat, according to Woodmorappe's up-to-date tabulations, while only about 11 percent would have been much larger than a sheep.

Germs?

Another problem often raised by atheists and theistic evolutionists is 'How did disease germs survive the Flood?' This is a leading question — it presumes that germs were as specialized and infectious as they are now, so all the Ark's inhabitants must have suffered from every disease on Earth today. But germs were probably more robust in the past, and may have only fairly recently lost the ability to survive in different hosts or independently of a host. In fact, even now many

The eggs of even the largest dinosaurs were no bigger than a football, so all young dinosaurs were quite small.

---

[7] McIntosh, J.S., 1992. Sauropoda. In: Wieshampel, D.B. *et al.*, *The Dinosauria*, University of California Press, Berkeley, CA, p. 345.

germs can survive in insect vectors or corpses, or in the dried or frozen state, or be carried by a host without causing disease. Furthermore, degeneration of hosts could allow microbes to cause disease where in the past the microbes may have lived in the host's gut, for example, without causing disease. Such loss of resistance would be consistent with the general degeneration of life since the Fall.[8]

Was the Ark large enough to carry all the necessary types?

The ark measured 300x50x30 cubits (Gen. 6:15) which is about 137x23x13.7 metres or 450x75x45 feet, so its volume was 43,200 m^3 (cubic metres) or 1.52 million cubic feet. To put this in perspective, this is the equivalent volume of 522 standard railroad stock cars, each of which can hold 240 sheep.

If the animals were kept in cages with an average size (some would be much bigger, others smaller) of 50x50x30 centimetres (20x20x12 inches), that is 75,000 cm^3 (cubic centimetres) or 4,800 cubic inches, the 16,000 animals would only occupy 1,200 m^3 (42,000 cubic feet) or 14.4 stock cars. Even if a million insect species had to be on board as well, it would not be a problem, because they require little space. If each pair was kept in cages of 10 cm (four inches) per side, or 1,000 cm^3, all the insect species would occupy a total volume of only 1,000 m^3, or another 12 cars. This would leave room for five trains of 99 cars each for food, Noah's family and 'range' for the animals, and air space. However, insects are not included in the meaning of *behemah* or *remes,* so Noah probably did not have to take them on board as passengers anyway.

Tabulating the total volume is fair enough, since this shows that there would be plenty of room on the Ark for the animals with ample left over for food, space to move, etc. It would be possible to stack cages, with food on top or nearby (to minimize the amount of food carrying the humans had to do), to fill up more of the Ark space, while

---

[8] Wieland, C., 1994. Diseases on the Ark. *CEN Technical Journal* **8**(1):16–18. Viruses often become much more infectious by random mutations causing changes in their protein coats. This makes it harder for the antibodies to recognize them, but there is no increase in information content, so no real evolution.

still allowing plenty of gaps for air circulation. We are discussing an emergency situation, not necessarily luxury accommodation. Although there is plenty of room for exercise, sceptics have overstated animals' needs for exercise anyway.

Even if we don't allow stacking one cage on top of another to save floor space, there still would be no problem. Woodmorappe shows from standard recommended floor space requirements for animals that all the animals together would have needed less than half the available floor space of the Ark's three decks. This arrangement allows for the maximum amount of food and water storage on top of the cages close to the animals.

Food requirements

The Ark would probably have carried compressed and dried foodstuffs, and a lot of concentrated food. Perhaps Noah fed the cattle mainly on grain, plus some hay for fibre. Woodmorappe calculated that the volume of foodstuffs would have been only about 15 % of the Ark's total volume. Drinking water would have taken up less than 10 % of the volume. This volume would be reduced further if rainwater were collected and piped into troughs.

Excretory requirements

How did Noah's family dispose of the waste of thousands of animals every day? The amount of labour could be minimized in many ways. Possibly they had sloped floors and/or slatted cages, where the manure

Simple sloped floors under cages with slatted floors would make them self-cleaning (from Woodmorappe,[2] used with permission).

could fall away from the animals and be flushed away (plenty of water around!) or destroyed by vermi-composting (composting by worms) which would also have provided earthworms as a food source. Very deep bedding can sometimes last for a year without needing a change. Absorbent material (e.g. sawdust, softwood shavings and especially peat moss) would have reduced the moisture content and hence the odour.

Hibernation

The space, feeding and excretory requirements were adequate even if the animals had normal day/night sleeping cycles. But hibernation is a possibility that would reduce these requirements even more. It is true that the Bible does not mention it, but it does not rule it out either. Some creationists suggest that God created, or enhanced, the hibernation instinct for the animals on the Ark, but we should not be dogmatic either way.

Some sceptics argue that food taken on board rules out hibernation, but this is not so. Hibernating animals do not sleep all winter, despite popular portrayals, so they would still need food occasionally.

Conclusion

We have shown here that the Bible can be trusted on testable matters like Noah's Ark. Many Christians believe that the Bible can only be trusted on matters of faith and morals, not scientific matters. But we should consider what Jesus Christ Himself told Nicodemus (John 3:12):

If I have told you earthly things and you do not believe, how shall you believe if I tell you heavenly things?

Similarly, if the Bible can be wrong on testable matters such as geography, history and science, why should it be trusted on matters like the nature of God and life after death, which are not open to empirical testing? Hence Christians should *'be ready always to give an answer to everyone who asks you a reason of the hope in you'* (1 Peter 3:15), when sceptics claim that the Bible conflicts with known 'scientific facts'.

Seeing that the Bible can be trusted on testable matters, nonbelievers disregard its warnings concerning future judgment at their own peril.

Chapter 14

How did fresh- and salt-water fish survive the Flood?

How did saltwater fish survive dilution of the seawater with freshwater, or how did freshwater types survive in saltwater? And how did plants survive?

IF the whole earth were covered by water in the Flood, then there would have been a mixing of fresh and salt waters. Many of today's fish species are specialized and do not survive in water of radically different saltiness to their usual habitat. So how did they survive the Flood?

Note that the Bible tells us that only land-dwelling, air-breathing animals and birds were on the Ark (Gen. 7:14,15, 21–23).

We do not know how salty the sea was before the Flood. The Flood was initiated by the breaking up of the *'fountains of the great deep'* (Gen. 7:11). Whatever the 'fountains of the great deep' were (see Chapter 9), the Flood must have been associated with massive earth movements, because of the weight of the water alone, which would have resulted in great volcanic activity.

Volcanoes emit huge amounts of steam, and underwater lava creates hot water/steam, which dissolves minerals, adding salt to the water. Furthermore, erosion accompanying the movement of water off the continents after the Flood would have added salt to the oceans. In other words, we would expect the pre-Flood ocean waters to be less salty than they were after the Flood.

The problem for fish coping with saltiness is this: fish in fresh water tend to absorb water, because the saltiness of their body fluids draws in the water (by osmosis). Fish in saltwater tend to lose water from their bodies because the surrounding water is saltier than their body fluids.

Saltwater/freshwater adaptation in fish today

Many of today's marine organisms, especially estuarine and tide-pool species, are able to survive large changes in salinity. For example, starfish will tolerate as low as 16–18% of the normal concentration of sea salt indefinitely. Barnacles can withstand exposure to less than one-tenth the usual salt concentration of sea-water.

Eels, like many sea creatures, can move between salt and fresh waters.

There are migratory species of fish that travel between salt and fresh water. For example, salmon, striped bass and Atlantic sturgeon spawn in freshwater and mature in saltwater. Eels reproduce in saltwater and grow to maturity in freshwater streams and lakes. So, many of today's species of fish are able to adjust to both freshwater and saltwater.

There is also evidence of post-Flood specialization within a kind of fish. For example, the Atlantic sturgeon is a migratory salt/freshwater species but the Siberian sturgeon (a different species of the same kind) lives only in freshwater.

Many families[1] of fish contain both fresh and saltwater species. These include the families of toadfish, garpike, bowfin, sturgeon, herring/anchovy, salmon/trout/pike, catfish, clingfish, stickleback, scorpionfish, and flatfish. Indeed, most of the families alive today have both fresh and saltwater representatives. This suggests that the ability to tolerate large changes in salinity was present in most fish at the time of the Flood. Specialization, through natural selection, may have resulted in the loss of this ability in many species since then (see Chapter 1, pp. 9–10).

Hybrids of wild trout (freshwater) and farmed salmon (migratory species) have been discovered in Scotland,[2] suggesting that the

---

[1] 'Family' is one of the main levels of classification for fish. In fish there is plenty of evidence for hybridization within families — the trout/salmon family, for example — suggesting that families may represent the biblical 'kind' in fish.
[2] Charron, B., 1995. Escape to sterility for designer fish. *New Scientist* **146**(1979):22.

differences between freshwater and marine types may be quite minor. Indeed, the differences in physiology seem to be largely differences in degree rather than kind.

The kidneys of freshwater species excrete excess water (the urine has low salt concentration) and those of marine species excrete excess salt (the urine has high salt concentration). Saltwater sharks have high concentrations of urea in the blood to retain water in the saltwater environment whereas freshwater sharks have low concentrations of urea to avoid accumulating water. When sawfish move from saltwater to freshwater they increase their urine output twenty fold, and their blood urea concentration decreases to less than one-third.

Major public aquariums use the ability of fish to adapt to water of different salinity from their normal habitat to exhibit freshwater and saltwater species together. The fish can adapt if the salinity is changed slowly enough.

So, many fish species today have the capacity to adapt to both fresh and salt water within their own lifetimes.

Aquatic air-breathing mammals such as whales and dolphins would have been better placed than many fish to survive the Flood, not being dependent on clean water to obtain their oxygen.

Many marine creatures would have been killed in the Flood because of the turbidity of the water, changes in temperature, etc. The fossil record testifies to the massive destruction of marine life, with marine creatures accounting for 95 %

Freshwater trout can hybridize with (saltwater) salmon.

of the fossil record.[3] Some, such as trilobites and ichthyosaurs, probably

---

[3] There is a huge number of marine fossils. If they really formed in the manner claimed by evolutionists (over hundreds of millions of years), then transitional fossils showing gradual change from one kind to another should be most evident here. But they are conspicuous by their absence. Furthermore, fossils of such things as jellyfish, starfish and clams are found near the bottom of the fossil record of multi-cellular organisms, and yet they are still around today, fundamentally unchanged.

became extinct at that time. This is consistent with the Bible account of the Flood beginning with the breaking up of the 'fountains of the great deep' (i.e. beginning in the sea; 'the great deep' means the oceans).

There is also a possibility that stable fresh and saltwater layers developed and persisted in some parts of the ocean. Freshwater can sit on top of saltwater for extended periods of time. Turbulence may have been sufficiently low at high latitudes for such layering to persist and allow the survival of both freshwater and saltwater species in those areas.

Survival of plants

Many terrestrial seeds can survive long periods of soaking in various concentrations of saltwater.[4] Indeed, saltwater impedes the germination of some species so that the seed lasts better in saltwater than freshwater. Other plants could have survived in floating vegetation masses, or on pumice from the volcanic activity. Pieces of many plants are capable of asexual sprouting.

Many plants could have survived as planned food stores on the ark, or accidental inclusions in such food stores. Many seeds have devices for attaching themselves to animals, and some could have survived the Flood by this means. Others could have survived in the stomachs of the bloated, floating carcasses of dead herbivores.

The olive leaf brought back to Noah by the dove (Gen. 8:11) shows that plants were regenerating well before Noah and company left the Ark.

Conclusion

There are many simple, plausible explanations for how fresh and saltwater fish and plants could have survived the Flood. There is no reason to doubt the reality of the Flood as described in the Bible.

Recommended reading: John Woodmorappe, 1996, *Noah's Ark: A feasibility study,* Institute for Creation Research, Santee CA, USA.

---

[4] Howe, G.F., 1968. Seed germination, sea water, and plant survival in the Great Flood. *Creation Research Quarterly* **5**:105–112. Ironically, Charles Darwin similarly proved that seeds could survive months of soaking in seawater.

Chapter 15

Where are all the human fossils?

Why are human fossils not found with trilobites, for example? If humans and dinosaurs lived at the same time, why aren't their fossils found together? How could the Flood produce the order in the fossil record?

THE Bible teaches (Genesis 1) that man was here from Day Six of the creation week — created the same day as land animals (which includes dinosaurs) and one day after the sea creatures and the birds.

Evolutionists claim that the order in the fossil record (e.g. trilobites deep down and humans near the top) is due to a succession of life forms on Earth, which occurred over many hundreds of millions of years. In this view, the rock strata represent huge periods of time.

On the other hand, creationists believe that most of the fossils were formed during the year-long global Flood recorded in Genesis chapters 6–9 (see Chapter 10, *Was the Flood Global?*). Thus creationists believe that the order in the fossil record is due to the order of burial during the Flood, and the local catastrophes that followed. So, sceptics ask, why are human fossils not found with dinosaur fossils, for example?

Do the rock strata represent eons of time?

There is a wealth of evidence that the rock strata do not represent vast periods of time. For example, the huge Coconino sandstone formation in the Grand Canyon is about 100 m thick and extends to some 250,000 km^2 in area. The large-scale cross-bedding shows that it was all laid down in deep, fast-flowing water in a matter of days. Other rock layers in the Grand Canyon indicate that they were rapidly deposited also, and without substantial time-breaks between the laying down of each unit.[1] Indeed, the whole Grand Canyon sequence is bent

---

[1] Austin, S.A., 1994. *Grand Canyon: Monument to Catastrophe,* Institute for Creation Research, San Diego, CA.

at the Kaibab Upwarp, in some spots quite radically, and without cracking. This indicates that the strata, which supposedly represent some 300 million years of evolutionary time, were all still soft when the bending occurred.[1,2] This is consistent with the layers being deposited and bent quickly, during the Genesis Flood.

Some other evidences for the non-existence of the eons of time and for the rapid deposition of the layers are:

● polystrate fossils — tree trunks, for example, running through strata supposedly representing many millions of years (these are common in coal) show that the strata must have been deposited in quick succession, otherwise the tops of the trunks would have rotted away;

● delicate surface features preserved on underlying rock units — such as ripple marks and footprints — indicate that there was no long time gap before the next unit was deposited;

● lack of fossilized soil layers in the rock strata, indicating no long time gaps;

● lack of erosion features in the rock layers or between the rock units

Photo: Andrew Snelling

There could have been no significant time between the deposition of these two geological formations, or there would have been erosion at the join between them (arrow). The join, or contact, is between the Coconino Sandstone (top) and the Hermit Shale (bottom), beside the Grandview Trail, Grand Canyon. The time gap is supposed to be 10 million years or more.

[2] Morris, J., 1994. *The Young Earth,* Creation-Life Publishers Inc., Colorado Springs, CO.

(any significant time break would result in channels being formed in the exposed strata from the action of water or wind);

● limited extent of unconformities. Although unconformities (clear breaks in deposition) indicate time breaks, such unconformities are localized, with no break evident in rocks of the same strata elsewhere, thus indicating that any time break was localized and brief;

● clastic dykes and pipes — where a sand/water mixture has squeezed up through overlying layers. Although the underlying sand is supposed to be millions of years older than the overlying layers, it obviously did not have time to harden.

● and much else.[2,3]

Uluru (Ayers Rock), in central Australia, is also supposed to have formed slowly over hundreds of millions of years, but the structure of the rock shows that it must have formed very quickly and recently (see pp. 165–166).[4]

The existence of many 'living fossils' also challenges the supposed hundreds of millions of years of 'Earth history'. For example, starfish, jellyfish, brachiopods, clams and snails, which are known as fossils dated by evolutionists as 530 million years old, look like those living today. Dr Joachim Scheven, a German scientist, has a museum with over 500 examples of such 'living fossils'. Furthermore, some of these fossils are missing from intervening strata that supposedly represent many millions of years of evolutionary time, again indicating that there were no time gaps.

Evidence that dinosaurs and humans co-existed

Much evidence suggests that people and dinosaurs lived together, not separated by 65 million years or more, as evolutionists believe:

● Many historical accounts of living animals, which were known as 'dragons', are good descriptions of what we call dinosaurs — such as *Triceratops, Stegosaurus, Tyrannosaurus* and *Ankylosaurus*. The video, *The Great Dinosaur Mystery* documents some of these.[5] The

---

[3] *Raging Waters,* video produced by Keziah Videos, 1998.

[4] Snelling, A., 1998. Uluru and Kata Tjuta. *Creation* **20**(2):36–40.

[5] Eden Films / Films for Christ. See also Chapter 19.

account in Job 40 of *behemoth* sounds like one of the big dinosaurs, such as *Apatosaurus* or *Brachiosaurus*.

● Unmineralized ('unfossilized') dinosaur bones.[6] How could these bones, some of which even have blood cells in them, be 65 million years or more old? It stretches the imagination to believe they are even many thousands of years old.

● Rocks bearing dinosaur fossils often contain very little plant material — e.g., in the Morrison formation in North America. This is another indication that the strata do not represent eras of life on Earth. If the strata represent an age of dinosaurs, what did they eat? A large *Apatosaurus* would need over three tonnes of vegetation per day, yet there is no indication of significant vegetation in many of these dinosaur-bearing strata. In other words, we see buried dinosaurs, not buried ecosystems or an 'Age of Dinosaurs'.

Out-of-sequence fossils

Many fossils and artefacts have been found 'out of place'.[7] That is, they are in strata that the evolutionist says represent a period of time when, for example, that organism did not live, or human artefacts could not have been made. There are plenty of examples; some published in respectable journals before the evolutionary paradigm became locked in. Such examples do not get published in modern standard evolutionary journals, possibly because it is inconceivable that such could exist in the evolutionary world-view. In another context, Nobel Prize winner Sir Fred Hoyle said,

'Science today is locked into paradigms. Every avenue is blocked by beliefs that are wrong, and if you try to get anything published by a journal today, you will run up against a paradigm, and the editors will turn it down.'[8]

---

[6] Wieland, C., 1999. Dinosaur bones: just how old are they really? *Creation* **21**(1):54–55), and references therein.

[7] For example: Howe, G.F., Williams, E. L., Matzko, G. T. and Lammerts, W. E., 1988. Creation Research Society studies on Precambrian pollen, Part III: A pollen analysis of Hakatai Shale and other Grand Canyon rocks, *Creation Research Society Quarterly* **24**(4):173–182.

[8] Horgan, J., 1995. Profile: Fred Hoyle. *Scientific American* **272**(3):24–25.

Forbidden Archeology, by Cremo and Thompson, lists some out-of-place human artefacts.[9] They wrote the book from a westernized Hindu perspective to show that humans were present from antiquity, as required for the eons of multi-cycles of re-incarnation of Hindu belief. (True Hindus are not concerned about such rationalizing, believing the physical world to be illusory.[10]) Cremo and Thompson are not worried about the millions of years, just whether humans were there. They are 'fellow-travellers' with creationists only in the sense that we also believe that people were here almost all along, except we do not accept the billions of years. Cremo and Thompson have done a thorough job, with the final work being 914 pages long.

Human fossils have been found, hundreds of them, but generally in deposits which most creationists would think were post-Flood (e.g. buried in caves during the post-Flood Ice Age — see Chapter 16). However, in at least one case, human bones have been found in 'older' strata.[11] Unfortunately, the lack of detailed documentation associated with their removal makes it impossible to say with certainty that they were not the result of subsequent intrusive burial, although nothing we know of suggests they were.

In regard to whether things found together necessarily lived and died together, paleontologists can inspect fossils for damage due to 're-working' for clues that the organisms did not necessarily live or die together. However, the 're-worked' or 'stratigraphic leak' (where something 'young' is found in 'old' rock) explanation is almost invariably invoked for 'out-of-place' fossils.

What about the general pattern?

Although the rock strata do not represent a series of epochs of Earth history, as is widely believed, they still follow a general pattern. For example, relatively immobile and bottom-dwelling sea creatures tend

---

[9] Cremo, M.A. and Thompson, R.L., 1993, *Forbidden Archeology.* Bhaktivedanta Institute, San Diego, CA, pp. 797–814.

[10] One reason why science flourished only in Bible-believing nations.

[11] Two human skeletons in a copper mine in Moab, Utah, in the (Cretaceous) Dakota Sandstone, which is supposed to be 'dinosaur age'. C. L. Burdick, 1973, Discovery of human skeletons in Cretaceous formation (Moab, Utah). *Creation Research Society Quarterly* **10**(2):109–10.

to be found in the lower strata that contain complex organisms, and the mobile land vertebrates tend to be found in the top layers. Consider the following factors:

Vertebrate fossils are exceedingly rare compared with invertebrate (without a backbone) sea creatures. The vast proportion of the fossil record is invertebrate sea creatures, and plant material in the form of coal and oil. Vertebrate fossils are relatively rare and human fossils are even rarer.[2]

If there were, say, 10 million people at the time of the Flood[12] and all their bodies were preserved and uniformly distributed throughout the 700 million cubic kilometres of fossil-bearing sedimentary rock layers, only one would be found in every 70 cubic kilometres of rock. Thus you would be unlikely to find even one human fossil.

A global Flood beginning with the breaking up of the fountains of the great deep would tend to bury bottom-dwelling sea creatures first — many of these are immobile, or relatively so. They are also abundant and generally robust (for example, shellfish).[13] As the waters rose to envelop the land, land creatures

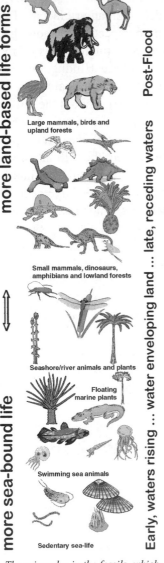

more land-based life forms

Large mammals, birds and upland forests

Small mammals, dinosaurs, amphibians and lowland forests

Seashore/river animals and plants

Floating marine plants

Swimming sea animals

Sedentary sea-life

more sea-bound life

Post-Flood

Early, waters rising ... water enveloping land ... late, receding waters

Possible phases of the Flood

There is order in the fossils, which would be expected from a global Flood.

---

[12] Woodmorappe, J., 1983. A diluviological treatise on the stratigraphic separation of fossils. *Creation Research Society Quarterly* **20**(4):133–185.
[13] However, the preservation of impressions of soft creatures such as jellyfish also occurs, and this testifies to the rapidity of burial.

would be buried last.[14] Also, water plants would tend to be buried before land-based swamp plants, which, in turn would be buried before upland plants.

On the other hand, land animals, such as mammals and birds, being mobile (especially birds), could escape to higher ground and be the last to succumb. People would cling to rafts, logs etc. until the very end and then tend to bloat and float and be scavenged by fish, with the bones breaking down rather quickly, rather than being preserved. This would make human fossils from the Flood exceedingly rare.

Further, the more mobile, intelligent animals would tend to survive the Flood longest and be buried last, so their remains would be vulnerable to erosion by the receding floodwaters at the end of the Flood and in the aftermath of the Flood. Hence their remains would tend to be destroyed. The intelligence factor could partly account for the apparent separation of dinosaurs and mammals such as cattle, for example.[15]

Another factor is the sorting action of water. A coal seam at Yallourn in Victoria, Australia, has a 0.5 m thick layer of 50 % pollen. The only way such a layer of pollen could be obtained is through the sorting action of water in a massive watery catastrophe that gathered the plant material from a large area and deposited it in a basin in the Yallourn area.

'Cope's Rule' describes the tendency of fossils (e.g. shellfish) to get bigger as you trace them upward through the geological strata. But why should evolution make things generally bigger? Indeed, living forms of fossils tend to be smaller than their fossil ancestors. A better explanation may be the sorting action of water.[16]

See geologist Woodmorappe's paper for an in-depth treatment of the fossil record of cephalopods (such as octopuses and squid) and how it concurs with Creation and the Flood.[17]

---

[14] The Bible suggests the Flood began in the 'great deep' (the sea). See p.157.

[15] Most creationists would regard large mammal fossil deposits, such as in the John Day County of Oregon, USA, as post-Flood.

[16] Although bigger rocks tend to be sorted to the bottom, larger shellfish, for example, are overall less dense than smaller ones and could be deposited after smaller ones in a sorting situation.

[17] Woodmorappe, J., 1978, The cephalopods in the creation and the universal Deluge. *Creation Research Society Quarterly* **15**(2):94–112.

These are some factors that could account for the patterns seen in the fossil record, including the general absence of human fossils in Flood deposits. Most of the fossil record does not represent a history of life on Earth, but the order of burial during the Flood. We would expect a pattern with a global Flood, but not an entirely consistent pattern, and this is what we find in the geological strata.

There are problems in reconstructing any historical event, but especially one that has no modern analogue. And such is the Flood.[18] So we have problems imagining the precise sequence of events by which the Flood eroded and deposited material, creating fossils. It may well be that some enterprising creationist scientists will come up with a model of the Flood that will fully account for the fossil and rock sequences.

Of interest in this regard is the TAB (**T**ectonically **A**ssociated **B**iological) provinces model of Woodmorappe.[12] Dr Tasman Walker has suggested a model of the Flood that also seems to explain much of the data.[19] The catastrophic plate tectonics model of Drs Austin, Baumgardner, and colleagues also looks interesting in explaining much of the fossil distribution (see Chapter 11). Other models are being developed which may also be helpful in explaining the evidence.[20]

One can be confident that the evolutionary view of Earth history is wrong and the record in the rocks and fossils, including the distribution of human fossils, makes much more sense in the light of the Bible's account of Creation, the Fall and the Flood.

When God pronounced judgment on the world, He said, '*I will destroy [blot out] man whom I have created from the face of the earth*' (Gen. 6:7). Perhaps the lack of pre-flood human fossils is part of the fulfilment of this judgment?

---

[18] Secular geologists wrongly assume that all Earth's history was shaped by the same processes we see happening *today* — this is the doctrine of *uniformitarianism,* which has directed geology for the last 200 years. As there is no global flood happening today, such thinking prevents most of today's geologists from seeing any evidence for the Flood — they try to explain the evidence seen in the present by the processes seen operating only in the present. The Bible has a prophecy, in 2 Peter 3:3–7, regarding this wrong approach to geology that denies miraculous creation and the Deluge.
[19] Walker, T., 1994. A biblical geologic model. *Proc. Third ICC,* pp. 581–92.
[20] Oard, Michael, personal communication.

Chapter 16

What about the Ice Age?

How many ice ages were there? Where does an ice age fit into the biblical account? How much of the earth was covered by ice? How long did it last? What about the frozen mammoths? How were people affected?

THE only clear evidence we have is for one Ice Age. We still see its remnants in such things as glaciers and the U-shaped valleys they carved. This ice age is said by evolutionists to have started about two million years ago and ended about 11,000 years ago. It was punctuated by relatively warm 'interglacial periods, which lasted about 10 % of the time. Most creationists, on the other hand, believe the Ice Age began soon after the Flood and continued for less than a thousand years. Indeed, as we shall see later, the biblical Flood provides a good basis for understanding how the *one* Ice Age developed. However, evolutionists have great difficulty accounting for any ice age.[1] In their understanding there would have been multiple ice ages, every 20–30 million years or so.

Earlier ice ages?

Using their principle that 'the present is the key to the past'[2] evolutionists claim that there is evidence for earlier ice ages. However, supposed similarities between the rocks in those geological systems and the special features produced in **the** Ice Age are not consistent.[3–5]

[1] Anon., 1997. Great science mysteries. *U.S. News and World Report,* Aug. 18.
[2] The Apostle Peter prophesied that in the latter days scoffers would claim that *'all things continue as they were from the beginning'* (2 Peter 3:3–7).
[3] Oard, M.J., 1997. *Ancient Ice Ages or Gigantic Submarine Landslides?* Creation Research Society Books, Chino Valley, Arizona.
[4] Molén, M., 1990. Diamictites: ice-ages or gravity flows? *Proc. Second ICC* **2**:177–190.
[5] Oard, M.J., 1990. *An Ice Age Caused by the Genesis Flood*, Technical Monograph, Institute for Creation Research, El Cajon, CA, pp. 135–149.

Arctic fox

Charcoal by Robert Smith.

Today, glaciers grind up the rock they travel over, creating deposits of fine and coarse material mixed together. This unsorted material is known as *till,* or *tillite* when it becomes bound together to form a rock unit. The grinding action of rocks embedded in the glacier also scores parallel grooves in the bedrock the glacier slides over — these grooves are called *striations.* When some melting occurs in summer, the glacier releases rock 'flour' which is washed into glacial lakes and settles to form fine and coarse alternating layers known as *varves.* Sometimes a piece of ice will break off the glacier or ice sheet and float into such a glacial lake, dropping embedded boulders as it melts. These 'dropstones' fall into the fine sediments (varves) on the lake floor, so that stones are sometimes found in the varves.

Geologists have claimed that these features have been found in ancient rock layers, proving that there had been **previous** ice ages over geologic time. Many lines of evidence now indicate that the observations have been misinterpreted:[3]

● The 'tillites' of lower rock layers are small in area, commonly thick, and probably all of marine origin, whereas those of modern glaciers are relatively large in area, thin and continental.

● There are limestones and dolomites frequently associated with these 'tillites' — carbonates which form today in warm water, not cold.

● The largest boulders in the ancient 'tillites' are much smaller than the larger boulders being deposited by glacial action today.

● Underwater mass flows can produce tillite-like deposits, as well as striated bedrock and striated stones in the 'tillite'. Such mass flows would be expected during Noah's Flood.

● Turbidity currents can deposit varve-like laminated sediments very quickly.[6] These sediments are more accurately called rhythmites. A varve is defined as a rhythmite deposited in one year. Lambert and Hsu have presented evidence from a Swiss lake that such varve-like rhythmites form rapidly by catastrophic, turbid water underflows.[7] At one location, five couplets of these varve-like rhythmites formed during a single year. At Mount St Helens in the USA, an 8 m (25 ft) thick stratified deposit consisting of many thin varve-like laminae was formed in less than one day (June 12, 1980).[8] Flow tank experiments have shown how laminations can form rapidly when two different grain sizes are carried together in flowing water.[9]

● The so-called 'dropstones' could not have been dropped into the ancient 'varvites'[10] because such a method of placement would result in tell tale disturbance of the laminations, which is rarely observed. The evidence suggests they were placed **with** the enclosing sediments by turbidity currents or other mass flows — again consistent with what would be expected during a global Flood. In other words the 'varvites' did not come from cyclical, annual, glacial lake deposition.

The extent of the ice

The effects of **the** Ice Age are still with us, particularly the giant ice sheets of Antarctica and Greenland, the alpine glaciers, and the

---

[6] A turbidity current is a dense mass of sediment-laden water travelling rapidly and violently down a slope underwater.

[7] Lambert, A. and Hsu, K.J., 1979. Non-annual cycles of varve-like sedimentation in Walensee, Switzerland. *Sedimentology* **26**:453–461.

[8] Austin, S.A., 1986. Mount St Helens and catastrophism. *Proc. First ICC*, Pittsburgh, PA **1**:3–9.

[9] Julien, P.Y., Lan, Y.Q. and Raslan, Y., 1998. Experimental mechanics of sand stratification. *CEN Technical Journal* **12**(2):218–221.

[10] 'Varves' of rhythmites which have become rock, or lithified.

glacial landforms and sediments. Because these effects are seen on the current land surface, it is clear that the Ice Age occurred after the Flood.

During the Ice Age, great ice sheets developed over Greenland and North America (as far south as the northern United States) and in northern Europe from Scandinavia to Germany and England (see diagram).

In the North American Rockies, the European Alps, and other mountain chains, permanent ice caps rested on the summits, and extensive valley glaciers descended down almost to the plains below.

In the Southern Hemisphere, another ice sheet covered most of Antarctica. Alpine ice caps developed on the mountains of New Zealand, Tasmania, parts of southeastern mainland Australia, and southern Chile. Some glaciers still remain in the high Southern Alps of New Zealand, and in the Andes Mountains, but glacial landforms are all that are left in New South Wales' Snowy Mountains, and in Tasmania, as a reminder of the action of the ice.

The approximate extent of the ice sheets at the peak of the Ice Age.

Nearly all textbooks used to claim that the Ice Age involved at least four advances and retreats of the ice, with relatively warm periods (called inter-glacials) in between. Based on the quest to find a cyclical pattern of ice ages, the number of ice ages during the past two million years of geological time has jumped to more than 20. However, the dense clay soils, old river terraces, and other phenomena, interpreted as evidence for multiple ice ages, can be more readily understood as resulting from advance and retreat phases of a *single* ice age after the Flood.[11]

The Ice Age and human habitation

It is important to realise that the ice never covered more than a third of the earth's land surface, even at its greatest extent. At the same time as there was glaciation in the upper latitudes, there was probably a period of higher rainfall in the lower latitudes. Such higher rainfall towards the equator would have assured an abundant water supply even in present-day desert areas such as the Sahara, the Gobi, and Arabia. Indeed, archaeological excavations have yielded abundant evidences of lush vegetation, human occupation and complex irrigation economies in these now desolate regions.

There is also evidence that human societies lived near the edge of the ice sheet in Western Europe throughout the Ice Age — the Neandertal peoples, for instance. Many anthropologists now recognize that their somewhat brutish appearance was at least partly due to disease (rickets, arthritis) caused by the dark, cold and damp climate of the region at that time. Their resulting lack of exposure to sunlight, which stimulates vitamin D synthesis necessary for normal bone development, and poor diet, would have caused rickets.[12]

Apart from highly questionable dating methods (see Chapter 4), there is no reason why Neandertals could not have lived at the same time as the advanced civilizations of Egypt, Babylonia, and others that were developing unhindered in the lower latitudes. The Ice Age can be better understood as lasting 700 years or so rather than two million years.

The biblical Flood: the trigger for the Ice Age

To develop an ice age, where ice accumulates on the land, the oceans need to be warm at mid- and high latitude, and the land masses need to

---

[11] Oard, Ref. 5, pp. 149–166.
[12] Ivanhoe, F., 1970. Was Virchow right about Neandertal? *Nature* **227**:577–579.

be cold, especially in the summer.[5,13–15] Warm oceans evaporate lots of water, which then moves over the land. Cold continents result in the water precipitating as snow rather than rain, and also prevent the snow from thawing during summer. The ice thus acculumates quickly.

Slow-and-gradual evolutionary scenarios[16] to explain the Ice Age

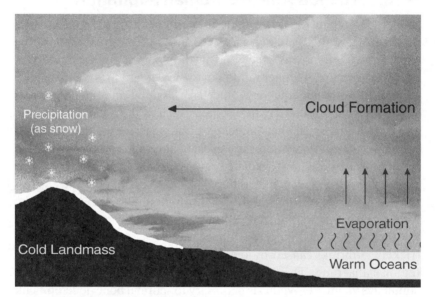

The Flood and its aftermath would provide the warm oceans and cold continents to get an 'Ice Age'.

do not work. Long-age theories involve a slow cooling down of the earth, but this will not generate an ice age. If the oceans gradually cooled, along with the land, by the time everything was cold enough so that the snow didn't melt during summer, evaporation from the oceans would be insufficient to produce enough snow to generate the massive ice sheets.[17] A frozen desert would result, not an ice age.

[13] Oard, M.J., 1979. A rapid post-Flood ice age. *Creation Research Society Quarterly* **16**(1):29–37.

[14] Oard, M.J., 1986. An ice age within the biblical time frame. *Proc. First ICC*, Pittsburgh, PA **2**:157–166.

[15] Wieland, C., 1997. Tackling the big freeze. *Creation* **19**(1):42–43.

[16] Oard, Ref. 5, pp. 1–22.

[17] The higher the water temperature the more the evaporation, because evaporation requires a lot of heat energy.

Charcoal by Robert Smith.

The polar bear is a species of the bear kind adapted to cold conditions.

However, the global Flood described in the Bible provides a simple mechanism for an ice age. We would expect warm oceans at the end of the global Flood, due to the addition of hot subterranean water to the pre-Flood ocean and heat energy released through volcanic activity. Oard and Vardiman point to evidence that the ocean waters were in fact warmer just before the Ice Age, as recorded by the oxygen isotopes in the shells of tiny marine animals called foraminifera.[18–20]

Large amounts of volcanic dust and aerosols from residual volcanic eruptions at the end of and after the Flood would have reflected solar radiation back into space, causing low temperatures over land, and especially causing the summers to be cold.[21] Dust and aerosols slowly settle out of the atmosphere, but continued post-Flood volcanism would have replenished these for hundreds of years following the Flood. In support of this, there is evidence of continued widespread volcanism in the large quantities of volcanic rocks among so-called 'Pleistocene'

[18] Vardiman, L., 1993. *Ice Cores and the Age of the Earth*, Technical Monograph, Institute for Creation Research, El Cajon, California.

[19] Vardiman, L., 1994. A conceptual transition model of the atmospheric global circulation following the Genesis Flood. *Proc. Third ICC*, Pittsburgh, PA, pp. 569–579.

[20] Vardiman, L., 1994. An analytical young-earth flow model of ice sheet formation during the 'Ice Age'. *Proc. Third ICC*, Pittsburgh, pp. 561–568.

[21] Oard, Ref. 5, pp. 33–38.

sediments, which probably formed soon after the Flood.

Vardiman[19,20] has shown, using standard knowledge of atmospheric circulation, that the warm oceans after the Flood, and the large rates of cooling at the poles, would have driven extreme atmospheric convection. This would have created an enormous polar hurricane-like storm system covering a large portion of the Arctic. This, he suggests, could have functioned for much of the 500-year period up to the glacial maximum (see next section). Such circulation patterns would have delivered to the higher latitudes the vast amounts of snow that would have quickly become ice sheets, spreading firstly over the continents, and then later over the oceans as the water cooled down towards the end of the glacial period.

How long an ice age?

Meteorologist Michael Oard[22] has estimated that it would have taken only about 700 years to cool the polar oceans from a uniform temperature of 30 °C at the end of the Flood to the temperatures observed today (average 4 °C). This 700-year period represents the duration of the Ice Age. The ice would have started accumulating soon after the Flood. By about 500 years after the Flood, the average global ocean temperature would have cooled to about 10 °C, and the resulting reduced evaporation would have caused much less cloud cover. This, combined with the clearing of the volcanic dust from the atmosphere, would have allowed more radiation to penetrate to the earth's surface, progressively melting the ice sheets. Thus the glacial maximum would have been about 500 years after the Flood.

Interestingly, there seem to be certain references to this Ice Age in the ancient book of Job (37:9–10, 38:22–23, 29–30), who perhaps lived in its waning years. (Job lived in the land of Uz, Uz being a descendant of Shem [Gen. 10:23], so that most conservative Bible scholars agree that Job probably lived at some time between the Tower of Babel and Abraham.) God questioned Job from a whirlwind, *'Out of whose womb came the ice? And the frost of the heavens, who fathered it? The waters are hidden like stone, and the face of the deep is frozen.'* (Job 38:29–30).

Such questions presuppose Job knew, either firsthand or by

---

[22] Oard, Ref. 5, pp. 109–119.

historical/family records, what God was talking about. This is probably a reference to the climatic effects of the Ice Age — effects not now seen in the Middle East.

In recent years the conventional age estimate for the Ice Age has been seemingly reinforced by claims that ice cores drilled from the Antarctic and Greenland ice sheets contain many thousands of annual layers. Layering is certainly visible in the uppermost section of such ice cores, but it only correlates with an annual pattern in the past few thousand years, as it should if it represents annual snow deposits since the end of the Ice Age. Lower down in the ice cores, the so-called annual layers become less distinct and can be understood as being caused by other mechanisms, such as individual storms.

Vardiman[18-20] has demonstrated that the ice core data support a long-age model only if they are interpreted that way. The ice-core data readily fit a young-earth model, with the bulk of the ice sheet thickness having been deposited by the hurricane-like circulation in the relatively brief 500-year period following the Flood. In this understanding, the oxygen isotope variations, for example, do not represent annual seasons but individual storms from different directions depositing water evaporated from oceans differing in temperature.[23]

The riddle of the frozen mammoths

The remains of hundreds of thousands of woolly mammoths are found across northern Europe, Siberia and Alaska. There was a lucrative trade in mammoth ivory for many years. At least a million mammoths must have lived in Siberia and Alaska.[24] The healthy appearance of carcasses indicates that they were well fed. But how could the frozen wastes of Siberia have ever produced enough food for the mammoths? And there were also woolly rhinoceros, bison, horses, musk ox, reindeer and antelopes in abundance. Even if the

Illustration by Steve Cardno

---

[23] The oxygen isotope concentrations of snow vary with the temperature of the ocean from which the water was originally evaporated.

[24] Oard, Ref. 5, p. 88

animals migrated there in summer, there would not have been enough food for them.

Furthermore, what did animals such as rhinoceros, bison and horses drink during the frozen winters? Such animals need large quantities of liquid water.

Evolutionists, with their eons of time and multiple ice ages, believe that Siberia and Alaska

The musk ox, probably of the cattle kind, is adapted to the cold.

are relatively warm at present,[25] compared with the time when mammoths lived there. So, how could these large populations of animals have lived in these areas?

It is estimated that about 50,000 carcasses or partial carcasses may still exist.[26] The vast majority show signs of substantial decay before they were buried and frozen, though about a half-dozen intact frozen carcasses have been found.

Some of the intact carcasses have been found with their stomach contents only partially digested. Some have claimed that an extraordinary snap-freeze would be needed to preserve such stomach contents. However, undigested stomach contents have been found in the remains of a non-frozen, non-fossilised mastodon in Ohio, USA. That most of the mammoth remains show that they were in various states of decay before they were buried shows that this was no instantaneous regional freeze. However, it still must have been fairly quick for the degree of preservation observed.

Some of the plant species identified in the stomach of the famous Beresovka mammoth now grow only in warmer climates. The evidence thus suggests a permanent, rapid change in climate in northern Siberia /Alaska. The mammoths lived there because the climate was much warmer, with more precipitation, than today. Mammoth remains have been found as far south as Mexico, showing that they were not adapted just to icy conditions.

---

[25] Evolutionists consider that we are presently in a warm 'interglacial' period.

[26] Oard, Ref. 5, p. 129.

Cave paintings of mammoths were obviously done by people living after the Flood.[27] Furthermore, since the mammoth remains are frozen in so-called 'muck', and in river terraces and deltas associated with river floods, on top of Flood sediments, they must have been frozen there at some time during the Ice Age, after the Flood. The mammoths must have been buried in the muck, sand and gravel, and frozen fast enough to preserve them up until the present.[28]

The burial and freezing of these mammoths cannot be accounted for with uniformitarian / evolutionary explanations of a slow-and-gradual onset of the Ice Age over thousands of years, and its slow waning over a similarly long period. However, while the mammoths are a big mystery to evolutionists, the biblical Flood / Ice Age model provides a framework for understanding the mammoths.

Oard proposes that the mammoths were buried and frozen towards the end of the post-Flood Ice Age.[15,29] It is significant that mammoth remains are most abundant close to the Arctic Ocean and in the islands off the coast. Also, they are mostly found south of the maximum southern limits of the ice sheets.

Oard suggests that as the continental ice sheets were melting and bringing in permanent climate change, there would have been catastrophic flooding events as ice dams failed and released huge lakes of cold, fresh water. There is published evidence of at least one such huge catastrophic dam burst in Siberia.[30] Such flooding could have buried the mammoths.

The Arctic Ocean at the end of the Ice Age, although below the freezing point of freshwater, would still have been warm enough for

---

[27] Distinctly mammoth-like elephants were recently discovered living in Nepal, suggesting that mammoths have not been extinct for as long as is commonly believed. See Wieland, C., 1997. 'Lost world' animals – found! *Creation* **19**(1):10–13.

[28] Oard, Ref. 5, pp. 86–91, 128–133.

[29] This means that there would be some 700 years for the populations of animals, including mammoths, to build up after the Flood. This is ample time to produce many millions of animals (with a conservative population doubling time of 17 years, a pair off the Ark could produce a population of more than a **billion** in 500 years).

[30] Baker, V.R., Benito, G. and Rudoy, A.N., 1993. Paleohydrology of late Pleistocene superflooding, Altay Mountains, Siberia. *Science* **259**:348–350.

the saltwater not to freeze. Thus a sudden flow of fresh water onto the sea would have caused the rapid formation of ice on the surface of the sea, cutting off evaporation from the sea. This would have resulted in the very rapid onset of very cold, dry weather in Siberia and Alaska, with temperatures dropping by up to 30 °C in about a week. This could explain the onset of sudden freezing weather in the area and hence the demise of so many mammoths, with their frozen carcasses.

The relatively warm Arctic Ocean would have kept the coastal lands habitable and productive during build up of the ice inland. Oard suggests that mammoths may have been in the habit of migrating north to these coastal regions near the Arctic Ocean during cold weather. However, with the freezing over of the sea, they moved in the wrong direction, into even colder weather. Some mammoths show evidence of death from suffocation or drowning and it is significant that very cold weather has been known to cause suffocation of cattle in North America.[31] Floods associated with the melting of the ice in the Asian mountains would have killed and buried many of the mammoths.

Hence, the biblical model easily accounts for the huge numbers of mammoth carcasses preserved along the Arctic Ocean coast.

The aftermath

Animals coming off the Ark multiplied in the centuries following the Flood. But with the development of the Ice Age and the onset of permanent climate change towards its end, many animals were unable to cope and became extinct. Some, like the woolly mammoths, died in catastrophes associated with these drastic changes.

As the ice retreated and the rainfall patterns changed yet again, many of the well-watered regions became arid, and so even more animals died out. The great cataclysm of the Flood, followed by the smaller related catastrophes of glaciation, volcanism, and eventual desiccation (drying out), drastically changed the character of the earth and its inhabitants to what we see today.

---

[31] The alveolar cells, which transfer oxygen in the lungs, are damaged by extreme cold, causing suffocation. Joggers in Canada have died from cold-induced suffocation at air temperatures of -20°C.

Chapter 17

How did animals get from the Ark to places such as Australia?

How did the animals get from remote countries to the Ark? After the Flood, did kangaroos hop all the way to Australia? What did koalas eat on the way?

LET us begin by reaffirming that God's Word does indeed reveal, in the plainest possible terms, that the whole globe was inundated with a violent, watery cataclysm — Noah's Flood. All land-dwelling, air-breathing creatures not on the Ark perished and the world was re-populated by those surviving on the Ark (see Chapter 10, *Was the Flood global?* pp. 137ff.).

How did the animals get to the Ark?

Sceptics paint a picture of Noah going to countries remote from the Middle East to gather animals such as kangaroos and koalas from Australia, and kiwis from New Zealand. However, the Bible states that the animals came to Noah; he did not have to round them up (Gen. 6:20). *God* apparently caused the the animals to come to Noah. The Bible does not state how this was done.

We also do not know what the geography of the world was like before the Flood. If there was only one continent at that time (see later in this chapter), then questions of getting animals from remote regions to the Ark are not relevant.

Animal distribution after the Flood

There are severe practical limitations on our attempts to understand the hows and whys of something that happened once, was not recorded in detail, and cannot be repeated.

Difficulties in our ability to explain every single situation in detail result from our limited understanding. We cannot go back in a time machine to check what happened, and our mental reconstructions of what the world was like after the Flood will inevitably be deficient. Because of this, the patterns of post-Flood animal migration present some problems and research challenges for the biblical creation model. However, there are clues from various sources which suggest answers to the questions.

Clues from modern times

When Krakatoa erupted in 1883, the island remnant remained lifeless for some years, but was eventually re-colonized by a surprising variety of creatures, including not only insects and earthworms, but birds, lizards, snakes, and even a few mammals. One would not have expected some of this surprising array of creatures to have crossed the ocean, but they obviously did. Even though these were mostly smaller than some of the creatures we will discuss here, it illustrates the limits of our imaginings on such things.

Land bridges

Evolutionists acknowledge that men and animals could once freely cross the Bering Strait, which separates Asia and the Americas.[1] Before the idea of continental drift became popular, evolutionists depended entirely upon a lowering of the sea level during an ice age (which locked up water in the ice) to create land bridges, enabling dry-land passage from Europe most of the way to Australasia, for example.

The existence of some deep-water stretches along the route to Australia is still consistent with this explanation. Evolutionist geologists themselves believe there have been major tectonic upheavals, accompanied by substantial rising and falling of sea-floors, in the time-period with which they associate an ice age. For instance, parts of California are believed to have been raised many thousands of feet from what was the sea-floor during this ice age period, which they call 'Pleistocene' (one of the most recent of the supposed geological periods). Creationist geologists generally regard Pleistocene sediments as post-Flood, the period in which these major migrations took place.

In the same way, other dry-land areas, including parts of these land

---

[1] Elias, S.A., Short, S.K., Nelson, C.H. and Birks, H.H., 1996. Life and times of the Bering land bridge. *Nature* **382**:60–63.

bridges, subsided to become submerged at around the same time.[2]

There is a widespread, but mistaken, belief that marsupials are found only in Australia, thus supporting the idea that they must have evolved there. However, living marsupials, opossums, are found also in North and South America, and fossil marsupials have been found on every continent. Likewise, monotremes were once thought to be unique to Australia, but the discovery in 1991 of a fossil platypus tooth in South America stunned the scientific community.[3] Therefore, since evolutionists believe all organisms came from a common ancestor, migration between Australia and other areas must be conceded as possible by all scientists, whether evolutionist or creationist.

Creationists generally believe there was only one Ice Age after, and as a consequence of, the Flood.[4] The lowered sea level at this time made it possible for animals to migrate over land bridges for centuries. Some creationists propose a form of continental break-up after the Flood[5], in the days of Peleg. This again would mean several centuries for animals to disperse, in this instance without the necessity of land bridges. However, continental break up in the time of Peleg is not widely accepted in creationist circles (see Chapter 11).

Did the kangaroo hop all the way to Australia?

How did animals make the long journey from the Ararat region? Even though there have been isolated reports of individual animals making startling journeys of thousands of kilometres, such abilities are not even necessary. Early settlers released a very small number of rabbits in Australia. Wild rabbits are now found at the very opposite corner (in fact, every corner) of this vast continent. Does that mean that an individual rabbit had to be capable of crossing the whole of Australia? Of course not. Creation speakers are sometimes asked mockingly, 'Did the kangaroo hop all the way to Australia?' We see by the rabbit example that this is a somewhat foolish question.

---

[2] Note that the region around the north of Australia to Southeast Asia is a tectonically active part of the world.

[3] Anon., 1992. Platypus tooth bites hard into long-held beliefs. *Creation* **14**(1):13, based on an article in *New Scientist,* August 24, 1991. A platypus is a monotreme (an egg-laying mammal).

[4] See Chapter 16, *What about the Ice Age?* pp. 187ff.

[5] See Chapter 11, *What about continental drift?* pp. 147ff.

Populations of animals may have had centuries to migrate, relatively slowly, over many generations. Incidentally, the opposite question (also common), as to whether the two kangaroos hopped all the way **from** Australia to the Ark, is also easily answered. The continents we now have, with their load of Flood-deposited sedimentary rock, are not the same as whatever continent or continents there may have been in the pre-Flood world.

Charcoal by Robert Smith

We also lack information as to how animals were distributed before the Flood. Kangaroos (as is true for any other creature) may not have been on an isolated landmass. Genesis 1:9 suggests that there may have been only one landmass. *('Let the waters under the heavens be gathered together into one place, and let the dry land appear.')* For all we know, kangaroos might have been feeding within a stone's throw of Noah while he was building the Ark.

It may be asked, if creatures were migrating to Australia over a long time (which journey would have included such places as Indonesia, presumably) why do we not find their fossils *en route* in such countries?

Fossilization is a rare event, requiring, as a rule, sudden burial (as in the Flood) to prevent decomposition. Lions lived in Israel until relatively recently. We don't find lion fossils in Israel, yet this doesn't prevent us believing the many historical reports of their presence. The millions of bison that once roamed the United States of America have left virtually no fossils. So why should it be a surprise that small populations, presumably under migration pressure from competitors and/or predators, and thus living in any one area for a few generations at most, should leave no fossils?

Unique organisms

Another issue is why certain animals (and plants) are uniquely found in only one place. Why is species x found only in Madagascar and species y only in the Seychelles? Many times, questions on this are phrased to indicate that the questioner believes that this means that species y headed only in that one direction, and never migrated anywhere else. While that is possible, it is not necessarily the case at all. All that the present situation indicates is that these are now the only places where x or y **still survive**.

The ancestors of present-day kangaroos may have established daughter populations in several parts of the world, most of which subsequently became extinct. Perhaps those marsupials only survived in Australia because they migrated there ahead of the placental mammals (we are not suggesting anything other than 'random' processes in choice of destination), and were subsequently isolated from the placentals and so protected from competition and predation.

Palm Valley in central Australia is host to a unique species of palm, *Livingstonia mariae*, found nowhere else in the world. Does this necessarily mean that the seeds for this species floated only to this one little spot? Not at all. Current models of post-Flood climate indicate that the world is much drier now than it was in the early post-Flood centuries. Evolutionists themselves agree that in recent times (by evolutionary standards) the Sahara was lush and green, and central Australia had a moist, tropical climate. For all we know, the *Livingstonia mariae* palm may have been widespread over much of Australia, perhaps even in other places that are now dry, such as parts of Africa.

The palm has survived in Palm Valley because there it happens to be protected from the drying out which affected the rest of its vast central Australian surrounds. Everywhere else, it died out.

Incidentally, this concept of changing vegetation with changing climate should be kept in mind when considering post-Flood animal migration — especially because of the objections (and caricatures) which may be presented. For instance, how could creatures that today need a rainforest environment trudge across thousands of kilometres of parched desert on the way to where they now live? The answer is that it wasn't desert then!

Livingstonia *palms in Palm Valley, central Australia*

The koala and other specialized types

The koala's preference for eucalyptus leaves is apparently due to an addiction. Young ones can be raised to eat other types of leaves.

Some problems are more difficult to solve. For instance, there are creatures that require special conditions or a very specialized diet, such as the giant panda of China and Australia's koala. We don't know, of course, that bamboo shoots or blue gum leaves[6] were not then flourishing all along their eventual respective migratory paths. In fact, this may have influenced the direction they took.

But, in any case, there is another possibility. A need for unique or special conditions to survive, may be a result of specialization, a downhill change in some populations. That is, it may result from a loss in genetic information, from thinning out of the gene pool or by degenerative mutation. A good example is the many modern breeds of dog, selected by man (although natural conditions can do likewise), which are much less hardy in the wild than their 'mongrel' ancestors. For example, the St Bernard carries a mutational defect, an overactive thyroid, which means it needs to live in a cold environment to avoid overheating.

This suggests that the ancestors of such creatures, when they came off the Ark, were not as specialized. Thus they were more hardy than their descendants, who carry only a portion of that original gene pool of information.[7] In other words, the koala's ancestors may have been

---

[6] Actually, the koala can eat other types of gum leaves. Australia has around 500 species of eucalypt (gum) trees. Koalas eat the leaves of about 20 species, with the blue gum a favourite. Recent work has shown that the koala's insistence on eucalypt is actually an **addiction** to certain chemicals in the leaf which it first eats in the mother's milk. Bottle-raised koalas can survive on a non-eucalypt diet (see *CEN Technical Journal* **8**(2):126). Also, the giant panda, which normally only eats bamboo shoots, has been known to eat small animals occasionally.

[7] See Chapter 18, *How did all the different races arise?* for an example of the

able to survive on a much greater range of vegetation. Such an explanation has been made possible only with modern biological insights. Perhaps as knowledge increases some of the remaining difficulties will become less so.

Iguanas have travelled hundreds of kilometres on rafts of vegetation created by storms.

Such changes do not require a long time for animals under migratory pressure. The first small population that formed would tend to break up rapidly into daughter populations, going in different directions, each carrying only a portion of the gene pool of the original pair that came off the Ark.

Sometimes all of a population will eventually become extinct; sometimes all but one specialized type. Where all the sub-types survive and proliferate, we find some of the tremendous diversity seen among some groups of creatures which are apparently derived from one created kind. This explains why some very obviously related species are found far apart from each other.

The sloth, a very slow-moving creature, may seem to require much more time than Scripture allows to make the journey from Ararat to its present home. Perhaps its present condition is also explicable by a similar devolutionary process. However, to account for today's animal distribution, evolutionists themselves have had to propose that certain primates have travelled across hundreds of miles of open ocean on huge rafts of matted vegetation torn off in storms.[8] Indeed, iguanas have recently been documented travelling hundreds of kilometres in this manner between islands in the Caribbean.[9]

The Bible suggests a pattern of post-Flood dispersal of animals and humans that accounts for fossil distributions of apes and humans, for example. In post-Flood deposits in Africa, ape fossils are found below human fossils. Evolutionists claim that this arose because

---

way in which a very light-skinned 'race' deriving from a mid-brown one is missing some of the information in the parent population.

[8] Anon., 1993. Hitch-hiking lemurs. *Creation* **15**(4):11, commenting on Tattersall, J., 1993. Madagascar's Lemurs. *Scientific American* **268**(1):90–97.

[9] Anon., 1999. Surfing lizards wipe out objections. *Creation* **21**(2):8.

humans evolved from the apes, but there is another explanation. Animals, including apes, would have begun spreading out over the earth straight after the Flood, whereas the Bible indicates that people refused to do this (Gen. 9:1, 11:1–9). Human dispersal did not start until Babel, some hundreds of years after the Flood. Such a delay would have meant that some ape fossils would be found consistently below human fossils, since people would have arrived in Africa after the apes.[10]

We may never know the exact answer to every one of such questions, but certainly one can see that the problems are far less formidable than they may at first appear.[11] Coupled with all the biblical, geological, and anthropological evidence for Noah's Flood, one is justified in regarding the Genesis account of the animals' dispersing from a central point as perfectly reasonable.[12] Not only that, but the biblical model provides an excellent framework for the scientific study of these questions.

---

[10] Dr Sigrid Hartwig-Scherer, paleoanthropologist, on the video, *The Image of God,* Keziah Videos.

[11] In recent literature about some of the problems of animal distribution, even within an evolutionary framework, there has been an occasional suggestion that early man may have been a much better boat-builder and navigator than previously thought. Various types of animals may thus have accompanied people on boats across the sea. This should be kept in mind as a possibility in some instances. Animals brought in this way to a new continent may have prospered, even though the accompanying people did not stay, or perished.

[12] For further reading: Whitcomb, J. and Morris, H., 1961. *The Genesis Flood,* Presbyterian and Reformed Publ. Co., Phillipsburg, New Jersey. Woodmorappe, J., 1990. Causes for the Biogeographic Distribution of Land Vertebrates After the Flood. *Proc. Second ICC,* Pittsburg, pp. 361–367.

Chapter **18**

How did all the different 'races' arise (from Noah's family)?

What is a 'race'? How did different skin colours come about? What are the consequences of false beliefs about 'race'? Are black people the result of a curse on Ham?

ACCORDING to the Bible, all humans on Earth today descended from Noah and his wife, his three sons and their wives, and before that from Adam and Eve (Gen. 1–11). But today we have many different groups, often called 'races', with what seem to be greatly differing features. The most obvious of these is skin colour. Many see this as a reason to doubt the Bible's record of history. They believe that the various groups could have arisen only by evolving separately over tens of thousands of years. However, as we shall see, this does not follow from the biological evidence.

The Bible tells us how the population that descended from Noah's family had one language and by living in one place were disobeying God's command to *'fill the earth'* (Gen. 9:1, 11:4). God confused their language, causing a break-up of the population into smaller groups which scattered over the earth (Gen. 11:8–9). Modern genetics shows how, following such a break-up of a population, variations in skin colour, for example, can develop in only a few generations. There is good evidence that the various people groups we have today have **not** been separated for huge periods of time.[1]

---

[1] World-wide variations in mitochondrial DNA (the 'Mitochondrial Eve' story) were claimed to show that all people today trace back to a single mother (living in a small population) 70,000 to 800,000 years ago. Recent findings on the rate of mitochondrial DNA mutations shorten this period drastically to put it within the biblical time-frame. See Loewe, L. and Scherer, S., 1997. Mitochondrial Eve: the plot thickens. *Trends in Ecology and Evolution* **12**(11):422–423; Wieland, C., 1998. A shrinking date for Eve. *CEN Technical Journal* **12**(1):1–3.

What is a 'race'?

There is really only one race — the human race. The Bible teaches us that God has *'made of one blood all nations of men'* (Acts 17:26). Scripture distinguishes people by tribal or national groupings, not by skin colour or physical features. Clearly, though, there are groups of people who have certain features (e.g., skin colour) in common, which distinguish them from other groups. We prefer to call these 'people groups' rather than 'races', to avoid the evolutionary connotations associated with the word 'race'.

All peoples can interbreed and produce fertile offspring. This shows that the biological differences between the 'races' are not very great. In fact, the DNA differences are trivial. The DNA of any two people in the world would typically differ by just 0.2 %.[2] Of this, only 6 % can be linked to racial categories; the rest is 'within race' variation.

> **'This genetic unity means, for instance, that white Americans, although ostensibly far removed from black Americans in phenotype, can sometimes be better tissue matches for them than are *other* black Americans.'**[2]

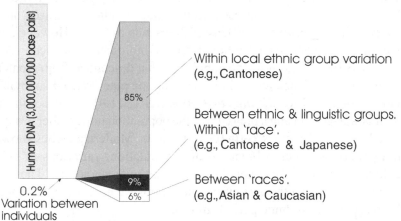

The variation in DNA between human individuals shows that racial differences are trivial.

Anthropologists generally classify people into a small number of main racial groups, such as the Caucasoid (European or 'white'),[3] the

---

[2] Gutin, J.C., 1994. End of the rainbow. *Discover,* November, pp. 71–75.
[3] However, people inhabiting the Indian subcontinent are mainly Caucasian and their skin colour ranges from light brown to quite dark. Even within Europe, skin colour ranges from very pale to brown.

Mongoloid (which includes the Chinese, Inuit or Eskimo, and Native Americans), the Negroid (black Africans), and the Australoid (the Australian Aborigines). Within each classification, there may be many different sub-groups.

Virtually all evolutionists would now say that the various people groups did not have separate origins. That is, different people groups did not each evolve from a different group of animals. So they would agree with the biblical creationist that all people groups have come from the same original population. Of course, they believe that such groups as the Aborigines and the Chinese have had many tens of thousands of years of separation. Most people believe that there are such vast differences between groups that there **had** to be many years for these differences to develop.

One reason for this is that many people believe that the observable differences arise from some people having unique features in their hereditary make-up which others lack. This is an understandable but incorrect idea. Let's look at skin colour, for instance. It is easy to think that since different groups of people have 'yellow' skin, 'red' skin, black skin, 'white' skin, and brown skin, there must be many different skin pigments or colourings. And since different chemicals for colouring would mean a different genetic recipe or code in the hereditary blueprint in each people group, it appears to be a real problem. How could all those differences develop within a short time?

However, we all have the same colouring pigment in our skin, melanin. This is a dark-brownish pigment that is produced in different amounts in special cells in our skin. If we had **none** (as do people called albinos, who inherit a mutation-caused defect, and cannot produce melanin), then we would have a very white or pink skin colouring. If we produced a little melanin, we would be European white. If our skin produced a great deal of melanin, we would be a very dark black. And in between, of course, are all shades of brown. There are no other significant skin pigments.[4]

---

[4] Other substances can in minor ways affect skin shading, such as the coloured fibres of the protein elastin and the pigment carotene. However, once again we all share these same compounds, and the principles governing their inheritance are similar to those outlined here. Factors other than pigment in the skin may influence the shade perceived by the observer in subtle ways, such as the thickness of the overlying (clear) skin layers, the density and

In summary, from currently available information, the really important factor in determining skin colour is melanin — the amount produced.

This situation is true not only for skin colour. Generally, whatever feature we may look at, no people group has anything that is essentially different from that possessed by any another. For example, the Asian, or almond, eye differs from a typical Caucasian eye in having more fat (see Figure 1). Both Asian and Caucasian eyes have fat —the latter simply have less.

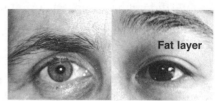

Figure 1. Caucasian and Asian eyes differ in the amount of fat around the eye.

What does melanin do?   It protects the skin against damage by ultraviolet light from the sun. If you have too little melanin in a very sunny environment, you will easily suffer sunburn and skin cancer. If you have a great deal of melanin, and you live in a country where there is little sunshine, it will be harder for you to get enough vitamin D (which needs sunshine for its production in your body). You may then suffer from vitamin D deficiency, which could cause a bone disorder such as rickets.

We also need to be aware that we are not born with a genetically fixed amount of melanin. Rather, we have a genetically fixed **potential** to produce a certain amount, and the amount increases in response to sunlight. For example, you may have noticed that when your Caucasian friends (who spent their time indoors during winter) headed for the beach at the beginning of summer they all had more or less the same pale white skin colour. As the summer went on, however, some became much darker than others.

---

positioning of the blood capillary networks, etc. In fact, 'melanin', which is produced by cells in the body called melanocytes, consists of two pigments, which also account for hair color. Eumelanin is very dark brown, phaeo-melanin is more reddish. People tan when sunlight stimulates eumelanin production. Redheads, who are often unable to develop a protective tan, have a high proportion of phaeomelanin. They have probably inherited a defective gene which makes their pigment cells 'unable to respond to normal signals that stimulate eumelanin production'. See Cohen, P., 1995. Redheads come out of the shade. *New Scientist* **147**(1997):18.

How is it that many different skin colours can arise in a short time? Remember, whenever we speak of different 'colours' we are referring to different shades of the one colour, melanin.

If a person from a very black people group marries someone from a very white group, their offspring (called mulattos) are mid-brown. It has long been known that when mulattos marry each other, their offspring may be virtually any 'colour', ranging from very dark to very light. Understanding this gives us the clues we need to answer our question, but first we must look, in a simple way, at some of the basic principles of heredity.

Heredity

Each of us carries information in our body that describes us in the way a blueprint and specifications describe a finished building. It determines not only that we will be human beings, rather than cabbages or crocodiles, but also whether we will have blue eyes, short nose, long legs, etc. When a sperm fertilizes an egg, **all** the information that specifies how the person will be built (ignoring such superimposed factors as exercise and diet) is already present. Most of this information is in coded form in our DNA.[5] To illustrate coding, a piece of string with beads on it can carry a message in Morse code:

The piece of string, by the use of a simple sequence of short beads, long beads (to represent the dots and dashes of Morse code), and spaces, can carry the same information as the English word 'help' typed on a sheet of paper. The entire Bible could be written thus in Morse code on a long enough piece of string.

In a similar way, the human blueprint is written in a code (or language convention) which is carried on very long chemical strings

---

[5] Most of this DNA is in the nucleus of each cell, but some is contained in mitochondria, which are outside the nucleus in the cytoplasm. Sperm contribute only nuclear DNA when the egg is fertilized. Mitochondrial DNA is inherited only from the mother, via the egg.

of DNA. This is by far the most efficient information storage system known, greatly surpassing any foreseeable computer technology.[6] This information is copied (and reshuffled) from generation to generation as people reproduce.

The word 'gene' refers to a small part of that information which has the instructions for only one type of enzyme, for example.[7] It may be simply understood as a portion of the 'message string' containing only one specification.

For example, there is one gene that carries the instructions for making hemoglobin, the protein that carries oxygen in your red blood cells. If that gene has been damaged by mutation (such as copying mistakes during reproduction), the instructions will be faulty, so it will often make a crippled form of hemoglobin, if any. (Diseases such as sickle-cell anemia and thalassemia result from such mistakes.)

So, with an egg which has just been fertilized — where does all its information, its genes, come from? One half comes from the father (carried in the sperm), and the other half from the mother (carried in the egg).

Genes come in pairs, so in the case of hemoglobin, for example, we have two sets of code (instruction) for hemoglobin manufacture, one coming from the mother and one from the father.

This is a very useful arrangement, because if you inherit a damaged gene from one parent that could instruct your cells to produce a defective hemoglobin, you are still likely to get a normal one from the other parent which will continue to give the right instructions. Thus only half the hemoglobin in your body will be defective. (In fact, each of us carries hundreds of genetic mistakes, inherited from one or the other of our parents, which are usefully 'covered up' by being matched with a normal gene from the other parent — see Chapter 8 on Cain's wife).

---

[6] Gitt, W., 1997. Dazzling design in miniature. *Creation* **20**(1):6.
[7] Incredibly, sometimes the same stretch of DNA can be 'read' differently, to have more than one function, by starting the reading process from different points. The creative intelligence behind such a thing is mind-boggling.

Skin colour

We know that skin colour is governed by more than one pair of genes. For simplicity, let's assume there are only two,[8] located at positions A and B on the chromosomes. One form of the gene, 'M', 'says' to make lots of melanin; another form of the gene,[9] 'm', says to only make a little melanin. At position A we could have a pair such as $M_A M_A$, $M_A m_A$ or $m_A m_A$[10] which would instruct the skin cells to make a lot, some, or little melanin.

Figure 2. A 'black' gene combination.

Similarly, at position B we could have the gene pairs $M_B M_B$, $M_B m_B$ or $m_B m_B$ instructing cells to make a lot, some or little melanin. Thus very dark people could have $M_A M_A M_B M_B$, for example (see Figure 2). Since both the sperm and eggs of such people could only be $M_A M_B$, (remember, only one of each A or B pair goes to each sperm or egg) they could only produce children with exactly the same combination of genes as themselves. So the children will all be very dark. Likewise, very light people, with $m_A m_A m_B m_B$, could produce children only like themselves (see Figure 3).

Let's look at what combinations would result from parents who are the type of brown-skinned person called a mulatto, or $M_A m_A M_B m_B$

---

[8] This simplification is not done to help our case — the more genes there are, the easier it is to have a huge range of 'different' colours. The principle involved can be understood by using two as an example.

[9] Variant forms of a gene are called 'alleles', but that is not important here.

[10] For the technically minded, this type of genetic expression, where allele dosage affects the trait, is called partial dominance.

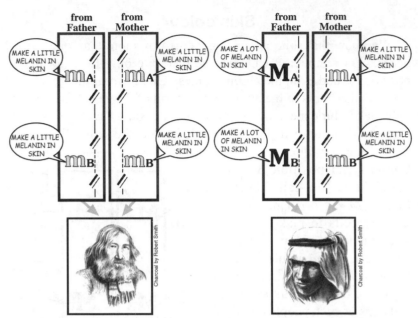

Figure 3. A 'white' gene combination.   *Figure 4. A 'brown' gene combination.*

(the offspring of an $M_A M_A M_B M_B$ and $m_A m_A m_B m_B$ union, for example; see Figure 4).

We can do this with a diagram called a 'punnet square' (see Figure 5). The left side shows the four different gene combinations possible in the sperm from the father and the top gives the combinations possible in the eggs from the mother (remember that a parent can only pass on one of each pair of genes to each sperm or egg). We locate a particular sperm gene combination and follow the row across to the column below a particular egg gene combination (like finding a location on a street map). The intersection gives the genetic makeup of the offspring from that particular sperm and egg union. For example, an $M_A m_B$ sperm and an $m_A M_B$ egg would produce a child with $M_A m_A M_B m_B$, just the same as the parents. The other possibilities mean that five levels of melanin (shades of colour) can result in the different offspring of such a mulatto marriage, as roughly indicated by the level of shading in the diagram. If three gene pairs were involved, seven levels of melanin would be possible.

Thus a range of 'colours', from very light to very dark, can result in only **one generation**, beginning with this particular type of mid-brown parents.

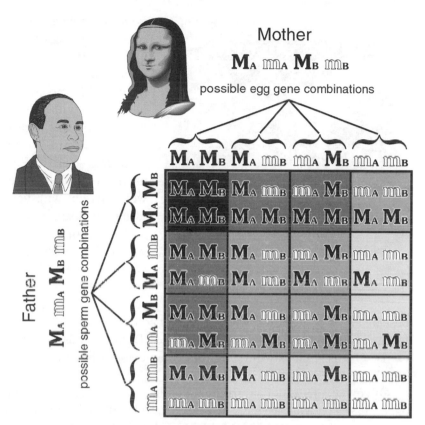

Figure 5. 'Punnet square' showing the possible offspring from 'mulatto' brown parents.

If people with $M_AM_AM_BM_B$, who are 'pure' black (in the sense of having no genes for lightness at all), were to intermarry and migrate to a place where their offspring could not marry people of lighter colour, all their descendants would be black — a pure 'black line' would result.

If 'white' people ($m_Am_Am_Bm_B$) were to marry only other whites and migrate to a place where their offspring could not marry darker people, a pure (in the same sense) 'white line' would result — they would have lost the genes needed to produce a large amount of melanin and be black.

It is thus easily possible, beginning with two middle-brown parents, to get not only all the 'colours', but also people groups with stable shades of skin colour.

But what about people groups that are permanently middle-brown,

MIXED DOUBLES

Two-tone twins

Figure 6. 'Britain's amazing twins'.

such as we have today? Again, this is easily explained. If those with genes $M_A M_A m_B m_B$ or $m_A m_A M_B M_B$, no longer intermarry with others, they will be able to produce only mid-brown offspring — as in Figure 4. (You may want to work this out with your own punnet square.)

If either of these lines were to interbreed again with the other, the process would be reversed. In a short time, their descendants would show a whole range of colours, often in the same family.   Figure 6 shows what were called Britain's most amazing twins. One is obviously quite light in complexion, while the other is clearly darker-skinned.

Of course, this is not amazing at all when you do the exercise on paper, based on what we have discussed. (A clue if you want to do it yourself: mother cannot be $M_A M_A M_B M_B$. Also, the twins are obviously not identical twins, which are derived from the same egg — that is, monozygous).

If all people on Earth were to intermarry freely, and then break into random groups that kept to themselves, a whole new set of gene combinations could emerge. It may be possible to have almond eyes with black skin, blue eyes with black frizzy short hair, etc. We need to remember, of course, that the way in which genes express themselves is much more complex than this simplified picture. For example, sometimes certain genes are linked together. However, the basic point is unaffected.

Even today, within a particular people group you will often see a feature normally associated with another people group. For instance, you will occasionally see a European with a broad flat nose, or a Chinese person with very pale skin, or Caucasian eyes. Most scientists now agree that, for modern humans, 'race' has little or no biological meaning. This also argues strongly against the idea that the people groups have been evolving separately for long periods.

What really happened?

We can now reconstruct the true history of the people groups, using:

● The information given by the Creator Himself in the book of Genesis.

● The background information given above.

● Some consideration of the effect of the environment.

The first created man, Adam, from whom all other humans are descended, was created with the best possible combination of genes — for skin colour, for example. A long time after Creation, a world-wide Flood destroyed all humans except a man called Noah, his wife, his three sons, and their wives. This Flood greatly changed the environment. Afterwards, God commanded the survivors to multiply and cover the earth (Gen. 9:1). A hundred years later, people chose to disobey God and to remain united in building a great city, with the Tower of Babel as the focal point of rebellious worship.

From Genesis 11, we understand that up to this time there was only one language. God judged the people's disobedience by imposing different languages, so that they could not work together against God. The confusion forced the people to scatter over the earth as God intended.

So all the people groups — black Africans, Indo-Europeans, Mongolians, and others — have come into existence since Babel.

Noah and his family were probably mid-brown, with genes for both dark and light skin, because a medium skin colour would seem to be the most generally suitable (dark enough to protect against skin cancer, yet light enough to allow vitamin D production). As all the factors for skin colour were present in Adam and Eve, they would most likely have been mid-brown as well, with brown eyes and brown (or black) hair. In fact, most of the world's population today is still mid-brown.

After the Flood, for the few centuries until Babel, there was only one language and one culture group. Thus, there were no barriers to marriage within this group. This would tend to keep the skin colour of the population away from the extremes. Very dark and very light skin would appear, of course, but people tending in either direction would be free to marry someone lighter or darker than themselves, ensuring that the average colour stayed roughly the same.

The same would be true of characteristics other than skin colour. Under these sorts of circumstances, distinct differences in appearance will never emerge. To obtain such separate lines, you would need to break a large breeding group into smaller groups and keep them separate, that is, prevent interbreeding between groups. This would be true for animal as well as human populations, as every biologist knows.

The effects of Babel

This is exactly what happened at Babel. Once separate languages were imposed, there were instantaneous barriers. Not only would people tend not to marry someone they couldn't understand, but entire groups which spoke the same language would have difficulty relating to and trusting those which did not. Thus, they would move away or be forced away from each other, into different environments. This, of course, is what God intended.

It is unlikely that each small group would carry the same broad range of skin colours as the original, larger group. One group might have more dark genes, on average, while another might have more light genes. The same thing would occur with other characteristics: nose shape, eye shape, etc. And since they would intermarry only within their own language group, these differences would no longer be averaged out as before.

As these groups migrated away from Babel, they encountered new and different climate zones. This would also have affected the balance of inherited factors in the population. However, the effects of the environment are nowhere near as important as the initial genetic mix of each group.

As an example, consider a group of people who moved to a cold region with little sunlight. Here, the dark-skinned members would not be able to produce enough vitamin D, and thus would be less healthy and have fewer children. So, in time, the light-skinned members would predominate. If several different groups went to such an area, and if one group happened to be carrying few genes for lightness, this particular group could in time die out. Thus, natural selection acts on the characteristics *already present,* and does not create new ones.

It is interesting to note that the Neandertals of Europe, now extinct but recognized as fully human, show evidence of vitamin D deficiency in that many of their bones were bent. In fact, this, plus a large dose of evolutionary prejudice, caused them to be classified as 'ape-men' for a long time. It is thus quite plausible that they were a dark-skinned people who were unfit for the environment into which they moved because of the skin colour genes *they began with*. Notice (again) that this natural selection, as it is called, does not *produce* skin colours, but only acts on the created capacity for making skin pigment that is *already there.*

Conversely, fair-skinned people in very sunny regions could easily be affected by skin cancer. Thus, in these regions dark-skinned people would more readily survive and come to predominate.

So we see that the pressure of the environment can (a) affect the balance of genes within a group, and (b) even eliminate entire groups. This is why we see, to a large extent, that the physical characteristics of people tend to match the environment where they live (e.g., Nordic people with pale skin, equatorial people with dark skin).

But this is not always so. The Inuit (Eskimo) have brown skin, yet live where there is not much sun. Presumably they all have a genetic makeup such as $M_A M_A m_B m_B$ which would not be able to produce lighter skin. On the other hand, native South Americans living on the equator do not have black skin. These examples confirm that natural selection does not create new information — if the genetic makeup of a group of people does not allow variation in colour toward the desirable, natural selection cannot create such variation.

Pygmies live in a hot area, but rarely experience strong sunshine in their dense jungle environment; yet they have dark skin. Pygmies may be a good example of another factor that has affected the racial history of man: discrimination.

People different from the 'norm' (e.g., a very light person in a dark people group), have historically been regarded as abnormal and rejected by the group. Thus, such a person would find it hard to get a marriage partner. This would further tend to eliminate light genes from a dark people, and vice versa. In this way, groups have tended to 'purify' themselves.

Also, in some instances, interbreeding within a small group can accentuate a commonly occurring unusual feature that would otherwise be swamped by marriage outside the group. There is a tribe in Africa whose members all have grossly deformed feet as a result of this inbreeding.

Let us return to the pygmies. If people possessing genes for short stature were discriminated against, a small group of them might seek refuge in the deepest forest. By marrying only each other they would ensure a pygmy 'race' from then on. The fact that pygmy tribes do not have their own languages, but instead speak dialects of neighbouring non-pygmy tribal languages, is good evidence to support this.

The effects of choice

Certain genetic characteristics may have influenced people groups to make deliberate (or semi-deliberate) choices concerning the environments to which they migrated. For instance, people with genes for a thicker, more insulating layer of fat under their skin would tend to leave areas that were uncomfortably hot.

Common memories

The evidence for the Bible's account of human origins is more than just biological and genetic. Since all peoples have descended from Noah's family, and a relatively short time ago, we would expect to find some memory of the catastrophic Flood in the stories and legends of many people groups. We may find the story distorted by time and retelling. In fact, an overwhelming number of cultures do have accounts that recall a world-destroying Flood. Often these have startling parallels to the true, original account (such as: eight people saved in a boat, the sending of birds, a rainbow, and more).

Conclusion

The dispersion at Babel broke up a large interbreeding group into small, inbreeding groups. This ensured that the resultant groups would have different mixes of genes for various physical features. By itself, this dispersion would ensure, in a short time, that there would be certain fixed differences in some of these groups, commonly called 'races'. In addition, the selection pressure of the environment would modify the existing combinations of genes so that the physical characteristics of each group would tend to suit their environment.

There has been no simple-to-complex evolution of any genes, for the genes were present already. The dominant features of the various people groups result from different combinations of previously existing created genes, plus some minor degenerative changes, resulting from mutation (accidental changes which can be inherited). The originally created (genetic) information has been either reshuffled or has degenerated, but has not been added to.

Consequences of false beliefs about the origin of races

● *Rejection of the Gospel*

The accuracy of the historical details of Genesis is crucial to the trustworthiness of the Bible and to the whole Gospel message.[11] So the popular belief that people groups evolved their different features, and could not all have come from Noah's family (contrary to the Bible), has eroded belief in the Gospel of Jesus Christ.

● *Racism*

One of the biggest justifications for racial discrimination in modern times is the belief that people groups have evolved separately. Thus different groups are at allegedly different stages of evolution, and so some people groups are more backward than others. Therefore, the other person may not be as fully human as you. This sort of thinking inspired Hitler in his quest to eliminate Jews and Gypsies and to establish the 'master race'.[12] Sadly, some Christians have been infected with racist thinking through evolutionary indoctrination that people of a different 'colour' are inferior because they are supposedly closer to the animals. Such attitudes are completely unbiblical (e.g. Acts 17:26, Col. 3:11), although out-of-context Bible verses are often conscripted in attempts to justify racist views (see Appendix 1).

● *Bad influence on missionary outreach*

Historically, the spread of evolutionary belief was associated with a slackening of fervour to reach the lost in far-away countries. The idea of savage, half-evolved inferior peoples somehow does not evoke the same missionary urgency as the notion that our 'cousins', closely linked to us in time and heredity, have yet to hear the Gospel.[13] Even many

---

[11] Ham, Ken, 1987. *The Lie: Evolution,* Creation-Life Publishers, San Diego, California, USA.

[12] Bergman, J., 1999. Darwinism and the Nazi race holocaust. *CEN Technical Journal* **13**(2):101–111.

[13] For example, Grigg, R., 1999. Darwin's quisling. *Creation* **22**(1):50–51.

of the finest of today's missionary organisations have been influenced, often unconsciously, by this deeply ingrained evolutionary belief of how other peoples and their religions came about.

All tribes and nations are descendants of Noah's family!

The Bible makes it clear that any newly 'discovered' tribe ultimately goes back to Noah. They are not a group of people who have never had superior technology or knowledge of God in their culture. Rather, their culture (going back to Noah) began with (a) a knowledge of God, and (b) technology at least sufficient to build a boat of ocean-liner size. Romans chapter 1 suggests the major reason for this technological loss and cultural degeneration (see Appendix II). It is linked to the deliberate rejection by their ancestors of the worship of the living God.

Therefore, the first priority in helping a 'backward' people group should not be secular education and technical aid, but first and foremost the Gospel.

In fact, most 'primitive' tribes still have a memory, in their folklore and religion, of the fact that their ancestors turned away from the living God, the Creator. Don Richardson, missionary of *Peace Child* fame, has shown that a missionary approach, unblinded by evolutionary bias, and thus looking for this link and utilizing it, has borne a bountiful and blessed harvest on many occasions.[14]

Jesus Christ, God's reconciliation in the face of man's rejection of the Creator, is the only truth that can set men and women of **every** culture, technology, people group or colour, truly free (John 8:32; 14:6).

ONE BLOOD
Acts 17:26

Adam & Eve
1 Corinthians 15:45
Genesis 3:20

Sons & Daughters
Genesis 5:4

Noah, Sons & Wives
Genesis 9:17-19

People at Tower of Babel
Genesis 11:8-9

Different People Groups/Cultures

---

[14] Richardson, D., 1986. *Eternity in Their Hearts,* Regal Books, Division of Gospel Light, Ventura, California, USA.

Appendix I. Are black people the result of a curse on Ham?

The previous discussion shows clearly that the blackness of, for example, black Africans, is merely one particular combination of inherited factors. This means that these factors themselves, though not in that combination, were originally present in Adam and Eve. The belief that the skin colour of black people is a result of a curse on Ham and his descendants is *nowhere taught in the Bible.* Furthermore, it was not *Ham* who was cursed, but his son, *Canaan* (Gen. 9:18,25, 10:6). Furthermore, Canaan's descendants were probably mid-brown skinned (Gen. 10:15–19), not black. False teaching about Ham has been used to justify slavery and other non-biblical racist practices. It is traditionally believed that the African nations are largely Hamitic, because the Cushites (Cush was a son of Ham: Gen. 10:6) are thought to have lived where Ethiopia is today. Genesis suggests that the dispersion was probably along family lines, and it may be that Ham's descendants were on average darker than, say, Japheth's. However, it could just as easily have been the other way around.

Rahab, mentioned in the genealogy of Jesus in Matthew 1, was a Canaanite. A descendant of Ham, she must have married an Israelite. Since this was a union approved by God, it shows that the particular 'race' she came from was not important. It mattered only that she trusted in the true God of Israel. Ruth, a Moabitess, also features in the genealogy of Christ. She expressed faith in the true God before her marriage to Boaz (Ruth 1:16). The only marriages God warns against are God's people marrying unbelievers.[15]

Appendix II. 'Stone Age' people?

Archaeology shows that there have been people who lived in caves and used simple stone tools. There are still people who do the same. We have seen that all people on Earth today are descended from Noah and his family. Before the Flood, Genesis indicates, there was at least enough technology to make musical instruments, farm, forge metal implements, build cities, and build a huge seaworthy vessel. After the dispersion from Babel, the hostilities induced by the new languages may have forced some groups to scatter rather rapidly, finding shelter

[15] Ham, K., 1999. Inter-racial marriage: is it biblical? *Creation* **21**(3):22–25.

where and when they could.

In some instances, the stone tools may have been used temporarily, until their settlements were fully established and they had found and exploited metal deposits, for example. In others, the original diverging group may not have taken the relevant knowledge with them. Ask an average family group today how many of them, if they had to start again, as it were, would know how to find, mine, and smelt metal-bearing deposits? Obviously, there has been technological (cultural) degeneration in many post-Babel groups.

In some cases, harsh environments may have contributed. The Australian Aborigines have a technology and cultural knowledge which, in relation to their lifestyle and need to survive in the dry outback, is most appropriate. This includes the aerodynamic principles used in making boomerangs (some of which were designed to return to the thrower, while others were not).

Sometimes we see evidence of degeneration that is hard to explain, but is real, nonetheless. For instance, when Europeans arrived in Tasmania, the Aborigines there had the simplest technology known. They caught no fish, and did not usually make and wear clothes. Yet recent archaeological discoveries suggest that earlier generations had more knowledge and equipment.

For instance, archaeologist Rhys Jones believes that in the Tasmanian Aborigines' distant past, these people had equipment to sew skins into complex clothes. This contrasts with the observations in the early 1800s that they just slung skins over their shoulders. It also appears that they were in fact catching and eating fish in the past, but when Europeans arrived, they had not been doing this for a long time.[16,17] From this we infer that technology is not always retained and built upon, but can be lost or abandoned.

Animist peoples live in fear of evil spirits and often have taboos against healthy practices like washing, and eating various nutritious foods. Again this illustrates how loss of knowledge of the true Creator-God leads to degradation (Rom. 1:18–32).

---

[16] Jones, R., 1987. Tasmania's Ice-Age hunters. *Australian Geographic*, No. 8, (Oct.–Dec.), pp. 26–45.
[17] Jones, R., 1977. The Tasmanian paradox. In: Wright, R.S.V. (ed.), *Stone Tools as Cultural Markers,* Australian Institute of Aboriginal Studies, Canberra.

Chapter **19**

What happened to the dinosaurs?

What does the Bible have to say about dinosaurs? Where did they come from? When did they live? What did they eat? Where did the fossils come from? What happened to them?

DINOSAURS are used more than almost anything else to indoctrinate children and adults in the idea of millions of years of Earth history. However, the Bible gives us a framework for explaining dinosaurs in terms of thousands of years of history, and solving the mystery of when they lived and what happened to them. Some key texts are Genesis 1:24–25 and Job 40:15–24.

Are dinosaurs a mystery?

Many think that the existence of dinosaurs and their demise is shrouded in such mystery that we may never know the truth about where they came from, when they lived, and what happened to them. However, dinosaurs are only a mystery if you accept the evolutionary story of their history.

According to evolutionists: Dinosaurs first evolved around 235 million years ago[1,2] — long before man evolved. No human being ever lived with dinosaurs. Their history is recorded in the fossil layers on the earth, which were deposited over millions of years. They were so successful as a group of animals, that they eventually 'ruled' the earth. However, around 65 million years ago something happened to change all of this — the dinosaurs disappeared. Most evolutionists believe some

---

[1] Horner, J.R. and Lessem, D., 1993. *The Complete* T. rex, Simon & Schuster, New York, p. 18.

[2] Norell, M.A., Gaffney, E.S. and Dingus, L., 1995. *Discovering Dinosaurs in the American Museum of Natural History,* Nevraumont Publ. Co. Inc., New York, p. 17, say that the oldest dino fossil is 'dated' at 228 million years.

sort of cataclysmic event — such as an asteroid impact — killed them. But, many evolutionists claim that some dinosaurs evolved into birds, and thus they are not extinct, but are flying around us today![3,4]

There is no mystery surrounding dinosaurs if you accept the Bible's totally different account of dinosaur history.

According to the Bible: Dinosaurs first existed around 6,000 years ago.[5-7] God made the dinosaurs, along with the other land animals, on Day Six of the Creation Week (Gen. 1:20–25, 31).[8] Adam and Eve were also made on day six — so dinosaurs lived at the same time as people, not separated by eons of time. Dinosaurs could not have died out before people appeared, because dinosaurs had not previously existed, and death, bloodshed, disease and suffering are a result of Adam's sin (Rom. 5:12,14, 1 Cor. 15:21–22).[8]

Representatives of all the **kinds** of air-breathing land animals, including the dinosaur kinds, went on board Noah's Ark (see Chapter 13, pp. 167ff.). All those left outside the Ark died in the cataclysmic circumstances of the Flood — many of their remains became fossils.

After the Flood (around 4,500 years ago), the remnant of the land animals, including dinosaurs, came off the Ark and lived in the present world, along with people. Because of sin, the judgments of the Curse and the Flood have greatly changed the earth. Post-Flood climatic change, lack of food, disease, and man's activities caused many types of animals to become extinct. The dinosaurs, like many other creatures, died out. Why the big mystery about dinosaurs?

---

[3] Gish, D.T., 1995. *Evolution: the Fossils Still Say No!* Institute for Creation Research, El Cajon, California. p. 129ff, discusses evolutionists' views from a creationist position.

[4] Norell, *et al.,* Ref. 2, p. 2. 'Dinosaurs belong to a group called Archosauria. ... The living Archosauria are the twenty-one extant crocodiles and alligators, along with the more than ten thousand species of living theropod dinosaurs (birds).'

[5] Morris, J.D., 1994. *The Young Earth*, Master Books, Green Forest, Arkansas.

[6] Morris, H.M., 1976. *The Genesis Record,* Baker Book House, Grand Rapids, Michigan, pp. 42–46.

[7] On the biblical chronology, see Ussher, James, 1658. *The Later Part of the Annals of the World,* E. Tyler for F. Crook and G. Bedell, London.

[8] See Chapter 2 on the days of creation.

Why such different views?

Where were you when I laid the foundations of the earth? (Job 38:4)

How can there be such totally different explanations for dinosaurs? Whether one is an evolutionist, or accepts the Bible's account of history, the evidence for dinosaurs is the same. All scientists have the same facts — they have the same world, the same fossils, the same living creatures, the same universe.

If the 'facts' are the same, then how can the explanations be so different? The reason is that scientists have only the present — dinosaur fossils exist only in the present — but scientists are trying to connect the fossils in the present to the past. They ask: 'What happened in history to bring dinosaurs into existence, wipe them out, and leave many of them fossilized?'[9]

The science that addresses such issues is known as *historical* or *origins science*, and it differs from the *operational science* that gives us cheap food, space exploration, electricity and the like. Origins science deals with the past, which is not accessible to direct experimentation, whereas operations science deals with how the world works in the here and now, which of course is open to repeatable experiments (see Chapter 1, p. 15). Because of difficulties in reconstructing the past, those who study fossils (paleontologists) have diverse views of dinosaurs.[9-12] As has been said:

'Paleontology [the study of fossils] is much like politics: passions run high, and its easy to draw very different conclusions from the same set of facts.'[13]

A paleontologist who believes the record in the Bible that claims to be the Word of God,[14] will come to different conclusions from an

---

[9] Benton, M., 1988. *Dinosaurs: An A–Z Guide,* Derrydale Books, New York, pp. 10–11.

[10] Lambert, D., and the Diagram Group, 1990. *The Dinosaur Data Book,* Avon Books, New York, pp. 10–35.

[11] Norell, 1995. Ref. 2, pp. 62–69.

[12] Sharpton, V.L. and Ward, P.D., Editors, 1990. *Global Catastrophes in Earth History,* The Geological Society of America, Special Paper 247.

[13] Lemonick, M.D., 1996. Parenthood, dino-style, *Time* January 8, p.48.

[14] Psalm 78:5, 2 Timothy 3:14–17, 2 Peter 1:19–21. God, who inspired the writing, has always existed, is perfect and never lies (Titus 1:2).

atheist who rejects the Bible. Wilful denial of God's Word (2 Peter 3:3–7) lies at the root of many disputes over 'historical science'.

Many people think the Bible is just a book about religion or salvation. It is much more than this. The Bible is the **History Book of the Universe** and tells us the future destiny of the Universe as well. It gives us an account of when time began (see Chapters 2–5 in this book), and the events of history such as the entrance of sin and death into the world (Chapter 6); the time when the **whole** surface of the globe was destroyed by water (Chapters 10–16); the giving of different languages at the Tower of Babel (Chapter 18); the account of the Son of God coming as man, His death and resurrection; and the new Heaven and Earth to come.

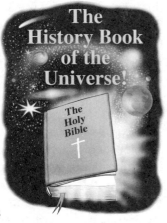

Ultimately there are only two ways of thinking: starting with the revelation from God (the Bible) as foundational to **all** thinking (biology, history, geology, etc.), resulting in a **Christian worldview;** or, starting with man's beliefs (for example, the evolutionary story) as foundational to **all** thinking, resulting in a **secular worldview**.

Most Christians have been indoctrinated through the media and education system to think in a secular way. They tend to take secular thinking **to** the Bible, instead of using the Bible to **build** their thinking (Rom. 12:1–2, Eph. 4:20–24).

The Bible says: *'The fear of the LORD is the beginning of knowledge'* (Prov. 1:7) and *'The fear of the LORD is the beginning of wisdom'* (Prov. 9:10).

If one begins with an evolutionary view of history (for which there were no witnesses or written record), then this way of thinking will be used to explain the evidence that exists in the present — thus the evolutionary explanation for dinosaurs above.

But if one begins with the biblical view of history from the written record of an eyewitness (God) to all events of history, then a totally different way of thinking, based on this, will be used to explain the **same** evidence. Thus the biblical explanation as given above.

Dinosaur history

Fossil bones of what we now call dinosaurs are found around the world. Many finds consist of just fragments of bones, but some nearly complete skeletons have been found. Scientists have been able to describe many different types of dinosaurs, based on distinctive characteristics such as the structure of the skull, limbs etc.[15] However, there appears to be variation in the definition of just what makes an animal a dinosaur.[16]

Where did dinosaurs come from?

The Bible tells us that God created different kinds of land animals on day six of creation week (Gen. 1:24–25). As dinosaurs were land animals, this must have included the dinosaur kinds.[17]

Evolutionists claim that dinosaurs evolved from some reptile that had originally evolved from amphibians. However, they cannot point to any clear transitional (in-between) forms to substantiate their argument. Dinosaur family trees in evolutionary books show many distinct types of dinosaurs, but only hypothetical lines join them up to some common ancestor. The lines are dotted because there is no fossil evidence. Evolutionists simply cannot prove their belief in a non-dinosaur ancestor for dinosaurs.

What did dinosaurs look like?

Scientists generally do not dig up a dinosaur with all its flesh intact. Even if they found **all** the bones, they still would have less than 40 % of the animal to work out what it originally looked like. The bones do not tell the colour of the animal, for example, although some fossils of skin impressions have been found, indicating the skin texture. As there is some diversity of colour among reptiles living today, dinosaurs may have varied greatly in colour, skin texture and so on. When reconstructing dinosaurs from bony remains, scientists make all kinds

---

[15] Lambert, D., 1983. *A Field Guide to Dinosaurs,* Avon Books, New York, p. 17.

[16] *Merriam-Webster's Collegiate Dictionary,* 1995. Merriam-Webster Inc., Springfield, Massachusetts, p. 326. Dinosaur '1: any of a group (Dinosauria) of extinct chiefly terrestrial carnivorous or herbivorous reptiles of the Mesozoic era. 2: any of various large extinct reptiles other than true dinosaurs.'

[17] If some dinosaurs were aquatic, then these would have been created on day five of creation week.

of guesses, and often disagree. For example, debate has raged about whether dinosaurs were warm- or cold-blooded. It is even difficult to tell whether a dinosaur is male or female from its bones. There is much speculation about such things.

Sometimes scientists make mistakes in their re-constructions that need correction when more bones are found. For instance, the famous *'Brontosaurus'* is not in newer dinosaur dictionaries. The original 'discoverer' put the wrong head on a skeleton of a dinosaur that had already been named *Apatosaurus*.[18]

Brontosaurus *was a mistake.*

Who discovered dinosaurs?

Secular books would tell you that the first discovery of what later were called dinosaurs was in 1677 when Dr Robert Plot found bones so big they were thought to belong to a giant elephant or a giant human.[19]

In 1822, Mary Anne Mantell went for a walk along a country road in Sussex. According to tradition, she found a stone that glittered in the sunlight, and showed it to her fossil-collecting husband. Dr Mantell, a physician, noticed that the stone contained a tooth similar to, but much larger than, that of modern reptiles. He concluded that it belonged to some extinct giant plant-eating reptile with teeth like an iguana. In 1825, he named the owner of the tooth *Iguanodon* (iguana tooth). It was Dr Mantell who began to popularise the 'age of reptiles'.[20]

From a biblical perspective, however, the above discoveries were actually when dinosaurs were **re-discovered!** Adam discovered dinosaurs first when he named the kinds of land animals God had created on the sixth day of Creation (Gen. 2:19–20).

---

[18] West, S., 1979. Dinosaur head hunt. *Science News* **116**(18):314–5.
Originally assembled wrongly with the head of a *Camarasaurus*-type dinosaur on an *Apatosaurus* skeleton and later corrected with the right head which was from 'the same family as its nearly identical cousin, *Diplodocus.*' p. 314.
[19] Benton, Ref. 9, p.14.
[20] Lambert, 1990. Ref. 10, p.279.

When did they live?

Evolutionists claim dinosaurs lived millions of years ago. But it is important to realise that, when they dig up a dinosaur bone, it does not have a label attached showing its date! Evolutionists obtain their dates by **indirect** dating methods that other scientists question, and there is much evidence against the millions of years.[21]

Does God tell us when He made *Tyrannosaurus rex*? Many would say no. But the Bible states that God made all things in six normal days.[22] He made the land animals, including dinosaurs, on day six (Gen. 1:24–25), so they date from around 6,000 years ago — the approximate date of Creation obtained by adding up the years in the Bible.[23] So, if *T. rex* was a land animal, and God made all the land animals on day six, then God made *T. rex* on day six!

Furthermore, from the Bible we see that there was no death, bloodshed, disease or suffering before sin.[24] If one takes Genesis to Revelation consistently, interpreting Scripture with Scripture, then death and bloodshed of man and animals came into the world only after Adam sinned. The first death of an animal occurred when God shed an animal's blood in the garden and clothed Adam and Eve (Gen. 3:21). This was also a picture of the atonement — foreshadowing Christ's blood that was to be shed for us. Thus, there could **not** have been bones of dead animals before sin — this would undermine the Gospel.

This means that the dinosaurs must have died after sin entered the world, not before, so dinosaur bones could **not** be millions of years old, because Adam lived only thousands of years ago.

T.rex

Does the Bible mention dinosaurs?

If people saw dinosaurs, you would think ancient historical writings, such as the Bible, should mention them. The King

---

[21] See Chapter 4 and Morris, Ref. 5, pp. 51–67.

[22] See Chapter 2.

[23] Morris, Ref. 6, pp. 4–6, Ussher, Ref. 7.

[24] See Chapters 2,3,4, also Stambaugh, J., 1996. Creation, suffering and the problem of evil. *CEN Technical Journal* **10**(3):391–404.

James Version was first translated in 1611.[25] Some people think that because the word 'dinosaur' is not found in this, or other translations, the Bible does not mention dinosaurs.

However, it was not until 1841 that the word 'dinosaur' was invented.[26,27] Sir Richard Owen, a famous British anatomist and first superintendent of the British museum (and a staunch anti-Darwinist),[28] on viewing the bones of *Iguanodon* and *Megalosaurus,* realised these represented a unique group of reptiles that had not yet been classified. He coined the term 'dinosaur' from Greek words meaning 'terrible lizard'.[29]

Thus, one would not expect to find the word 'dinosaur' in the King James Bible — the word did not exist when the translation was done.

Is there another word for 'dinosaur'? There are *dragon* legends from around the world. Many 'dragon' descriptions fit the characteristics of specific dinosaurs. Could these actually be accounts of encounters with what we now call dinosaurs?

The Hebrew word commonly translated 'dragon' in the KJV (Hebrew: *tan, tannin, tannim, tannoth*) appears in the Old Testament some 30 times. There are passages in the Bible about 'dragons' that lived on the land: *'he [Nebuchadnezzar] has swallowed me like a dragon'* (Jer. 51:34), *'the dragons of the wilderness'* (Mal. 1:3). Many biblical creationists believe that in many contexts these could refer to what we now call dinosaurs.[30] Indeed, *Strong's Concordance* lists 'dinosaur' as one of the meanings of *tannin/m.*

---

[25] The KJV most often used today is actually the 1769 revision by Benjamin Blayney of Oxford.

[26] Dixon, D., Cox, B., Savage, G.J.G. and Gardiner, B., 1988. *The Macmillan Illustrated Encyclopedia of Dinosaurs and Prehistoric Animals,* Macmillan Publishing Co., New York, p. 92.

[27] Grigg, R.M., 1990. Dinosaurs and dragons: stamping on the legends! *Creation* **14**(3):11.

[28] Norman, D., 1985. *The Illustrated Encyclopedia of Dinosaurs,* Salamander Books Limited, London, p. 8.

[29] The meaning of 'terrible lizard' has helped popularize the idea that dinosaurs were all gigantic savage monsters. This is far from the truth. Had Owen known about the **smaller** dinosaurs, he may never have coined the word.

[30] The Hebrew words have a range of meanings, including sea monster (Gen. 1:21, Job 7:12, Psalm 148:7, Isa 27:1, Eze. 29:3, 32:2) and serpent (Ex. 7:9 cf. Ex. 4:3 and Hebrew parallelism of Deut. 32:33). *Tannin/m* are fearsome

In Genesis 1:21, the Bible says: *'And God created the great sea monsters and every living creature that moves, with which the waters swarmed, after their kind...'* The Hebrew word here for 'sea monsters' ('whales' in KJV) is the word translated elsewhere as 'dragon' (Hebrew *tannin*). So, in the first chapter of the first book of the Bible God may be describing the great sea dragons (sea-dwelling dinosaur-type animals) He created.

There are other Bible passages about dragons that lived in the sea: *'the dragons in the waters'* (Psalm 74:13), *'and he shall slay the dragon that is in the sea'* (Isa. 27:1). Though the word 'dinosaur' strictly only refers to animals that lived on the land, the sea reptiles and flying reptiles are often grouped with the dinosaurs. The sea-dragons could have included dinosaur-type animals such as the *Mosasaurus*.[31]

Job 41 describes a great animal that lived in the sea, *Leviathan,* that even breathed fire. This 'dragon' may have been something like the mighty 17 metre long *Kronosaurus*[32], or the 25 m long *Liopleurodon*.

There is also a mention of a flying serpent in the Bible: the *'fiery flying serpent'* (Isa. 30:6). This could be a reference to one of the pterodactyls, which are popularly thought of as flying dinosaurs, such

---

creatures, inhabiting remote, desolate places (Isa 34:13, 35:7, Jer. 49:33, 51:37, Mal. 1:8), difficult to kill (Isa. 27:1, Isa. 51:9), and/or serpentine (Deut. 32:33 cf. Psalm 91:13), and/or having feet (Eze. 32:2). However, *tannin* are referred to as suckling their young (Lam. 4:3), which is not a feature of reptiles, but of whales, for example (sea monsters?). The word(s) seem to refer to large, fearsome creatures that dwelt in swampy areas or in the water. The term could include reptiles and mammals. Modern translators often render the words as 'jackals', but this seems inappropriate because jackals are not particularly fearsome, or difficult to kill, and don't live in swamps.

[31] Some have suggested that a carcass of a marine creature found off the coast of New Zealand was a plesiosaur. However, a thorough analysis of all the data suggests it was a basking shark. See Jerlström, P. and Elliott, B., 1999. Let rotting sharks lie: further evidence for shark identity of the Zuiyo-maru carcass. *CEN Technical Journal* 13(2):83–87. Nevertheless, paintings of 'Yarru', clearly a plesiosaur-like creature, by tribespeople in northern Australia suggest that plesiosaurs have been living quite recently: see Driver, R., 1999. Australia's aborigines — did they see dinosaurs? *Creation* 21(1):24–27.

[32] Czerkas, S.J. and Czerkas, S.A., 1996. *Dinosaurs: A Global View,* Barnes and Noble Books, Spain, p. 179.

as the *Pteranodon, Rhamphorhynchus or Ornithocheirus.*[33,34]

Not long after the Flood, God was showing a man called Job how great He was as Creator, by reminding Job of the largest land animal He had made:

> *Behold now behemoth, which I made with you; he eats grass like an ox. See now, his strength* is *in his loins, and his force* is *in the muscles of his belly. He moves his tail like a cedar: the sinews of his thighs are knit together. His bones* are *like tubes of bronze; his limbs* are *like bars of iron. He* is *the chief of the ways of God: his maker brings near his sword.* (Job 40:15–19).

The phrase *'chief of the ways of God'* suggests this was the largest land animal God had made. So what kind of animal was 'behemoth'?

Bible translators, not being sure what this beast was, often transliterated the Hebrew, and thus the word *'behemoth'* (e.g., KJV, NKJV, NASB, NIV). However, in many Bible commentaries, and Bible footnotes, 'behemoth' is said to be 'possibly the hippopotamus or elephant'.[35] Some Bible versions actually translate 'behemoth' this way.[36] Besides the fact that the elephant and hippo were **not** the largest land animals God made (some of the dinosaurs far eclipsed these), this description does not make sense, since the tail of behemoth is compared to a cedar tree (verse 17).

Illustration by Steve Cardno

Was 'behemoth', seen by Job, one of the big dinosaurs?

Now an elephant's tiny tail (or a

[33] Norman, Ref. 28, pp. 170–172.

[34] Wellnhofer, P., 1991. *Pterosaurs: The Illustrated Encyclopedia of Prehistoric Flying Reptiles,* Barnes and Noble, N.Y., pp. 83–85, 135–136.

[35] E.g. *NIV Study Bible,* 1985. Zondervan, Grand Rapids, Michigan.

[36] *New Living Translation: Holy Bible,* 1996. Tyndale House Publishers, Wheaton, Illinois. Job 40:15: 'Take a look at the mighty hippopotamus'.

hippo's tail that looks like a flap of skin!) is quite unlike a cedar tree! Clearly the elephant and the hippo could not possibly be 'behemoth'. No **living** creature comes close to this description. However, behemoth is very like *Brachiosaurus*, one of the large dinosaurs.

Some English Bible versions have a footnote that Behemoth, which had a tail like a cedar, was possibly an elephant or a hippopotamus.

Are there other ancient records of dinosaurs?

One of the oldest books of British history, *The Anglo-Saxon Chronicles,* records encounters people had with dragons — and many of the descriptions fit well-known dinosaurs.[37] The emblem on the flag of Wales (United Kingdom) is a dragon.

> **Many historical descriptions of 'dragons' fit specific types of dinosaurs.**

In the film, *The Great Dinosaur Mystery,*[38] a number of dragon accounts are presented:

● A Sumerian story dating back to 2,000 BC or more tells of a hero named Gilgamesh, who, when he went to fell cedars in a remote forest, encountered a huge vicious dragon which he slew, cutting off its head as a trophy.

● When Alexander the Great (c. 330 BC) and his soldiers marched into India, they found that the Indians worshipped huge hissing reptiles that they kept in caves.

● China is renowned for its dragon stories, and dragons are prominent

---

[37] Cooper, Bill, 1995. *After the Flood,* New Wine Press, West Sussex, England, pp. 130–161.

[38] Taylor, P.S., 1991. *The Great Dinosaur Mystery,* Films for Christ, Mesa, Arizona. See also the book: Taylor, P., 1989. *The Great Dinosaur Mystery and the Bible,* Accent Publications Inc., Denver, Colorado.

**Dragons:
Dinosaurs in History**

on Chinese pottery, embroidery and carvings.

● England has its story of St George, who slew a dragon that lived in a cave.

● There is the story of a 10th century Irishman who wrote of his encounter with what appears to have been a *Stegosaurus*.

● In the 1500s, a European scientific book, *Historia Animalium,* listed several animals that we would call dinosaurs, as still alive. A well-known naturalist of the time, *Ulysses Aldrovandus,* recorded an encounter between a peasant named *Baptista* and a dragon whose description fits that of the small dinosaur *Tanystropheus.* The encounter was on May 13, 1572, near Bologna in Italy, and the peasant killed the dragon.

Petroglyphs (drawings carved on rock) of dinosaur-like creatures have also been found.[39]

Summary: People down through the ages have been very familiar with dragons. The descriptions of these animals fit with what we know about dinosaurs. The Bible mentions such creatures, even ones that lived in the sea and flew in the air. There is a tremendous amount

Ancient Indian rock drawings, like this one of a sauropod dinosaur from White River Canyon, Utah, show that dinosaurs co-existed with man.

of other historical evidence that such creatures have lived beside people.

What do the bones say?

There is also physical evidence that dinosaur bones are not millions of years old. Scientists from the University of Montana found *T. rex* bones that were not totally fossilized. Sections of the bones were like fresh bone and contained what seems to be blood cells and hemoglobin.

---

[39] Swift, D., 1997. Messages on stone. *Creation* **19**(2):20–23.

If these bones really were millions of years old, then the blood cells and hemoglobin would have totally disintegrated.[40] Also, there should not be 'fresh' bone if it were really millions of years old.[41,42] A report by these scientists stated the following:

'A thin slice of *T. rex* bone glowed amber beneath the lens of my microscope . . . the lab filled with murmurs of amazement, for I had focused on something inside the vessels that none of us had ever noticed before: tiny round objects, translucent red with a dark center ... Red blood cells? The shape and location suggested them, but blood cells are mostly water and couldn't possibly have stayed preserved in the 65-million-year old tyrannosaur... The bone sample that had us so excited came from a beautiful, nearly complete specimen of *Tyrannosaurus rex* unearthed in 1990 ... When the team brought the dinosaur into the lab, we noticed that some parts deep inside the long bone of the leg had not completely fossilized ... So far, we think that all of this evidence supports the notion that our slices of *T. rex* could contain preserved heme and hemoglobin fragments. But more work needs to be done before we are confident enough to come right out and say, "Yes, this *T. rex* has blood compounds left in its tissues".'[43]

Unfossilized duck-billed dinosaur bones have been found on the North Slope in Alaska.[44] Also, creationist scientists collected such (unfossilized) frozen dinosaur bones in Alaska.[41] Evolutionists would not say that these bones had stayed frozen for the many millions of years since these dinosaurs supposedly died out (according to evolutionary theory). Yet the bones could not have survived for the millions of years unmineralized. This is a puzzle to those who believe in an 'age of dinosaurs' millions of years ago, but not to someone who builds their thinking on the Bible.

---

[40] Wieland, C., 1997. Sensational dinosaur blood report. *Creation* 19(4):42–43.
[41] Batten, D., 1997. Buddy Davis — the Creation Music Man (who makes dinosaurs). *Creation* 19(3):49–51.
[42] Helder, M., 1992. Fresh dinosaur bones found. *Creation* 14(3):16–17.
[43] Schweitzer, M. and Staedter, T., 1997. The real Jurassic Park. *Earth,* June, 1997, pp. 55–57. See report in *Creation* 19(4):42–43, which describes the careful testing that showed that hemoglobin was present.
[44] Davies, K., 1987. Duckbill dinosaurs (Hadrosauridae, Ornithischia) from the north slope of Alaska. *Journal of Paleontology* 61(1):198–200.

What did dinosaurs eat, and how did they behave?

Movies like *Jurassic Park* and *The Lost World* portray most dinosaurs as aggressive meat eaters. But the mere presence of sharp teeth does **not** tell you how an animal behaved, or necessarily what food it ate — only what kind of teeth it had (for ripping food, etc.). However, by studying fossil dinosaur dung (coprolite),[45] scientists have been able to determine the diet of some dinosaurs.

Originally, before sin, **all** animals, including the dinosaurs, were vegetarian. Genesis 1:30 states: *'And to every beast of the earth, and to every bird of the air, and to every thing that creeps upon the earth, which* has *life,* I have given *every green herb for food: and it was so.'*

This means that even *T. rex,* before sin entered the world, ate only plants. Some people object to this by pointing to the big teeth that a large *T. rex* had, insisting they must have been used for attacking animals. However, just because an animal has big sharp teeth does not mean it eats meat. It just means it has big sharp teeth.[46]

Many animals today have sharp teeth but are basically vegetarian. The giant panda has sharp teeth like a meat eater, but it eats bamboo. Perhaps the panda's teeth were beautifully designed to eat bamboo. To 'explain' why a giant panda has teeth like many meat eaters today, yet it eats bamboo, evolutionists have to say that the giant panda evolved as a meat eater, and then switched to bamboo.[47]

Different species of bats variously eat fruit, nectar, insects, small animals and blood, but their teeth do not clearly indicate what they eat.[48] Bears have teeth similar to those of a big cat (e.g., a lion), but some bears are vegetarian, and many, if not most, are mainly vegetarian.

Before sin, God described the world as *'very good'* (Gen. 1:31). Some cannot accept this concept of perfect harmony, because of the food chain that they observe in today's world. However, one cannot look at the sin-cursed world, and the resultant death and struggle, and

---

[45] Lucas, S.G., 1994. *Dinosaurs: The Textbook,* Wm C. Brown Publishers, Dubuque, Iowa, pp. 194–196.

[46] Marrs, D. and Kylberg, V., 1991. *Dino Cardz. Estemmenosuchus* was a large mammal-like reptile. 'Despite having menacing-looking fangs it apparently was a plant-eater.' They possibly concluded this from its rear teeth.

[47] Brandes, K., 1974. *Vanishing Species,* Time-Life Books, N.Y., p. 98.

[48] Weston, P., 1999. Bats: sophistication in miniature. *Creation* **21**(1):28–31.

use this to reject the Genesis account of history. Everything has changed because of sin. That's why Paul describes the present Creation as *'groaning'* (Rom. 8:22). One must look at the world through Bible 'eyes' to understand it. [49]

Brown bears have teeth similar to a big cat's but are mainly vegetarian.

In the beginning, God gave Adam and Eve dominion over the animals: *'And God blessed them, and God said to them, be fruitful, and multiply, and fill the earth, and subdue it, and have dominion over the fish of the sea, and over the birds of the air, and over every living thing that moves on the earth'* (Gen. 1:28). Looking at today's world we are reminded of Hebrews 2:8: *'You have put all things in subjection under his feet. For in order that he put all things under him, he left nothing that is not put under him. But now we do not see all things put under him.'* Man's relationship with all things changed because of sin — they are not 'under him' as they were originally.

Most people, including most Christians, tend to observe the world as it is today, with all its death and suffering, and then take that observation to the Bible and interpret it in that light. But we are sinful, fallible human beings, observing a sin-cursed world (Rom. 8:22) and thus we need to start with divine revelation,[14] the Bible, to begin to understand.

So how did fangs and claws come about? Dr Henry Morris states:
'Whether such structures as fangs and claws were part of their original equipment, or were recessive features which only became dominant

---

[49] Some argue that people or animals would have been hurt even in an 'ideal' world. They contend that even before sin, Adam, or an animal, could have stood on small creatures, or scratched himself on a branch. Now these sorts of situations are true of today's **fallen** world — the present world is **not** perfect; it is suffering from the effects of the Curse (Rom. 8:22). One cannot look at the Bible through the world's 'eyes' and insist that the world before sin was just like the world we see today. We do not know what a perfect world, continually restored and totally upheld by God's power (Col. 1:17,

due to selection processes later, or were mutational features following the Curse, or exactly what, must await further research.'[50]

After sin entered the world, everything changed. Maybe some animals started eating each other at this stage. By the time of Noah, God described what had happened this way: *'And God looked upon the earth, and, behold, it was corrupt; for all flesh had corrupted its way upon the earth'* (Gen. 6:12).

Also, after the Flood, God changed the behaviour of animals. We read (Gen. 9:2), *'And the fear of you and the dread of you shall be upon every beast of the earth, and upon every bird of the air, upon all that moves on the earth, and upon all the fishes of the sea. Into your hand they are delivered.'* Thus man would find it much more difficult to carry out the dominion mandate given in Genesis 1:28.

Why do we find dinosaur fossils?

Fossil formation requires a sudden burial. When an animal dies, it usually gets eaten or decays until there is nothing left. To form a fossil, unique conditions are required to preserve the animal and replace it with minerals, etc.

Heb. 1:3), would have been like — we have never experienced perfection (only Adam and Eve did before sin). But, we do get little glimpses from Scripture: in Deut. 8:4, 29:5 and Neh. 9:21, we are told that when the Israelites wandered in the desert for 40 years, their clothes and shoes did not wear out, nor did their feet swell. When God upholds things perfectly, wearing out or being hurt in any way is not even an option. Think of Shadrach, Meshach, and Abednego (Dan. 3:26–27) — they came out of the fire without even the smell of smoke on them. Again, when the Lord upholds perfectly, being hurt is **not** possible. In a perfect world, before sin and the curse, God would have upheld **everything,** but in this cursed world things run down. Many commentators believe the description in Isa. 11:6–9 of the wolf and lamb, and lion that eats straw like an ox, is a picture of the new Earth in the future restoration (Acts 3:21), when there will be no more curse or death (Rev. 21:1, 22:3). The animals described are living peacefully as vegetarians (this is also the description of the animal world before sin — Gen. 1:30). Today's world has been changed dramatically because of sin and the Curse. The present food chain and animal behaviour (which also changed after the Flood — Gen. 9:2–3) **cannot** be used as a basis for interpreting the Bible — the Bible explains **why** the world is the way it is!

[50] Morris, Ref. 6, p. 78. See also Chapter 6, *How did bad things come about?*

Evolutionists once claimed that the fossil record was formed slowly as animals died and were gradually covered by sediment. But they have acknowledged more recently that the fossil record must involve catastrophic processes.[51] To form the billions of fossils world-wide, in layers sometimes kilometres thick, the organisms, by and large, must have been buried quickly. Many evolutionists now say the fossil record formed quickly, in spurts interspersed by millions of years!

According to the Bible, as time went on, the earth became full of wickedness, so God determined He would send a world-wide Flood *'to destroy all flesh, in which is the breath of life, from under the heavens'* (Gen. 6:17).

God commanded Noah to build a very large boat into which he would take his family and representatives of every kind

Dinosaur graveyards testify to catastrophic burial conditions, consistent with the Flood.

of land-dwelling, air breathing animals (that God Himself would choose and send to Noah — Gen. 6:20). This must have included two of each kind of dinosaur.

How did dinosaurs fit on the Ark?

Many people think of dinosaurs as large creatures that would never have fitted into the Ark. But the average size of a dinosaur (based on the skeletons found over the earth) is about the size of a sheep.[52,53] Indeed, many dinosaurs were relatively small. For instance, *Struthiomimus* was the size of an ostrich, and *Compsognathus* was no

---

[51] For example, Ager, D., 1993. *The New Catastrophism*, Cambridge U.P.
[52] Crichton, M., 1995. *The Lost World,* Ballantine Books, New York, p. 122. 'Dinosaurs were mostly small ... People always think they were huge, but the average dinosaur was the size of a sheep, or a small pony.'
[53] Horner, 1993. Ref. 1, p. 124. 'most dinosaurs were smaller than bulls.'

bigger than a rooster. *Mussaurus* ('mouse reptile') was not much bigger than a mouse. Only a few dinosaurs grew to extremely large sizes (e.g., *Brachiosaurus, Apatosaurus),* but even they were not as large as the largest animal in the world today, the blue whale. (Reptiles have the potential to grow as long as they live. Thus, the large dinosaurs were probably very old ones.)

Dinosaurs laid eggs, and the biggest fossil dinosaur egg found is about the size of a football.[54] Even the largest dinosaurs were very small when first hatched. Remember that the animals that came off the boat were to re-populate the earth. Thus it would have been almost essential to choose young adults, which would soon be in the prime of their reproductive life, to go on the Ark. So it is realistic to assume that God would have sent young adults to the Ark, not fully grown creatures.

Some might argue that the 600 or more named species of dinosaurs could not have fitted on the Ark. But Genesis 6:20 states that representative *kinds* of land animals boarded the Ark. The question then is, what is a 'kind' (Hebrew *min*)? Biblical creationists have pointed out that there can be many 'species' descended from a 'kind'.[55] For example, there are many types of cats in the world, but all cat 'species' probably came from only a few 'kinds' of cats originally.[56] The cat varieties today have developed by natural and artificial selection acting on the original variation in the information (genes)[57] of the original cats. This has produced different combinations and subsets of information, and thus different types of cats. Even 'speciation' could occur through these processes.[58] Thus only a few feline pairs would have been needed on Noah's Ark.

---

[54] Lambert, D., 1983. *A Field Guide to Dinosaurs,* Avon Books, New York, p. 127.

[55] See Chapter 13, *How did all the animals fit on the Ark?* pp. 167ff.

[56] Mehlert, W., 1995. On the origin of cats and carnivores. *CEN Technical Journal* **9**(1):106–120.

[57] Mutations (errors in copying of the genes during reproduction) can also contribute to the variation, but the changes caused by mutations are 'down-hill', causing loss of the original information.

[58] This speciation is **not** 'evolution', since it is based on the created information *already present*, and is thus a limited, 'downhill' process, not involving an upward increase in complexity. See Chapter 1, pp. 15–16.

Dinosaur names have tended to proliferate, with new names being given to just a few pieces of bone, or a skeleton that looks similar to one that is a different size, or in a different country. There were probably fewer than 50 distinct groups or kinds of dinosaurs that had to be on the Ark.[55]

Also, it must be remembered that Noah's Ark was extremely large and quite capable of carrying the number of animals needed, including dinosaurs.

The land animals (including dinosaurs) that were not on the Ark drowned. Many were preserved in the layers formed by the Flood — thus the millions of fossils. Presumably many of the dinosaur fossils were buried at this time, around 4,500 years ago. Also, after the Flood, there would have been considerable catastrophism, including such events as the Ice Age (see Chapter 16), resulting in some post-Flood formation of fossils also.

The contorted shapes of these animals preserved in the rocks, the massive numbers of them in fossil graveyards, their wide distribution, and some whole skeletons, all provide convincing evidence that they were buried rapidly, testifying to massive flooding.[59-61]

Why don't we see dinosaurs today?

At the end of the Flood, Noah, his family and the animals came out of the Ark (Gen. 8:15–17). The dinosaurs thus began a new life in a new world. Along with the other animals, the dinosaurs came out to breed and re-populate the earth. They would have left the landing place of the Ark and spread over the earth's surface. The descendants of these dinosaurs gave rise to the dragon legends.

But the world they came out to re-populate differed from the one they knew before Noah's Flood. The Flood had devastated it. It was now a much more difficult world in which to survive.

After the Flood God told Noah that from then on the animals would fear him, and man could eat their flesh (Gen. 9:1–7). Even for man,

---

[59] For example, reptiles drowned in a flash flood 200 million years ago, according to the interpretation put upon the reptile fossils discovered in Lubnock Quarry, Texas. *The Weekend Australian*, Nov. 26–27, 1983, p. 32.

[60] Norell, *et.al.,* Ref. 2, Figure 56, pp. 86–87.

[61] Czerkas and Czerkas, Ref. 32, p. 151.

the world had become a harsher place. To survive, the once easily obtained plant nutrition would now have to be supplemented by animal sources.

Both animals and man would find their ability to survive tested to the utmost. We can see from the fossil record, from the written history of man, and from experience over recent centuries, that many forms of life on this planet have not survived that test.

We need to remember that many plants and air-breathing, land-dwelling animals have become extinct **since** the Flood — either due to man's action or competition with other species, or because of the harsher post-Flood environment. Many groups are still becoming extinct. Dinosaurs seem to be numbered among the extinct groups.

Why then are people so intrigued about dinosaurs, and have little interest in the extinction of the fern *Cladophebius,* for example? It's the dinosaurs' appeal as monsters that excites and fascinates people.

Evolutionists have capitalised on this fascination, and the world is awash with evolutionary propaganda centred on dinosaurs. This has resulted in the thinking of even Christians being permeated by evolutionary philosophy. As a result, they tend to single out the dinosaurs as something mysterious.

If you were to ask at the zoo why they have endangered species programs, you would probably get an answer something like this: 'It's obvious. We've lost lots of animals from this Earth. Animals are becoming extinct all the time. Look at all the animals that have gone forever. We need to act to save the animals.' If you then asked, 'Why are animals becoming extinct?' You might get an answer like this: 'It's obvious! People killing them; lack of food; man destroying the environment; diseases; genetic problems; catastrophes like floods — there are lots of reasons.'

If you then asked, 'Well, what happened to the dinosaurs?' The answer would probably be, 'We don't know! Scientists have suggested dozens of possible reasons, but it's a mystery.'

Maybe one of the reasons dinosaurs are extinct, is that we did not start our endangered species programs early enough! The factors that cause extinction today, which came about because of man's sin — the Curse, the aftermath of the Flood (a judgment) etc. — are the same factors that caused the dinosaurs to become extinct.

Are dinosaurs really extinct?

One cannot prove an organism is extinct without having knowledge of every part of the earth's surface simultaneously. Experts have been embarrassed when, after having declared animals extinct, they were discovered alive and well. For example, explorers recently found elephants in Nepal that have many features of mammoths.[62]

Scientists in Australia found some living trees that they thought had become extinct with the dinosaurs. One scientist said, '... it was like finding a "live dinosaur".'[63,64] When scientists find animals or plants they thought were extinct long ago, they call them 'living fossils'. There are hundreds of 'living fossils', a big embarrassment for those who believe in millions of years of Earth history.[65]

Explorers and natives in Africa have reported sighting dinosaur-like creatures, even recently.[66–68] These have usually been confined to out-of-the-way places such as lakes deep in the Congo jungles. Descriptions certainly fit those of dinosaurs.[69]

Cave paintings by native Americans seem to depict a dinosaur[70] — scientists accept the mammoth drawings in the cave, so why not the dinosaur drawings? Evolutionary indoctrination that man did not live at the same time as dinosaurs stops most scientists from even considering that the drawings are of dinosaurs.

It certainly would be no embarrassment to a creationist if someone

---

[62] Wieland, C., 1996. 'Lost World' animals found! *Creation* **19**(1):10–13.

[63] Anon., 1995. Sensational Australian tree ... like 'finding a live dinosaur'. *Creation* **17**(2):13.

[64] See also, Anon., 1980. *Melbourne Sun*, Feb. 6. More than 40 people claimed to have seen plesiosaurs off the Victorian coast (Australia) over recent years.

[65] Scheven, J., *Living Fossils: Confirmation of Creation,* Creation Videos, Answers in Genesis, Queensland, Australia.

[66] Anon, 1981. Dinosaur hunt. *Science Digest* **89**(5):21.

[67] Regusters, H.A., 1982. Mokele-Mbembe: an investigation into rumours concerning a strange animal in the republic of Congo, 1981. *Munger Africana Library Notes,* Issue 64, pp. 2–32.

[68] Agmagna, M., 1983. Results of the first Congolese Mokele-Mbembe expedition. *Cryptozoology,* **2**:103 — as cited in *Science Frontiers* No. 33, 1983.

[69] Catchpoole, D., 1999. Mokele-Mbembe: a living dinosaur? *Creation* **21**(4):24–25.

[70] Swift, D., 1997. Messages on stone. *Creation* **19**(2):20–23.

discovered a dinosaur living in a jungle. However, this should embarrass evolutionists.

And no, we could not clone a dinosaur, as in the movie *Jurassic Park*, even if we had dinosaur DNA. We would also need a living female dinosaur. Scientists have found that to clone an animal they need an egg of a living female, as there is 'machinery' in the cytoplasm of the egg that is necessary for the new individual to develop.[71]

Birdosaurs?

Many evolutionists do not really think dinosaurs are extinct anyway!

In 1997, at the entrance to the bird exhibit at the Cincinnati zoo in Ohio, USA, we read the following on a sign:

'Dinosaurs went extinct millions of years ago — or did they? No, birds are essentially modern short-tailed feathered dinosaurs.'

In the mid-1960s, Dr John Ostrom from Yale University in the USA, began to popularize the idea that dinosaurs evolved into birds.[72] However, not all evolutionists agree with this. 'It's just a fantasy of theirs,' says Alan Feduccia, an ornithologist at the University of North Carolina at Chapel Hill, and a leading critic of the dino-to-bird theory. 'They so much want to see living dinosaurs that now they think they can study them vicariously at the backyard bird feeder.'[73]

There have been many attempts to indoctrinate the public to believe that modern birds are really dinosaurs. *TIME* magazine on April 26, 1993, had a front page cover of a 'birdosaur', now called *Mononykus*, with feathers, (a supposed transitional form between dinosaurs and birds) based on a fossil find that had **no** feathers. In the same month, *Science News* had an article suggesting this animal was a digging creature more like a mole.[74,75]

In 1996, newspapers reported a find in China of a reptile fossil that supposedly had feathers.[76] Some of the media reports claimed that, if

---

[71] Wieland, C., 1997. Hello Dolly! *Creation* **19**(3):23.

[72] Norell, 1995. Ref. 2, p. 13.

[73] Morell, V., 1997. Origin of birds: the dinosaur debate. *Audubon*, March/April, p. 38.

[74] Anon., 1993. New 'birdosaur' NOT missing link! *Creation* **15**(3):3.

[75] Anon., 1993. 'Birdosaur' more like a mole. *Creation* **15**(4):7.

[76] Browne, M.W., 1996. Downy dinosaur reported. *Cincinnati Enquirer*, Oct. 19, p. A13.

it were confirmed, it would be 'irrefutable evidence that today's birds evolved from dinosaurs'.[77] One scientist stated 'You can't come to any conclusion other than that they're feathers.'[77] However, in 1997, the Academy of Natural Sciences in Philadelphia sent four leading scientists to investigate this find.[78] They concluded they were **not** feathers. The media report stated, concerning one of the scientists, 'He said he saw "hair-like" structures — not hairs — that could have supported a frill, or crest, like those on iguanas.'[78]

No sooner had this report appeared, than another media report claimed that 20 fragments of bones of a reptile found in South America showed dinosaurs were related to birds![79]

Birds are warm-blooded and reptiles are cold-blooded, but evolutionists who believe dinosaurs evolved into birds would like to see dinosaurs as warm-blooded to support their theory. But Dr Larry Martin, of the University of Kansas opposes this idea:

'[R]ecent research has shown the microscopic structure of dinosaur bones was "characteristic of cold-blooded animals", Martin said. "So we're back to cold-blooded dinosaurs".'[78]

Sadly, the secular media have become so blatant in their anti-Christian stand and pro-evolutionary propaganda, that they are bold enough to make such ridiculous statements as 'Parrots and hummingbirds are also dinosaurs.'[79]

Several new reports have fuelled the bird/dinosaur debate among evolutionists. One concerns research on the embryonic origins of the fingers of birds and dinosaurs, showing that birds could **not** have evolved from dinosaurs![80] A study of the so-called feathered dinosaur from China revealed that the dinosaur had a distinctively reptilian lung and diaphragm, which is distinctly different from the avian lung.[81]

---

[77] Anon., 1997. Remains of feathered dinosaur bolster theory on origin of birds. Associated Press, New York.

[78] Stieg, Bill, 1997. 'Did birds evolve from dinosaurs?' *The Philadelphia Inquirer*. March.

[79] Recer, Paul, 1997. Birds linked to dinosaurs. *Cincinnati Enquirer*, May 21, p. A9.

[80] Burke, A.C. and Feduccia, A., 1997. Developmental patterns and the identification of homologies in the avian hand. *Science* **278**:666–668.

[81] Ruben, J.A., Jones, T.D., *et al.*, 1997. Lung structure and ventilation in theropod dinosaurs and early birds. *Science* **278**:1267–1270.

Another report said that the frayed edges that some thought to be 'feathers' on the Chinese fossil are similar to the collagen fibres found immediately beneath the skin of sea snakes.[82]

There is **no** credible evidence dinosaurs evolved into birds.[83,84] Dinosaurs have always been dinosaurs and birds have always been birds!

What if a 'dinosaur' fossil *was* found with feathers on it? Would that prove that birds evolved from dinosaurs? No — a duck has a duck bill and webbed feet, as does a platypus, but no one believes that this proves that platypuses evolved from ducks. Reptilian scales on the way to becoming feathers, that is, transitional, would be impressive evidence for the belief that reptiles (or dinosaurs) evolved into birds, but not fully-formed feathers. A dinosaur-like fossil with feathers would just be another curious mosaic, like the platypus, and part of the pattern of similarities placed in creatures to show the hand of the one true Creator God Who made everything.

Why does it matter?

Although dinosaurs are fascinating, some readers may say, 'Why are dinosaurs such a big deal? Surely there are many more important issues to deal with in today's world such as: abortion, family breakdown, racism, promiscuity, dishonesty, homosexual behaviour, euthanasia, suicide, lawlessness, pornography, and so on. In fact, we should be telling people about the Gospel of Jesus Christ, not worrying about side issues like dinosaurs!'

Actually the evolutionist teachings on dinosaurs that pervade society *do* have a great bearing on why many will not listen to the Gospel, and thus why the social problems mentioned above abound today.

The implications

If we accept the evolutionists' teachings on dinosaurs, then we must accept that the Bible's account of history is false. If the Bible is wrong in this area, then it is not the Word of God and we can ignore everything else it says that we find inconvenient.

---

[82] Gibbons, A., 1997. Plucking the feathered dinosaur. *Science* **278**:1229.
[83] Sarfati, J., 1998. Dino-bird evolution falls flat. *Creation* **20**(2):41.
[84] Oard, M.J., 1998. Bird-dinosaur link challenged. *CEN Tech. J.* 12(1):5–7.

If everything made itself through natural processes — without God — then God does not own us and has no right to tell us how to live. In fact, God does not really exist in this way of thinking, so there is no absolute basis for morality. Without God, anything goes — concepts of right and wrong are just a matter of opinion. And without a basis for morality, there is no such thing as sin. And no sin means that there is no judgment to fear from God and there is no need for the Saviour, Jesus Christ.

Millions of years and the Gospel

The teaching that dinosaurs lived and died millions of years before man directly attacks the foundations of the Gospel in another way. The fossil record, of which dinosaurs form a part, documents death, disease, suffering, cruelty, and brutality. It is a very ugly record. Allowing for the millions of years for the fossil layers means accepting death, bloodshed, disease and suffering before Adam's sin.

However, the Bible makes it clear that death, bloodshed, disease and suffering are a **consequence of sin.** God warned Adam in Genesis 2:17, that if he ate of the *'tree of the knowledge of good and evil'*, he would *'surely die'*. The Hebrew translated 'you shall surely die' actually means, 'dying, you will die'. In other words, immediate spiritual death would be followed by a process of physical decay, ending eventually in bodily death.

> **As soon as one allows millions of years for dinosaur fossils, one has accepted death, disease and suffering before Adam sinned and brought death and suffering into God's creation.**

After Adam disobeyed God, the LORD clothed Adam and Eve with *'coats of skins'* (Gen. 3:21). To do this He must have killed and shed the blood of at least one animal. The reason for this can be summed up by Hebrews 9:22:

And by the law almost all things are cleansed with blood; and without shedding of blood there is no remission.

God required the shedding of blood for the forgiveness of sins. What happened in the Garden of Eden was a picture of what was to come in Jesus Christ, who shed His blood on the cross as *'the Lamb of*

God, who takes away the sin of the world' (John 1:29).

Now if the shedding of blood occurred before sin, as would have happened if the garden were sitting on a fossil record of dead things millions of years old, then the foundation of the atonement would be destroyed.

This 'big picture' also fits with Romans 8, which says that the whole creation 'groans' because of the effects of the fall of Adam — it was not 'groaning' with death and suffering before Adam sinned.

Jesus Christ suffered physical death and shed His blood because death was the penalty for sin. Paul discusses this in detail in Romans 5 and 1 Corinthians 15.

Revelation chapters 21 and 22 make it clear that there will be a *'new heaven and a new earth'* one day where there will be *'no more death'* and *'no more curse'* — just like it was before sin changed everything. Obviously, if there are going to be animals in the new Earth, they will not die or eat each other, or the redeemed people!

Thus, the teaching of millions of years of death, disease and suffering before Adam sinned is a direct attack on the foundation of the message of the cross.

Conclusion

If we accept God's Word, beginning with Genesis as being true and authoritative, then we can explain dinosaurs and make sense of the evidence we observe in the world around us. In doing this, we are helping people see that Genesis is absolutely trustworthy and logically defensible, and is what it claims to be — the true account of the history of the universe and mankind. And what one believes concerning the book of Genesis will ultimately determine what one believes about the rest of the Bible. This in turn will affect how a person views him or herself, and fellow human beings, and what life is all about, including their need for salvation.

Chapter 20

What can I do?

MAYBE, having read *The Answers Book,* you have realized for the first time that the Bible is indeed the written revelation of Almighty God to man — it is our Creator's message to us, His creatures.

As His creatures, He owns us and we are accountable to Him for how we live our lives (Romans 14:12, Hebrews 9:27). The Bible tells us that we all, like Adam, have departed from God's ways; we have gone our own way, living life as if we were God, in effect. This, the Bible calls 'sin'. We have all sinned (Romans 3:23).

The Bible also tells us that God will hold us accountable for our sin. Like Adam, we all deserve God's judgment for our sin. As descendants of Adam, we all suffer physical death at the end of this earthly life. The Bible calls this death a curse and 'the last enemy' (Genesis 3:19, 1 Corinthians 15:26). It came about because of Adam's sin, when he by his actions effectively told God that He was not needed — Adam was going to be his own god. However, each one of us has effectively endorsed Adam's action, in ourselves rejecting God's rule over us (Romans 5:12).

The Good News is that God has provided a way of escape from the curse of death and the judgment to come. *'For God so loved the world that He gave his only begotten Son, that whoever believes in Him should not perish, but have everlasting life'* (John 3:16).

Jesus Christ came into the world, born of a woman, to take upon Himself the curse and penalty for our sins. As God in the flesh (Colossians 2:9), the God-man Jesus lived a sinless life (Hebrews 4:15) and willingly gave Himself to suffer death for us, in our place (Romans 5:8, 1 Peter 3:18). He took upon himself the punishment for our sins. As He was God (as well as man), His life was of sufficient value to pay for the sins of any number of people.

God offers this free gift of salvation to all who will receive it. He

calls upon all to turn away from their sinful ways and trust in what
Christ has done for us. There is nothing we can do to remove our guilt
before God. Doing good things does not remove our sin, and since we
are all sinners, nothing we can do can undo that; it is only by the
mercy of God that we can be saved through what He has done
(Ephesians 2:8,9).

On the other hand, whoever spurns God's offer will suffer His wrath
in the judgment to come, which the Bible clearly warns. This is a
terrifying prospect (2 Thessalonians 1:8–9). Jesus spoke much of this,
warning people of their fate. The book of Revelation uses graphic
imagery to depict the dreadful future of those who reject God's mercy
here and now.

How can I be saved?

If God has shown you that you are an unworthy sinner, deserving
of God's condemnation, in need of His forgiveness, then the Bible
says that you must have *'repentance toward God and faith toward our
Lord Jesus Christ'* (Acts 20:21). *Repentance* means a complete change
of heart and mind regarding sin — that you agree with God about your
sin and now want to live a life pleasing to Him. *Faith* in Jesus Christ
entails accepting who He is, *'the Son of the living God'*, that *'Christ
died for the ungodly'* and that He conquered death in His resurrection
(1 Corinthians 15:1–4,21,22). You must believe that He is able to
save you, and you must put your trust in Christ alone to make you
right with God.

If God has shown you your need and given you the desire to be
saved, then turn to Christ now. Speak to Him, admitting that you are
a guilty, helpless sinner, and ask Him to save you and be Lord of your
life, helping you to leave behind your sinful ways and live for Him.
The Bible says, *'if you confess with your mouth the Lord Jesus, and
believe in your heart that God raised Him from the dead, you shall be
saved'* (Romans 10:9).

If you have prayed in this manner, then you should find some
Christians who hold to the Bible as God's Word (as the authors of this
book do) and ask them to help you as you learn to live as God wants
you to live. Perhaps someone gave you this book to read — that person
might be able to advise you as to how to contact a group of such
Christians.

How can I spread the Creation/Gospel message?

● *Use* **Creation** *magazine to keep informed* — subscribe for yourself and keep up to date with what is happening so that you are ready to share with anyone who *'asks you a reason for the hope that is in you'* (1 Pet. 3:15). Many a person has been converted through a friend sharing things learned from *Creation* magazine. It encourages and equips Christians, and challenges non-Christians as to where they stand with Christ. The magazine helps both young and old. Testimonies from children to professors show that it is understandable, but also biblically and scientifically accurate. A special children's section caters for younger children.

Schoolteachers find that *Creation* magazine gives them great up-to-date material, and illustrations, for the classroom. The magazine helps teachers to keep up to date so that the best of current science is being taught, and not outmoded arguments[1] (science is always changing). The evolutionists are always 'shifting the goal posts' and we need to keep re-directing our aim in sharing the Creation/Gospel message, so as to be most effective.

● *Lend* **Creation** *magazines* to your friends, relatives, workmates, pastor, youth leader, etc. If someone asks about something that *Creation* magazine has an article about, lend them the whole magazine, not just the photocopied article. They will almost certainly read the whole lot and be challenged. There are many testimonies of folk converted because someone gave them *Creation* magazines to read. Donate subscriptions to church leaders, school libraries, local government libraries, friends, relatives, etc.

---

[1] For example, the Japanese 'plesiosaur', or lack of moon dust as evidence for a young creation.

● *Put* **Creation** *magazines in waiting rooms* at doctors' surgeries, dentists, hairdressers, automotive repair shops, etc. People will read them — they are so colourful and attractive — instead of the shallow magazines that is so often available to read in those places.

● *Lend, or give, someone a tract or a book.* Good books to give are *Stones and Bones* (Wieland) and *The Lie: Evolution* (Ham). The book *Refuting Evolution* (Sarfati) deals with the major scientific arguments in an excellent manner. Some testify to having been converted through *The Answers Book,* as they found answers to problems that they thought were insoluble (like *Who was Cain's wife?*). Of course, if you have read them first, you will be better able to know which book is suitable for the person you are trying to reach!

Good books are an excellent way to inform yourself and spread the message

● *Show videos.* Many people will not read much these days, but they might watch a video, especially if you invite them around to your home and show genuine hospitality. Some good videos are *Creation and the Christian Faith,* featuring Ken Ham, which is good for awakening Christians to the issues. *Evolution: Fact or Belief* is a good one-off video on evidences for the biblical account of Creation and the Flood and is particulary suitable for showing to non-Christians. In this video, several scientists are asked why they do not believe in evolution.

A good video for young people in high school is *When Two Worldviews Collide,* featuring geologist Dr John Morris. The series of videos, *Answers in Genesis,* with Ken Ham and Dr Gary Parker, contain more than 10 hours of teaching, and provide a wonderful overview, especially for Christians. A study book is available to use with the videos, either for individual use or group study. A new series of half-hour videos, *Answers with Ken Ham,* gives much teaching in a compact format.

There are many other videos suitable for various levels of interest. When presenting a video to a group of Christians, it is important to encourage them to obtain their own resources, particularly *Creation* magazine, so that they can also become equipped to share the message with others.

● *Sponsor a visiting speaker* — you could act as a local support person or organiser for a visiting speaker. Speak to your pastor about the possibility and then ask for a visiting speaker when one is available, distributing promotional material before the meeting. You may have to encourage your pastor to understand the importance of the issue — your own testimony can be powerful here, as well as videos that explain the foundational importance of the Genesis accounts of Creation, the Fall and the Flood.

Ken Ham, one of many creationist speakers available around the world.

● *Give creation talks* — this is recommended only if you really know the issues and you are able to teach. If those senior to you who know you best do not actively affirm that you are able to teach, please consider that your gifts may lie elsewhere. However, continue sharing the message on a one-on-one personal basis — everyone can do that.

Jesus said,

> *All authority is given to Me in heaven and on earth. Therefore go and teach all nations, baptizing them in the name of the Father and of the Son and of the Holy Spirit, teaching them to observe all things, whatever I commanded you. And, behold, I am with you all the days until the end of the world* (Mat. 28:18–20).

Index

About the authors

Don Batten, B.Sc. (Hons), Ph.D. (Editor)

Dr Batten graduated B.Sc.Agr., majoring in horticultural science, with first class honours, in 1973. He was awarded a Ph.D. by the University of Sydney in 1977 for research on the physiology of root initiation in plant cuttings. Don worked for the New South Wales Department of Agriculture from 1976-1994 researching newer sub-tropical fruit crops such as lychee and custard apple. He travelled to India, Thailand, Taiwan and China to study fruit crops and collect varieties. Don has collaborated with scientists at universities in Australia and overseas, as well as with CSIRO scientists. Major research interests include floral biology, environmental adaptation and breeding. Don once tried to harmonize the Bible with popular beliefs by way of 'theistic evolution', but came to see that this did not work. He now works full-time for *Answers in Genesis*, which sees him speaking at various locations throughout Australia and overseas, as well as researching and writing to spread the Gospel/creation message.

Ken Ham, B.Sc. Dip. Ed.

Ken Ham is the founder and executive director of *Answers in Genesis* in the USA. He is one of the most sought-after Christian speakers in North America. Ken is the author or co-author of many books, including *The Lie: Evolution, The Genesis Solution, Genesis and the Decay of the Nations, What Really Happened to the Dinosaurs, A is for Adam, D is for Dinosaur, Creation Evangelism for the New Millennium,* and *One Blood: the Biblical Answer to Racism.* He is heard daily on the radio program *Answers ... with Ken Ham*, on more than 300 radio stations worldwide. Ken also features on various videos, including the series *Answers in Genesis,* with Dr Gary Parker and the 12-part series of 28-minute videos, *Answers ... with Ken Ham.* Ken's teaching is clear, true to the Bible, engaging and challenging. Many have found salvation, and others have been encouraged and equipped to reach others with the Gospel through Ken's ministry.

Jonathan D. Sarfati, B.Sc. (Hons), Ph.D., F.M.

Dr Sarfati was born in Ararat, Australia, but spent most of his life in New Zealand. He obtained a B.Sc. (Hons.) in chemistry (with two physics papers substituted) and a Ph.D. in physical chemistry from Victoria University of Wellington. He has co-authored papers in mainstream scientific journals on high temperature superconductors and selenium-containing ring and cage molecules. To help Christians defend the faith, Dr Sarfati was a co-founder of the Wellington Christian Apologetics

Society. Since August 1996, he has worked full-time with *Answers in Genesis* in Brisbane, where he writes and reviews articles for *Creation* magazine and *CEN Technical Journal*, answers technical correspondence and contributes to the *AiG* website. He is also a former New Zealand Chess Champion, and represented New Zealand at the World Junior Champs and in three Chess Olympiads.

Carl Wieland, M.B., B.S.

Dr Wieland is the Chief Executive Officer of *Answers in Genesis*, Brisbane, Australia. Carl also serves as a Director of the affiliated *Answers in Genesis* creation ministries in the U.K. and U.S.A. A former Adelaide, South Australia, medical practitioner (past president of the South Australian Christian Medical Fellowship), Carl is in great demand as a speaker on the scientific evidence for creation/Flood, and its relevance to Christianity. He has lectured extensively in Australia and overseas. Carl has written many

articles on the subject of creation, evolution and Genesis. He is the author of the popular *Stones and Bones*, which has been translated into five other languages. He is also co-author of *One Blood: The Biblical Answer to Racism*. In 1978 he founded *Creation* magazine, of which he is managing editor. The magazine now goes to over 140 countries.

CREATION EVANGELISM FOR THE NEW MILLENNIUM

Ken Ham

This new book by Ken Ham presents a revolutionary approach to evangelism in our sceptical, post-Christian society! Here is a fresh approach to successfully reach today's evolutionistic, humanistic world with the Gospel. Endorsed by Dr D. James Kennedy of Evangelism Explosion, this book will revolutionize your own witnessing! 176 pages.

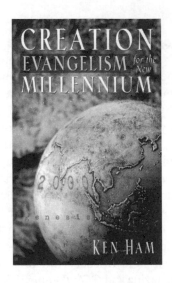

REFUTING EVOLUTION

Dr Jonathan Sarfati

Refuting Evolution is a hard-hitting critique of the most up-to-date arguments for evolution to challenge educators, students and parents. It is a powerful, yet concise summary of the arguments against evolution and for creation. It should stimulate much discussion and help students and teachers think more critically about origins. 176 pages.

AUSTRALIA
Answers in Genesis,
PO Box 6302,
Acacia Ridge DC, Qld 4110

NEW ZEALAND
Answers in Genesis,
PO Box 39005,
Howick 1730, Auckland

UK/EUROPE
Answers in Genesis,
PO Box 5262,
Leicester LE2 3XU, UK

USA
Answers in Genesis,
PO Box 6330,
Florence, Kentucky 41022

CANADA
Answers in Genesis,
5–420 Erb Street West,
Suite 213,
Waterloo, ON 2NL 6K6

OTHER COUNTRIES
Answers in Genesis,
PO Box 6302, Acacia Ridge DC,
Qld 4110, Australia

Visit our website: www.AnswersinGenesis.org